DEEP DECEPTION

JUSTINE McCARTHY is an award-winning journalist and a frequent broadcaster. She works for *The Sunday Times* and is the author of *Mary McAleese: The Outsider*, a biography of the president.

DEEP DECEPTION

IRELAND'S SWIMMING SCANDALS

JUSTINE MCCARTHY

PB

THE O'BRIEN PRESS
DUBLIN

First published 2009 by The O'Brien Press Ltd,
12 Terenure Road East, Rathgar, Dublin 6, Ireland.
Tel: +353 1 4923333; Fax: +353 1 4922777
E-mail: books@obrien.ie
Website: www.obrien.ie

ISBN: 978-1-84717-082-8

A catalogue record for this title is available from the British Library

1 2 3 4 5 6 7 8
09 10 11 12 13 14

Layout and design: The O'Brien Press Ltd
Printing: Cox & Wyman Ltd

Picture permissions:
Derry O'Rourke, Judge Roderick Murphy & Fr Ronald Bennett ©
Collins Photo Agency. George Gibney & Michelle Smith-de Bruin ©
Photocall Ireland. Photograph of Chalkie White used by kind
permission of Chalkie White. Photographs of Gary & Aidan O'Toole
used by kind permission of Gary O'Toole. Photographs of Jessica
McCann, the McCann family Communion & Esther McCann used by
kind permission of Marian Leonard. Photograph of Frank McCann ©
The Sunday Tribune.

Extract from 'Flood' by Brian Barker used with permission.

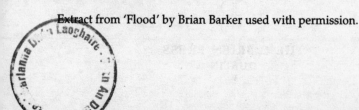

CONTENTS

Introduction   9

1. The Trial of Derry O'Rourke   15
2. Chalkie's Story   29
3. The Beginning of the End for George Gibney   36
4. The Swimmers' Stories   61
5. 'Fatal Fire Investigated'   74
6. A Black Year for Irish Swimming   93
7. Derry O'Rourke & King's Hospital   113
8. 'The Most Devious Psychopath'   146
9. 'He's Always There'   151
10. On the Run   164
11. 'Who Knew?'   177
12. Fr Ronald Bennett   202
13. 'Why Did Victims Not Complain?'   215
14. Was There A Paedophile Ring?   237
15. Where Are They Now?   252

Two Mexican boys drift by on the current
In a dead-man's float, shirtless, their bodies
Dark as skates. Just as they pass,
They roll over onto their backs
Laughing before they hit the spot where the rapids
Begin to wheel and surf out of sight.

(From the poem, 'Flood', by Brian Barker)

The dead man's float is a survival technique recommended to swimmers. The swimmer is required to adopt a vertical position in the water, face down with only the back of the head breaching the surface. The swimmer allows his or her arms and legs to dangle and raises his or her head regularly to breathe in oxygen. It is the air in the lungs that keeps the swimmer afloat. Although the name is derived from the common position in which human corpses are found in water, the technique is recognised as a method of prolonging endurance. The smaller the swimmer's limbs — a child's, for instance — the more likely the person is to float facing upwards, and to survive.

Introduction

I was a staff features writer for the *Irish Independent* in the mid-1990s when I was drawn to a story that was to occupy my life for years to come – the story of the sexual abuse of children within Irish swimming. At that time, I knew Chalkie White only by his newspaper byline as he was the *Irish Independent's* swimming correspondent. Our paths did not cross until he sought me out in the office one night with the quintessential journalist's bait: 'I've got a story for you that's going to be massive when it breaks,' he promised, or words to that effect.

The names Derry O'Rourke, George Gibney and Frank McCann are now notorious, but this was still two years before Derry O'Rourke would be jailed for the first time for sex offences involving child and teenage swimmers. George Gibney had fled the state after charges against him of indecent assault and unlawful carnal knowledge of young swimmers collapsed on a technicality. Frank McCann was in jail awaiting trial for the murder of his wife and foster daughter. At that stage, the macabre events tearing swimming apart were still the sport's dirty little secret. A secret that Chalkie White was determined to expose.

Chalkie would collect me in his car at night after we had both finished work; it was on these night-time excursions that he introduced me to survivors of child sexual abuse in the sport of swimming. Through him I first met the swimmer whom George Gibney had locked into a Florida hotel room and raped five years before. Two years before the night we were introduced, she had made her first attempt to kill herself, but she was clinging to life and – for the purpose of our meeting – to her anonymity in her suburban home, flanked by her loving parents. She talked with machine-like detachment, as if her mind had managed to disengage even if she could not make her body stop living.

Despite the enforced silence of the survivors – or possibly, because of it – there is an enduring *esprit de corps* between survivors of George Gibney and survivors of Derry O'Rourke. Many of them had been elite swimmers whose lives overlapped in the pool. It was Chalkie, on his mission to expose George Gibney, who introduced me to Bart Nolan, the doughtiest pursuer of justice you could hope to meet. Through Bart, I came to know eight of the women who had been abused by Derry O'Rourke. On every encounter over the years, my admiration for their dignity and strength of character has been renewed. I feel they are my friends.

The people whose stories have combined to create this book had their voices taken from them as children. By telling their stories, they are taking their voices back. Those abused by George Gibney, Derry O'Rourke and Fr Ronald Bennett were warned to say nothing. They grew up saying nothing. Their friends, their neighbours, their extended families and work colleagues have never known about the childhood torments that haunt them. In some cases, their parents went to their graves still oblivious. Though they all, apart from Chalkie, remain anonymous, they are men and women of singular fortitude and I thank them for their courage.

In the early days, when the survivors were unable to speak even off the record, others spoke for them. Gary O'Toole, the world-beating swimmer, has been an even greater champion behind the scenes than he was in the water. He took personal risks beyond the normal human obligations to ensure that good eventually triumphed. Were it not for Gary, his father, Aidan, and his mother, Kaye, these tragedies might have been brushed under the carpet. Another hero is Johnny Watterson, now a sports journalist with *The Irish Times*, who, along with a plucky editor and a dash of pragmatic legal advice, exploded the taboo of naming George Gibney as a child sexual abuser in the *Sunday Tribune* after the State's criminal justice system failed to do so.

These people have been invaluable sources of information to me, contributing by way of interviews, correspondence, photographs and a wealth of documents. Because so many cannot be named, it has not been consistently possible to identify sources of specific information throughout the narrative. Others, such as Carole Walsh, who privately advocated on behalf of two of George Gibney's victims, have been wholeheartedly committed to ensuring the story is told. Marian Leonard, the sister of Esther McCann, who was murdered along with her beloved little Jessica by Frank McCann, has tirelessly told and re-told her story so that it can reach the widest possible audience. I thank Marian and her daughter – named Esther in honour of her aunt – for all their help and for their bravery.

Val White was one of the many indirect victims of the secret crimes in swimming. I thank her especially for her courage in telling how her marriage to a man she loves to this day disintegrated under the strain of Gibney's legacy.

When Michael O'Brien of The O'Brien Press initially approached me to write a book on child abuse in swimming I had reservations; I was concerned that the book would become just another true crime book, dependent on shock value. But when I ran the idea by some of the survivors, they unanimously decided that the book had to be written, for all sorts of reasons: catharsis, truth, vindication, but most of all to safeguard the children of future generations. For more than two years, they willed this book on, figuratively sitting on my shoulder and tapping the keys of this laptop. When we hit wall after wall, the text messages, emails, phone calls and catch-up cups of coffee with 'K', and swimmers 'A', 'B', 'C', 'D', Bart and Aidan *et al* kept the momentum going. We've toasted a wedding, a new baby and a class action High Court settlement in the lacunae.

And so I, along with the survivors of these swimming scandals, want to say thank-you, finally, to The O'Brien Press for treating the story of their lives with sensitivity.

To you the reader, we ask only that you read it. And, please, don't ever forget.

Justine McCarthy,
August 2009

Note on reported speech

One of the traits many of those who were abused have in common is their minutely detailed recollection of the events that have dominated their lives. They remember them as if they happened yesterday. It is a characteristic shared with those who campaigned on their behalf and also suffered for doing so. While this has proven a valuable resource, it also presents a dilemma. They remember whole conversations and relate them as if verbatim. The information imparted by their remembered conversations is, no doubt, correct but it is unlikely that the dialogue is always word-for-word accurate. Therefore, throughout the book, these remembered conversations appear, not in conventional quotation marks, but preceded by dashes. Any conversation presented within quotation marks comes either from written statements or from recorded conversations.

1. The Trial of Derry O'Rourke

They link arms like a wind-breaker braced for a storm. The grey light of a dank January morning reveals faces pulled tight with apprehension. Far-away voices drift along the corridors, the shrill of their business-like assuredness sounding incongruous in the hush enveloping the women. Many of them are in their twenties, some in their thirties. One is only seventeen, a blow-in from a different generation, snared by a flattering letter written long ago by the coach to her parents, so admiring of her talent that they moved house to be closer to the swimming pool.

'If someone had done something then, when it was happening to them,' she thinks, looking at the older women and feeling again the burning indignation that, on one occasion, rescued her from his groping intentions, 'I would have been saved.'

None of the women had ever entered a courtroom before filing into the Four Courts to pursue some fragment of affirmation that, once upon a time, they were little girls with dreams. They speak soft words of mutual encouragement, their glances darting to the entrance with growing frequency as more and more newcomers congregate outside the shut courtroom door. Some more of the women stand apart in scattered islands buffered by mothers and fathers, husbands and lovers, sisters and brothers, and friends and supporters, many of whom have themselves been ostracised and denounced for insisting that the truth be told. Of the eleven women, one has returned from her new home overseas to share with the judge the childhood secret that to this day, she has not told her parents; her mother died six years ago. Another kept her secret for sixteen years believing she had learned to live with it. The day her brother invited her to be godmother to his first-born child, however, her joy turned to panic. He told that her old swimming coach, who had previously sold life insurance to him and his wife, had visited his house to inquire if the couple would add the baby's name to the policy. It was then that she had gone to the Gardaí.

So many of them drifted away in the years since they left school and the club and swimming, not daring to look back. They snatch glimpses of one another and recognise, beneath the adult masks of cosmetics and practised inscrutability, girls who once were their friends and swam in the lanes beside them, morning after morning, while their fathers slept in their cars outside. Never knowing.

'Our mothers made tea in flasks for them and they'd sleep in sleeping bags in the cars while we trained at five o'clock in the morning. Our parents made big sacrifices for us. It cost £300 a year to be a member of the club, plus you had all the gear and the away trips and my dad was on the dole. To think of all those dads outside asleep in the car. When they found out, it broke their hearts. And that's what breaks my heart.'
(Swimmer D)

When he appears, they are paralysed. He looks no different from the coach who used to tell smutty jokes and get the boys to compete in spitting competitions in the pool. Back comes the old fear that he will single out one girl; catch her eye, crook his finger and summon her to the 'chamber of horrors'.

'You can't put into words the fear, the fear. I can never forgive myself

for the day my best friend begged me for help with her eyes before turning and following him into that room. It was at the far end of the pool. She was begging to me and I didn't go and I have to live with that for the rest of my life. We called it the "chamber of horrors" even then. What was it like? It was very dark.' (Swimmer C).

Even peripheral players in their story, the milling lawyers, reporters and court staff, who have not seen him enter know that he has arrived, alerted by the stiffened atmosphere. A big man at one time, now he is devoured by his herringbone tweed coat. There is a gold band on his wedding finger. A holy medal glints in his lapel. There are rumours that he has taken to wearing religious emblems, promoting prayer meetings and peppering his language with references to the Almighty since the Garda investigation commenced. In appearance he is unexceptional; a father of six and a grandfather. He does not cast the women an eye as he and his retinue cross the hall to establish their station until the heavy courtroom doors will open. He betrays neither bravado nor contrition. Beside him stands a slight woman with lank grey pigtails and Barbie-pink clothes.

– That's the wife, a whisper goes around.

Presently, an elderly man in Derry O'Rourke's entourage hands him a sheet of paper and a biro and he begins to write something down. When he finishes, he gives the paper back and the older man, attired in the conventional clerical garb of black suit and white stock, breaks away from the entourage. The priest shuffles between the waiting knots of people dispersed around the hallway, proffering his pen and paper while the word goes round that he is here to give character evidence for O'Rourke in his appeal for the court's leniency. Colour drains from the faces of those he approaches when they read the paper and discover it is an anti-abortion petition. Their shock turns to anger when they see O'Rourke's name at the top of the page.

The fifty-one-year-old family man, daily mass-goer and self-confessed child rapist has appended the address of his parents' house in Crumlin where he grew up. The self-confidence of the signature evinces his imperviousness to these obscenely warped circumstances but, as the courtroom doors open and the hall empties, the women themselves are philosophical. They have known the depths of Derry O'Rourke's depravity.

In the courtroom, he sits impassive and unflinching in a front row seat as Detective Garda Sarah Keane, from the Sexual Assault Unit in Harcourt Square, recounts his orgy of sexual abuse of children in his care over two decades. He raped three of these eleven women before they were teenagers. The testimony of the young detective is littered with blunt labels like oral sex, hypnosis, digital penetration, intimidation, assault, rape. The women's sobbing is audible from the gallery of seats at the back of the room, but O'Rourke might as well be listening to a recitation of the Dublin Bus timetable. His face is unreadable. The former two-pound-a-week clerk in Donnelly's Coal Yard on Sir John Rogerson's Quay keeps his gaze trained on the witness stand. Five years after the Garda investigation began in January 1993, and after he tried to convert every loophole in the law books into an escape hatch from justice, he finally surrendered. He had originally been charged on 10 July 1995 with ninety offences against girls aged eleven to fifteen. Nearly two and a half years later, in December 1997 in the Dublin Circuit Criminal Court, he pleaded guilty to twenty-nine sample charges, a common mechanism in child sexual abuse cases where the sheer volume of complainants and charges is often too unwieldy for each one to be prosecuted efficiently. After pleading guilty in December, he went home for a month, celebrating Christmas and seeing in the New Year with his family while the court awaited victim impact reports. Now it is January 29,

1998 and he stands convicted of unlawful carnal knowledge, sexual assault and indecent assault of eleven girls, between 1976 and 1992.

Much of the abuse, says Detective Keane, was committed in the boardroom, a storage area for floatation aids located off the poolside. This was the room the girls knew as the 'chamber of horrors'. It was here that he hypnotised them, before violating them. He would instruct them to imagine themselves lying on a sun-drenched beach and to imagine a boyfriend lying down with them. The boy, he told them, was touching parts of their bodies and he would name each body part as he touched it. He said the hypnosis was a scientific technique designed to relax them and improve their swimming. If the hypnosis did not work, he pretended he was measuring their muscle development while he fondled them. He would rebuke them for poor performances in the pool and ply them with insistent questions about their menstrual cycles. These interrogations often targeted girls who were too young to have begun menstruating. When he summoned a girl to his 'chamber of horrors', he would order her to raise her hands onto an overhead shelf and he would proceed to feel her breasts under her togs. He would then tell her to lower her togs to her waist to allow him 'to get a better measure'. Sometimes, his hand would move inside the bottom half of the togs and he would touch the girl there. One girl, the seventeen-year-old, said that she had grown braver by the time she reached fifteen and she told him to stop 'molesting' her. He did. Another time, she and her best friend hid his measuring tape. When it was found, a female swimming official marched the girls into the showers but, instead of reprimanding them as they expected, she announced: – From now on, I'll be measuring you.

Usually he perpetrated the rapes in his Mazda car. He was in the habit of giving club members lifts home from training, by prior arrangement with their parents. Ten minutes or so after driving away from the prestigious Dublin boarding school where he was employed as pool manager, he would park the car in a side-road and rape his victim.

'You'd be sitting in the car shitting yourself and your stomach going up and down and wanting to tell your mam but not wanting to tell her because you wouldn't be able to go swimming anymore.'(Swimmer C).

He raped one girl in his own bed after bringing her to his house on the pretext that he needed to talk to her about her swimming. He called another girl, aged thirteen, to his office and made her sit astride him on his lap, facing him. He told her to shut her eyes and, when she obeyed, he unwrapped a condom and raped her. He asked her if it hurt. She said it did and she asked him to stop, please. He asked her did she know what happened. She said 'yes' and ran crying from the room. In her statement to Gardaí years later she acknowledged that she had not understood that what he had done to her constituted sexual intercourse.

Detective Keane says that O'Rourke has shown no remorse throughout the five-year investigation. She says he did not co-operate when she questioned him. He had sworn to Judge Peter Kelly in his application to the High Court to have the prosecution struck out that, if it went ahead, he would plead not guilty to all the charges and rigorously defend himself. As it turns out, his 'guilty' response before Christmas to the twenty-nine sample charges has rendered a hearing of the evidence against him unnecessary. All that is to be done now is to determine how long he must spend in jail.

Beside him in the front row in Court Number 23, Julie, the wife he courted when they were both young and she was a clerk in Sheridan's coal yard in Hanover Hill, keeps her grey head bowed. She is flanked by a son and a daughter, each holding one of her hands in a tableau of grief. The son's mouth moves incessantly, as if he is incanting the same prayer over and over into his mother's ear.

When the formal evidence is concluded, the first of the women walks from the back of the courtroom, enters the witness stand, takes the Bible in her right hand and swears to tell the truth. She sits facing the judge.

'I want to tell you how Derry O'Rourke destroyed my life,' she begins, addressing the wigged figure of authority. She tells the judge how her swimming coach violated her in her school uniform and raped her in his car three times a week, starting when she was twelve years of age. She is holding a sodden tissue and occasionally dabbing tears from her cheeks, but she is coherent and her voice is resolute. The judge tells her she does not have to put herself through the ordeal of telling her story: O'Rourke has been convicted; he will be punished, he assures her.

'I must,' she replies.

'I am a man. I was never a woman. It must be a horrible experience. I sympathise with you, but this isn't the worst case of its kind that I've heard. I've heard much worse, actually. Get on with your life,' Mr Justice Kieran O'Connor advises her, seemingly oblivious to the gasps emanating from the back of the courtroom where the other women are seated. 'Get counselling.'

'I can't bring myself to go for counselling for fear that the anger will come out and ruin my marriage and my children. I didn't know until I was seventeen that what he did to me was sexual intercourse. I left my home town to avoid him and never went back. To this day, I cannot perform with my husband in ways I would like to.'

The man standing by the door being cradled like a baby by a friend is her husband. He watches his wife step down from the witness box and walk towards him, past O'Rourke, who does not look up. She stares into O'Rourke's face as she goes by and as she reaches her husband's side and he puts his arms around her, the judge is saying that the court will sit again in the morning to determine sentence. The judge alone seems unaware that something has snapped and that he has been the catalyst. Until today, there had been a loose arrangement among the women that only one of them would give a victim impact statement at the sentence hearing, but that may no longer hold. As O'Rourke walks from the courtroom for his last night of freedom, the women hold each other and determine that any mandatory diminution of his sentence as a reward for pleading guilty will only be decided after they have fully informed the judge of their suffering.

And so the next day, Friday 30 January, when Mr Justice Kieran O'Connor arrives on the bench to resume the hearing, a queue of women is waiting to occupy the witness stand. Six more will have their say before their abuser is led away to the prison van despite renewed efforts by the judge to shush them.

Today, O'Rourke is wearing a homespun jumper – the sort middle-aged men receive as Christmas presents – under a sports jacket. In his lapel, once again, is the holy medal, but there is no sighting of the priest. O'Rourke will not look at the first woman to take her seat in the witness box, who the judge is advising with avuncular concern to take up a hobby. He recommends, among other pursuits, swimming.

'Get it out of your system and get on with your life,' he urges her.

'It's important for me to let him know what he has done to me,' she persists. 'He cruelly took away my childhood. I trusted him. My parents trusted him. But he abused that trust. I had to tell my mother when I was twenty-four what he did to me and I made my mother cry.'

Turning to face the coach whom she and the other girls used to call

'God', she speaks to him directly. 'You made my mother cry.'

Another woman takes her place. Again, Judge O'Connor cautions against what he calls unnecessary agony.

'I chose to come and say what I have to say and I chose to because I feel I need this man to understand the effect his crime has had on me,' she explains. Then looking straight at the judge, she adds: 'And I'm sorry if my distress upsets you.'

The applause that erupts in the courtroom is the noise of a long silence rupturing.

The seventeen-year-old girl is next. She speaks with the same compelling dignity as the others.

'He ruined my life and all the prayers in the world won't change that. I remember sitting in the car, knowing I was going to be measured. I remember my best friend begging me to go in after her and I didn't and that guilt has lived with me. For me, the way to cope as a teenager and in my early twenties was through drinking and hiding behind drink.'

You can feel the courtroom tensing when it is his turn to offer mitigation in his defence. His senior counsel, Patrick Gageby, has appealed to the judge to take into account that 'the worst of the offences happened sixteen to twenty-one years ago'. His main argument is that there were no 'sexual intercourse offences' after 1983 and that there did not seem to be 'any offending from 1983 to 1991'. He urges the judge to deal with his client 'based on the character he is now'.

O'Rourke enters the witness box, takes the Bible in his right hand and swears to tell the truth.

His voice is steady and strong. 'I consider it a blessing that when I was first interviewed [by Gardaí] the first thing I did was to pray for the young people I offended,' he tells the judge. The past five years, he says, have been 'as close to hell as you can get'. He apologises to the women he abused and says that he prays for them. He apologises to his family for the shame he has brought upon them. He apologises to his employers for having abused his position of trust. The sound of his victims' weeping fills the pauses in his public act of contrition. 'The only thing I can add is that, in all sincerity, I ask everyone I have hurt, in the name of Jesus Christ, to forgive me.'

Next to take the oath is Julie, his petite, ashen-faced wife, followed by their daughter, Kirsty.

Both women attest to what a good father and provider he has been down through the years.

'You have a wonderful family whom you don't deserve,' the judge rebukes him. He praises Julie for being 'the bravest woman I have ever had in this court.' If the unintended insult goes unremarked by some of the women seated together in the back it is because they sense that O'Rourke's punishment is about to be announced and nothing will distract them from this denouement.

Mr Justice O'Connor is saying that he is obliged, following a ruling by the superior courts, to regard the convicted man's guilty plea as mitigation. 'The only thing I can find in your favour is that you pleaded guilty and saved your victims the horrible trauma of having to relive their dreadful experience of what you did to them all those years ago. ... All that has been said in this case can only lead me to the conclusion that your behaviour was the planned pursuit of sexual perversion against young girls on whom you visited sex in a cruel and brutal way.'

Next he addresses the victims. 'To all those girls, I say it was a horrible experience. Go on now and live your lives in the hope you will recover as best you can from a foul deed perpetrated on your young bodies.'

As he passes sentence, the crowded courtroom struggles to keep abreast of the arithmetic.

Two terms of twelve years each for unlawful carnal knowledge of girls under fifteen; two separate terms of seven years and five years plus eight terms of six years for indecent assault; five three-year terms for the sexual assaults, and ten terms of one year each for other indecent assaults. The women at the back of the room and the O'Rourke family at the front are so engrossed in calculating the length of the sentence that many of them do not hear the judge declare all the sentences are to run concurrently. Patrick McCarthy, senior counsel for the DPP, asks that the media ban on identifying O'Rourke be lifted, at the request of the victims whose own names, ages and occupations should remain confidential. The judge acquiesces.

As the court rises and the judge leaves the bench, the words, 'a hundred and nine years' are repeated in a babel of disbelief and awe. Some of the jubilant women and their supporters climb onto the courtroom seats and applaud, tears streaming down their faces. Two uniformed prison officers approach O'Rourke. The steel handcuffs glint as they are slipped around his wrists. There is a sudden hush. The click of the cuffs is audible. He does not flinch.

'No pain, no gain,' cries out the mother of one of his victims, repeating his favourite training mantra. People around her clap, a tentative applause of the kind you hear in a theatre when the audience is unsure if the drama is concluded. When he is led from the room, the women crowd around the windows in the corridor outside and watch attentively as he is loaded into a prison van.

'I have waited a long, long time for this moment,' says a woman aloud, to herself.

By the time of his release from the Midlands Prison in Portlaoise after nine years, on Thursday, March 1, 2007, he will have been convicted, in three separate tranches of prosecutions, on fifty-five charges of sexually abusing eighteen girls, amounting to cumulative prison sentences of 130 years. His youngest victim, it will be established by the law courts, was ten.

'I know for a fact that he abused more than us. He behaved as if he was invincible. We've talked about it and we think there could have been a hundred girls or more. We had our picture taken for the Irish Press *one time for a gala and he had his hand under my top, and the photographer there with his camera. He didn't give a shit.' (Swimmer B)*

On the same day in the Dublin Circuit Criminal Court, Fr Ivan Payne, a fifty-four-year-old priest of the archdiocese of Dublin and a former chaplain to Our Lady's Hospital for Sick Children, has pleaded guilty to the sexual abuse of eight boys from 1968 to 1987. It was revealed five years earlier that the Archbishop of Dublin, Dr Desmond Connell, approved a loan of IR£27,500 from diocesan funds for the priest to pay damages in settlement of a claim brought by a former altar boy, Andrew Madden, whom Payne started abusing when the boy was eleven. The name of Ivan Payne was to become a landmark in the slow unravelling of the Catholic Church's sheltering of paedophile priests.

But it is Derry O'Rourke who will become the most notorious paedophile in the jurisdiction and his jailing will come to be seen as a defining event for Irish society. His name will, overnight, become a byword for the exposure of a series of macabre, multiple-paedophile scandals within the sport of swimming, sparking speculation that an organised ring may have been secretly operating within the State-funded sport. Yet, despite his notoriety, by the time he will have served his sentence and be freed back into society nine years later, the survivors of his crimes will still not have received a cent in compensation. Nor will the authorities who entrusted their care to Derry O'Rourke have issued an apology to them.

'Nobody has said sorry. Nobody. Nobody. Even now, seeing my kids in their togs, I can feel the cold in that room. I used to count the phone books on the shelf and the certificates on the wall, once the door closed. When I went for counselling, I started counting things in the counseller's office. I remember being so depressed as a child, and wanting to die and going to the top of our back garden and saying "Please, Lord, take me. Don't take anybody else. Just me".' (Swimmer D).

But on this day of triumph in Court 29 of the Dublin Circuit Criminal Court, the future looks bright. Outside the courthouse, on the footpath beside the Liffey, the women gather around a woman solicitor who has been engaged by one of them to keep a watching brief at the trial. She gives them a synopsis of their rights and entitlements and their faces, pressed close to one another in concentrated audience, glow with relief. The solicitor offers to meet them again before they depart in groups and pairs to begin the rest of their lives, the sounds of renewed camaraderie trailing in their wake betoken the lifelong friendships that might have been.

'We should have been at each other's birthdays and weddings and debs, but we lost all that. We had been so close. He took our friendships and our childhood and our dreams. I grieve for that; for the child I was.' (Swimmer B).

Swimmer A takes a short-cut along the riverside to the family-owned business where her parents and other relations are waiting for her. 'You were bloody brilliant,' her aunt greets her as she comes through the doorway. Swimmer A accepts the congratulations from her family, but she does not linger for long to bask in the euphoria. She moves to a small office at the back. She flicks opens a telephone directory, finds the number she wants and taps it out on the phone. 'Hello, I'd like to speak to the Minister for Sport, please,' she says. She listens politely while a voice at the other end explains that the minister is in Donegal and unable to take her call.

'Ah, but I think he will want to talk to me,' she answers confidently. 'Tell him I'm one of Derry O'Rourke's victims.'

2. Chalkie's Story

On 26 December 1990, Chalkie White was 35,000 feet high in the night sky, somewhere between London and Singapore. The plastic meal trays had been cleared away and passengers were reading airport paperbacks, watching the movie or dozing under skimpy blankets. Chalkie looked across at where Gary O'Toole was sitting in the window-seat of an otherwise vacant row of seats, his feet tucked under him, the overhead light illuminating his concentration on an electronic chess board. Chalkie could not see George Gibney, but he guessed that, as the national swimming coach, he would be seated towards the front of the plane with the travelling blazers from the Irish Amateur Swimming Association, all buoyed with inflated expectations for the World Championships in Perth. Gibney, the most powerful figure in Irish swimming, was a member of the Association's technical committee, giving him the casting vote in the selection of the national swimming team. Up front with him would be Derry O'Rourke, swimming's admiral-in-waiting, who was accompanying his club's golden girl, Michelle Smith, to the Australian games.

Chalkie stood up and walked over to Gary, kick-starting what the older man would later describe as 'the blackest period of my life'.

– How's it going? Are you looking forward to this? he asked lightly, hunkering down in the seat beside Gary.

– I dunno. I've been training hard. Maybe over-training.

Gary was all chlorine-bleached, sparkling good looks, unbowed by expectations that he would secure, at minimum, a fourth place in the breaststroke in Perth. It was hard to dislike him and the few who did were inclined towards envy. As the leading Irish performer in the pool since the mid-1980s, he was awarded a £5,000 'elite athlete's grant' in 1990 by Cospóir, the State sports organisation. He had been swimming since he was a small boy, first in his hometown club, Bray Cove, and, from the age of nine, under George Gibney's tutelage at the prestigious Trojan Swimming Club in Blackrock, County Dublin. He had competed in the Seoul Olympics in 1988, along with Michelle Smith from Trojans' foremost rival club, King's Hospital in west Dublin, with Gibney as Irish Olympic coach. Neither swimmer had progressed beyond the heats but, in 1989, Gary sensationally won a silver medal at the European Championships in Bonn and the hopes of a gloomy, pre-Celtic Tiger nation hungry for international applause were impelling him towards the winners' podium at the Barcelona Olympics in 1992. The World Championships in Perth, from January 3 to 13, 1991, would be a significant test of the twenty-one-year-old UCD medical student's potential to achieve the ultimate sporting dream.

– Do you get on ok with George? wondered Chalkie.

– Yeah, fine. It's just professional, you know. We wouldn't be bosom buddies or anything, if that's what you mean. I don't know where he lives and I wouldn't have his phone number.'

– Did he ever do anything to you?'

– He's been a bit of a prick alright, and he's upset me the odd time, yeah, Gary admitted.

– No, I mean has he ever done anything untoward?

– What're you talking about?

– Has he ever abused you?

– You mean, sexually abused me?

– Yeah, said Chalkie, intensely aware of how the half-light and the high-backed seats screened the pair of them from the other passengers.

– No. Why are you asking me this?

– Because he did it to me.

At thirty-five, Francis 'Chalkie' White was fourteen years older than Gary O'Toole. He was married with two young sons and worked full time as an IT consultant with a multinational company. He was travelling to Perth as a member of the coaching staff, having prepared one of his Glenalbyn Club swimmers, Aileen Convery, for competition in the Seoul Olympics in 1988. He began swimming with the Guinness club at the age of nine. When he won the Liffey Swim, an arduous 1,800 metre handicapped race through Dublin city centre, as a pale, slender eleven-year-old for the first of his two successive victories, his English-born coach, Eddie Ince, had cheered, 'Well done, Chalkie, m'lad,' as he emerged dripping from the water in front of clamouring reporters and photographers. The following day's newspapers reported that a boy from Clondalkin, name of Chalkie White, had surged to victory in the Liffey Swim. After that, nobody ever called him Francis again. It was as Chalkie White that he went on to swim for Ireland and won a sports scholarship to Villanova University in Pennsylvania where he roomed with fellow Irish sports scholarship student, the Olympic runner Eamonn Coghlan. Sixteen years after his life-defining conversation with Gary on board the flight to Perth he would be formally inducted into the university's hall of fame.

Chalkie's prowess in the sport was implicitly acknowledged by his appointment as the *Irish Independent*'s swimming correspondent, in addition to his day job. He had also commenced writing a regular column for *Swim* magazine in the autumn of 1990. In his inaugural column for a special World Championships issue, he singled out Gary's silver medal in Bonn for special mention.

Chalkie's record as an outstanding swimmer was in stark contrast with George Gibney's personal accomplishments in the water. When one of the national coach's protégés pushed Gibney into the pool for a lark one day, the country's elite swimmers had stood on the deck and watched with appalled mirth as their coach doggy-paddled to the side and held on, gasping and spluttering. The truth was out. The top coach in the country could not swim to save his life. Not that it detracted from his reputation as a brilliant motivator who delivered results. Among his earliest trophies had been Chalkie White.

Gibney had been orphaned young by the early deaths of his parents. He lived for some time with an uncle in Athlone and, for a short while, with a great-aunt in a Guinness-owned house in Derravaragh Road in Terenure. At the age of nineteen, he was sharing a house in Dublin with his brother. It was around the time he took Chalkie under his wing, in the late 1960s. The house stood in a humble row of artisan red-bricks called Greenville Terrace, off South Circular Road, close to the Guinness brewery, where he worked as a fitter and coached swimmers in the company pool. In his bedroom, he kept a pull-out sofa which he used as a bench for work-outs and it was here that he brought Chalkie, aged eleven, for weight-training sessions. What the child noticed was that the curtains were always drawn, even in daylight. One weeknight before Christmas 1967, Chalkie was stretched out on the sofa bed after completing his exercises, when Gibney switched off the overhead light and came and lay on top of him.

– What would you do if I was a girl? he asked.

Twice a week for the next three years, the coach routinely sexually abused him, not stopping until the boy turned fourteen. Almost all the incidents happened in the Greenville Terrace house. An exception was in the summer of 1968, when Chalkie was thirteen and attending a residential swimming camp at the fee-paying boarding school, Gormanston College in County Meath. The swimmers at the camp were sleeping one to a cubicle. One night, after Gibney finished supervision duty in the dormitory, he got into bed with Chalkie in his cubicle and stripped off his own pyjamas.

– What would you do if I was a girl? he asked, as always.

In the soporific ambience of the big airliner, Chalkie poured his story out to Gary in unsparing detail. The young swimmer listened quietly as a memory returned to him. He was eleven years old and feeling homesick during a training camp in California in June 1980. His coach, the mighty George Gibney, came tiptoeing into his bedroom. Gary feigned sleep. He could smell the coach standing beside his bed. Then he felt his hand on his leg and realised he was trying to get into bed with him. Gary remembered how he had told him to go away and how his coach had offered him an apple and slunk off, never to seek him out again. He told Chalkie this story and, inside him, Chalkie's heart shrivelled with the realisation that 'nothing had happened to Gary other than that he had refused; he'd been strong'. A dread entered him that this plea for help would evaporate, once again.

For he had sought help once before. Upon returning home to Dublin from his scholarship at Villanova with a business finance degree he had commenced training with Derry O'Rourke, club coach at King's Hospital in Palmerstown and Olympic coach-designate for Moscow 1980. Despite reaching the qualifying standard for the 1976 Olympics in Montreal, Chalkie had not been picked for the team and would ultimately be declared too old to participate in Moscow in 1980. On a day in 1978, while sitting at the poolside with O'Rourke at the end of a training session, the now twenty-two-year-old swimmer felt disgust build inside him as his new coach delivered a stream of lascivious comments about the young girl swimmers arriving in their swimsuits for a class.

– Nice little bit of stuff, ho, ho, O'Rourke leered at one of the children.

Fury welled inside Chalkie.

– What are you going on about? he demanded.

– I'm only looking at the kids and wondering what they'll be like when they grow up.

Perhaps it was a combination of anger and frustration and the pain of all the years, or maybe it was a simple recognition of the deceitfulness mirrored in O'Rourke's line of defence that made Chalkie utter his next words.

– I had a relationship with George when I was a kid, he blurted out.

O'Rourke looked nonplussed.

– Well, all I can say is that's something I'd keep to myself if I were you.

– Why?

– Maybe people would start asking questions about you, saying you were gay. You know, being at the pool where there are boy swimmers going round in tight little togs.

What most alarmed Chalkie about the conversation with his coach was not that O'Rourke failed to act on the information that his colleague had engaged in sex with a minor, but the tacit admission that it was standard practice for adult coaches to regard young swimmers as sexual objects.

This time, however, he had chosen his confidante well. As Chalkie went on talking quietly in the slumbering plane, Gary made two seismic decisions. The first one was that he believed what he was hearing. 'I believed him absolutely', he recalls. 'I'm not saying my loyalty to George immediately evaporated but I looked at Chalkie's eyes and I knew it was deeply personal.'

He informed Chalkie of his second decision.

– I guarantee you, as soon as the Olympics are over, I'll do something about this. You have my word.

As the wheels of the airliner touched down in Singapore, before the final leg of the journey to Australia, the process for the exposure of some of the most prolific paedophiles in Ireland had been set in motion. As he disembarked, Gary was acutely aware of the danger he was facing. 'I was a medical student. I hadn't even graduated. If I was to go around making these allegations and they turned out not to be true, my career would be over before it began.'

Chalkie too understood that a road had been taken during the flight to south-east Asia from which there would be no turning back. Many years later, Val White, his wife of twenty-eight years, would discover a jotter filled with a detailed memoir of his conversation with Gary in the course of a spring clean of their home. She found it after Chalkie left home.

3. The Beginning of the End for George Gibney

The high hopes for Gary O'Toole's performances at the World Championships in Perth sank like pirate treasure. Instead of the third or fourth placings he had aspired to, his best finish left him trailing in eleventh. To the dismayed public, it was an inexplicable failure, but not to the swimmer.

'I'm being told my split times by a coach I know has been acting the way Chalkie's told me and I'm thinking, "If he did that to Chalkie, what about X and what about Y? Is that why she left the club suddenly the way she did?" I was thinking that I'd never thought to ask those people who vanished from Trojans [five senior swimmers left the club between December 1990 and January 1991] what was wrong. When I was fourteen or fifteen, there were girls of thirteen or fourteen being abused by him. As a male, there were girls you were trying to date and, when they said no, you just left them alone. You didn't ask why because you didn't have the confidence. You didn't know these were girls who had been warned not to have anything to do with any other males.'

Chalkie too was starting to feel the pangs of apprehension, fearing nothing would come from his conversation with Gary. The pair talked often during those three weeks in Perth, always conscious that George Gibney was watching them. For Chalkie knew that Gibney knew that Chalkie had reached a crisis in his life.

Only weeks earlier, at the beginning of December 1990, Chalkie had inadvertently walked in on a meeting of the Irish Amateur Swimming Association (IASA). He saw Gibney sitting at the table and heard a snatch of the conversation that clearly showed the topic on the agenda was the selection of IASA coaches for the World Championships. Chalkie left the room, furious. He waited outside the door trying to control himself as the realisation sank in that Gibney had double-crossed him by excluding him from the meeting and, ergo, from the trip to Perth. He thought: 'I've just got screwed by this guy again.' With that, he opened the door, re-entered the meeting and let loose a tirade against the esteemed national coach, causing what he classifies as 'a bit of a kerfuffle'. He accused Gibney of conspiring against him, of deliberately misleading him and of being a master manipulator. Chalkie was more shocked than anybody by his outburst. For a long time, he had managed to convince himself that he could leave the past undisturbed and work alongside his abuser as a fellow Leinster-based coach with Glenablyn Club in nearby Stillorgan, County Dublin.

'When George became national coach, he started giving me coaching jobs to do for big events but, after a year of working beside him, I could see he hadn't changed. I began to see the deceitfulness in him. I thought: "You're thirty-five. What possessed you to believe in him? He manipulated me when I was younger and now he's doing it again." It caused me real big headaches; probably more than he had actually done to me before. I knew I couldn't handle it anymore.'

He felt torn between reminders of Gibney's duplicity and auguries that he was a reformed character. The transformation never seemed more convincing than when, in 1989, Chalkie suffered serious injuries in a mountain fall in Chiasso, close to the Italian border in southern Switzerland, where he was Irish team manager for an Eight Nations swimming competition. In the fall, his head struck a rocky outcrop, the trauma causing a haematoma that required eight hours of emergency surgery in a Swiss hospital. George Gibney, who was not on that trip, was the one who took charge back at home. It was he who broke the news to Chalkie's family, arranging air travel and finances and acquiring an emergency passport for Chalkie's wife, Val, to fly to Switzerland.

The good impression quickly receded on Chalkie's return to Ireland. He watched with growing apprehension as his old coach revelled in the power invested in him by the sport's governing body. Gibney had been appointed national swimming coach by the Irish Amateur Swimming Association in 1981. In 1988, when the newly-established National Lottery provided the Department of Education with the finances to fund a national Director of Swimming, Gibney got the job. It was the same year he was Olympic coach for the games in Seoul. In the twelve months preceding the games, he brought his elite swimmers on numerous training and acclimatisation camps overseas, including trips to Mission Bay in Florida, Canet in France, Edinburgh and Honolulu. After the previous Olympics in Los Angeles, he had produced a four-year plan entitled 'Our Goal Is Seoul', ensuring his position as team manager for South Korea. In the following year, 1989, he was granted an honorary life membership of the IASA on the nomination of the Connaught branch. He tendered his resignation from the Director of Swimming position in May 1990, arguing that the duties involved were too onerous, whereupon the IASA abolished the position. Gibney stayed on as the all-powerful national coach.

He was further assimilated into the sport's national governance by his appointment to the IASA's medical committee, its technical committee and to its education and coaching committee. In 1990, he was awarded the Sports Manager of the Year accolade, sponsored by the Irish Life Assurance Company. Thanks to his assiduous cultivation of influential social contacts, many sourced from Trojans, where the members and the parents of competitive swimmers comprised a pantheon of Ireland's professional class, he enjoyed extensive political promotion. He kept a well-thumbed copy of *How to Make Friends and Influence People* within arm's reach in his office, embracing the essential ethos between its covers that pleasing others is the most effective route to success. Trojans, with an active membership of 450 people, was housed in the sports complex attached to Newpark Comprehensive School on Newtownpark Avenue in Blackrock, a leafy residential heartland of the well-to-do. It was ripe for Gibney's go-getter love-bombing.

'He very deliberately courted influential people,' recalls sports journalist Johnny Watterson, a former pupil at Newpark College. 'For instance, his kids went to school in St Andrews in Booterstown and so did the kids of a lot of influential people. He was always offering those kids lifts to and from school to ingratiate himself with their parents. He was your clichéd creep. He used to stop on the road after school and offer the girls from Newpark School lifts. He always looked pervy. Maybe it was the bottle glasses and the unctuous nature. He had this creepy way about him in school that kids picked up on but that the parents, who sent their kids to be coached by him, missed. He was driven, convincing, and intelligent. He was a good communicator. There were no questions from the parents.'

Newpark was a liberal, pioneering school; the first in Ireland to introduce a transition year in its calendar. The school that was originally built on the eight-acre site, the Protestant-managed Avoca School, had merged with Kingstown School, a small Presbyterian school based in Dun Laoghaire, in the mid-1960s and was run for a few years as a private venture. Its progressive cachet attracted many sons and daughters from south Dublin's self-employed and senior civil service strata. They were motivated parents with a can-do attitude to their offsprings' education. One such mother was Utta Jytte, a dynamic Dane in whose memory the school's theatre hall is named. It was Jytte who spearheaded the construction of a twenty-five-metre indoor, heated swimming pool in the grounds in 1972, contained in a multi-purpose sports complex complete with gym and hockey pitch. When the Department of Education took the school over and reinvented it as Newpark Comprehensive School it agreed to provide funding for the pool on condition that it would be self-financing. The parents, who boasted some of the capital's leading accountants and lawyers, set up a company called Swim Plan to operate the sports complex and to pay for insurance cover. By the early 1990s, the annual insurance premium was costing about £25,000. The Department of Education paid capitation fees to the school for its students' use of the pool for swimming lessons. The rest of the time, it was available for use by the public, by a local club called Otter, and by Trojan Swimming Club. The latter was George Gibney's brainchild. He founded it in 1976, when he was taken on by Swim Plan as manager of Newpark Sports Centre. He sourced most of his first in-take of competitive swimmers from Glenalbyn Swimming Club in nearby Stillorgan, where he had previously coached. Trojans was formally affiliated with the IASA in December 1976 and had its debut away trip to Holland the next year. It has produced half-a-dozen Olympians since its inception.

Landing the manager's job in Newpark was a serious career fillip for Gibney. He had begun adult life as a fitter with Guinness and a fledgling swim coach at the world famous James' Gate brewery, under the wing of Eddie Ince, Chalkie's first coach. This was followed by a spell working for another world-famous brand name. Waterford Glass had constructed a fine swimming pool in its grounds for employees and public alike, but the facility was proving to be a financial drain on the company. Gibney was hired to turn it into a proper business venture. He spent a couple of years in the Munster city, organising galas and structured coaching sessions. The pool soon started to show a profit, enhancing Gibney's reputation as a go-getter. On returning to Dublin, he coached at Marian College pool in Ballsbridge and Glenalbyn, but left the latter under a cloud. Officially, he was sacked for 'insubordination', a cryptic misdemeanour that only compounded his image as a strong, indomitable coach whereas the true reason his contract was terminated was 'lack of accountability to the committee regarding the number of swimmers attending and the return of fees paid'. The job at Newpark came about after he secured part-time work teaching technical drawing in the school. His credentials for the sports manager's job were impressive, having made history by being the first person awarded an Irish masters degree in swimming.

'He copied the thesis for the degree from a paper done by the parent of one of the young swimmers in Trojans,' recalls Aidan O'Toole, Gary's father. 'I remember because I was in his house until about five o'clock in the morning arranging it for him. He was very impressive. He had the gift of the gab. He used to start working on the IASA's incoming president a year before he'd take office. A lot of the executive were in awe of his power and influence. He ran Trojans as his own fiefdom. There was no real committee in the club, as was required under the rules.'

As manager of Newpark Sports Centre, Gibney was in charge of half-a-dozen staff and the centre's accounts, reporting to once-a-term board meetings attended by the school principal and Swim Plan's directors. Each year, Swim Plan held a dinner at such upper crust venues as the Royal St George Yacht Club in Dun Laoghaire andFitzwilliam Lawn Tennis Club in Leeson Park. 'George would have been a tad uncomfortable in those places,' remembers Newpark Comprehensive teacher Derek West, who later became the school's principal.

Gibney's influence spread beyond Newpark and the small pond of Irish swimming. In the mid-1980s, he and Frank McCann, future president of the Leinster Branch of the Irish Amateur Swimming Association, were appointed directors of the City of Dublin Swim Team, established to exploit the tourism potential of Ireland's participation in the European Championships. The project enjoyed the patronage of the Lord Mayor of Dublin. After the 1989 general election, Gibney was appointed by the Minister for Education, Mary O'Rourke, to the Irish Coaching Bureau and to the Selection Committee, both established under the auspices of the Department of Sport, where the junior minister was Frank Fahey. The brief for the two boards was to devise curriculums and to define the roles of coaches across the spectrum of all sport. Gibney counted a Garda sergeant among his follow board members. He was, in addition, a director of the National Training & Coaching Centre at the University of Limerick and was a member of the Committee of Elite Sports persons, the grant-allocation body that gave him enormous clout and kudos. He befriended many eminent people on his way to the top who could never have imagined his secret life.

'We used to go to meetings with officials in the Department,' Derek West recalls. 'He had this plan to have the pool extended to 50 metres so that it would be the first Olympic-size pool in the country. He had a BMW car, which was unusual in those days. Mine was a Datsun Sunny. When you got an offer of a lift in a BMW, you took it. So he used to drive us to town for the meetings. The car always smelt of talcum powder. He was very affable and charismatic. Sometimes when I think of George, I think of Squealer in *Animal Farm*, the pig with the persuasive tail. He was very effective.'

Gibney's ambition was unquenchable. In 1989, through a swimming contact who was friendly with the Minister for Labour, Bertie Ahern, he swung a private audience with Charles Haughey, the Taoiseach of the day and the most intimidating politician of the modern era. Gibney arrived at Government Buildings armed with charts, graphs, mathematical projections and a specially-commissioned video to make the pitch for his 50-metre pool. The magnificent edifice housing the Taoiseach's office had been dubbed Chateau Charlemagne by the chattering classes because of the exorbitant taxpayers' money expended on its refurbishment during an economic recession. Haughey liked to see himself as a cultured man and a visionary. He sanctioned the regeneration of Temple Bar, the refurbishment of Dublin Castle and the Royal Hospital Kilmainham, and the creation of the International Financial Services Centre in Dublin's moribund docklands. The Fianna Fáil-led coalition government was planning to build a national sports stadium near the Custom House in Dublin's docklands, complete with pool, but the depressed economy and huge Exchequer borrowings eventually put paid to the plans. Haughey remained steadfastly unimpressed with Gibney's ode to an Olympic-size pool. Having been dismissed with the hollow silence of indifference, the swim coach was not going be put off. He wrote repeatedly to Haughey thereafter and pestered Fianna Fáil backbenchers to inveigle the Taoiseach to change his mind until, finally, Haughey summoned his minister, Bertie Ahern, in whose constituency the doomed national stadium was to be located; 'Get that man off my back', or words to that effect, Haughey reputedly instructed his future successor.

By the time Chalkie White phoned George Gibney some days after chancing upon the secret IASA meeting and invited him to his house on Seafield Road in Killiney, south Dublin, the coach who had abused him from the age of eleven held vast sway over the swimming world.

He arrived in the afternoon, a short man with a goatee and over-sized, tinted prescription glasses. He sat in an armchair positioned in front of the sitting room window. His face, haloed by the backlight of a winter sun, was smug. 'He knew he'd rattled me at the meeting,' says Chalkie. 'I can still see him in that chair looking at me with this … this casualness.' Gibney's superior demeanour wiped any doubts from Chalkie's mind.

– All the things you did to me years ago are beginning to come back to me, he began. You know what I mean?

– No, said Gibney, flippantly.

– Look, I lost control at that meeting. I'm afraid of what I might say the next time. I might say something that could land you in jail. Do you know what I mean?

– No.

Chalkie tried again.

– I've got to do something about it. Do you understand what I'm talking about?

– Not really, answered the voice that was a blend of Dublin's streets and a hint of America.

– OK, let me be blunt. When you got into bed with me as a kid is now coming back to haunt you. Now do you understand me?

– Yes.

There was no act of contrition, no remorse. It seemed to Chalkie that nothing discommoded the man in the armchair across the room.

His attitude was that this was some sort of operational hitch that required to be addressed with an expedient solution.

– OK, I'll go to the World Championships in Australia and, when I come back, I'll resign as national coach and just concentrate on Trojans. Does that suit you?

Chalkie felt despair. 'That was a million times worse,' he recalls. 'Now he was going to spend all his time in the club where he had total power and access to lots of vulnerable kids. Besides, I thought we were going to have a discussion about what he did to me and how I could be helped to get over it. He left the house, and I was no better. A few days later I wrote a letter to the IASA saying I would take the coach's position going to the World Championships.'

And that was how Chalkie had been bound for Perth on St Stephen's Day, 1990. It was the reason too why he felt deeply pessimistic, despite Gary O'Toole's pledge to him on the plane. And it was why he spontaneously adopted a scatter-gun solution to the problem, in the belief that the more people he told, the more likely something would be done about George Gibney.

He says it was around eleven o'clock one morning during the World Championships when he spotted Dr Moira O'Brien, the IASA's and the Leinster branch's medical advisor, sitting alone at a café near the pool in Perth. As a professor of anatomy in Trinity College Dublin and an expert in sports medicine, she was widely respected in sports and medical circles. She had served as president of the IASA in 1982 and was friendly with George Gibney, having worked with him and five other contributors on an academic paper, 'A Study of Blood Lactate Profiles Across Different Swim Strokes', using a £4,000 lactate-testing machine supplied by BM Browne, a medical company in Sandyford, County Dublin. (The paper was listed on Gibney's curriculum vitae, under 'Published Work', without credit to his collaborators). When Trinity set up a master's degree in sports medicine, the university appointed Moira O'Brien Emeritus Professor of the course. Over the coming years, she would serve as president of the Osteoporosis Society and as a member of the State's Forum on Fluoridation. Chalkie approached her at the Perth poolside and asked to talk to her about something important. For the second time in a couple of weeks, he poured out the story of what George Gibney had done to him as a child.

He remembers that she advised him to put it behind him and get on with his life as it would be his word against Gibney's.

'I think the thing that had bothered me throughout my life was that I was going to die and nobody was going to find out about it.'

At the time, there was very little public knowledge of paedophilia; the climate was markedly different to the one that subsequently evolved, following successive child abuse scandals that raised public awareness of the crime and prompted the state and institutions to introduce guidelines for the handling of complaints. Seven years later, a state-appointed inquiry chaired by senior counsel Roderick Murphy recorded that Dr O'Brien (who is referred to in the inquiry report as the Honorary Medical Officer) maintained the conversation happened prior to departure for Perth, that Chalkie was 'confused, and emotionally unstable, as a result of a head injury', that he did not want her to report the matter and that a doctor-patient relationship existed. The report stated that Dr O'Brien was unaware of any other allegations of abuse until November 1994. Murphy concluded that there was 'no conflict of evidence in relation to the conversation' between Chalkie White and Moira O'Brien and that it had been governed by doctor-patient confidentiality.

Asked by the author to recount her recollection of the conversation, Moira O'Brien replied: 'I gave evidence at the Murphy

Tribunal and I have nothing further to add.'

By the end of the World Championships, Gibney had already left Australia, returning to Ireland prematurely without an explanation offered to the swimmers. Gary O'Toole headed for Sydney and a three-week holiday, staying with a cousin who lived there. His head was a jumble of disappointment over his performances in Perth and anxiety about what Chalkie had told him.

'I didn't really appreciate the awfulness of it at the time. My first concern was how this was going to affect me and my swimming,' he admits. 'I felt that Chalkie was ok because I knew he was getting some counselling.'

It was February 1991 by the time Gary got home. The World Student Games were looming, and the Olympics lay on the horizon beyond that. He went to see George Gibney and informed him that he was quitting his team of elite swimmers. For the national coach to lose the country's number one swimmer amounted to losing his *raison d'être*. Gibney wanted to know why.

'I think you know why,' Gary replied. He walked out the door and went to train with Triton Swimming Club based in the Presentation College in Bray. His new coaches were his father, Aidan, Alex Moraghan, whose son, Shane, was a water polo international, and Chalkie White. (Gary won gold in the 200 metres breaststroke at the World Student Games).

The story that he had deserted Gibney was the lead item in all the sports sections of the newspapers. 'I'm leaving because thirteen years is a long time with the same coach,' Gary told reporters, 'and my career needs a fresh input.'

Within days, George Gibney had resigned as national swimming coach. To the majority in the sport who remained unaware of the allegations of child sexual abuse, his resignation in the year before the Barcelona Olympics was bewildering, but no explanation was forthcoming from the sport's authorities. An impression was conveyed that he was simply taking temporary leave with the intention of returning reinvigorated for the Olympic Games in July 1992. More mystery was added when Gibney appeared on Bibi Baskin's chat show on RTE television, with Gary O'Toole as his fellow guest, and claimed that he had been inundated with offers of work abroad, but because he loved Ireland so much he did not intend leaving his homeland. He had gleaned endless column inches of positive publicity from his association with Baskin, the Irish-speaking Donegal native and TV personality-of-the-moment. After a lifetime of aquaphobia, it was Gibney who had finally taught her to swim, prompting a myriad of 'lifestyle' media features in the newspapers about conquering one's fear of water.

Gibney was replaced as national coach by his rival at King's Hospital, Derry O'Rourke. 'It was George who put Derry's name forward as national coach,' says Carole Walsh, an age-group swim coach who worked closely with Gibney in Trojans. 'I was in George's office when he was talking to Celia Millane [the IASA's PRO] on the phone and he mentioned Derry. He put the phone down and I said, "Nominating somebody who isn't as good as you, that's a good move – so when you want to go back you'll be able to say he isn't doing a good job". He said: "You're getting to know me very well."'

When the *Sunday Tribune* asked Chalkie White why he had not applied for the national coach's job, he replied: 'It's a whole lot of hassle and I'd have a part to play as a politician. People have to be manipulated and won over within the swimming association. There are too many people in the IASA interested in power, people who are working for themselves. Personally, I don't think it's worth it. My only interest is what goes on in the pool.'

After Gary walked out of Trojans, Gibney did an interview for a sports programme on Century Radio, Ireland's first licensed independent national station, in which he lambasted the young swimmer's performances in Perth, accusing him of allowing his love life to interfere with his swimming. The allegation was repeated in an article in the *Sunday Independent.*

Gary's parents, Kaye and Aidan O'Toole, were incensed at the vilification of their son, though they still did not know what was motivating Gibney's attacks. It would be nearly a year after the fateful flight to Perth before Gary would finally tell them what Chalkie had told him. On eventually hearing the full story, it triggered something in Aidan's memory about a swimming gala in Cork when Gary was nine. He had heard 'a commotion' during the night in the hotel where the swimmers were staying, but when he enquired about it the next morning he was assured there was nothing to worry about. Only later did he hear on the grapevine that 'there had been some incident' with one of the girl swimmers.

'I got legal advice from a solicitor about Gibney's outlandish accusations towards Gary and he said it would be very hard to prove a case against Gibney,' says Aidan O'Toole, himself a sports-complex manager who spent eighteen years coaching swimmers and eight years as a selector. It was Aidan who had first asked Gibney to take Gary on as one of his swimmers. 'I made a pledge when the boys were born that I would teach them to swim early. Gary took part in the Community Games when he was six or seven. The second year, he won the under-eights easily. Kaye used to save the children's allowance for the swimming costs. I thought George was a very good coach and very ambitious, but over the years he never gave us any favours, even though Gary was probably the best swimmer he ever had. In a way, his achievements probably gave Gibney even more power.'

On 15 February 1991, Aidan wrote to the secretary of the Irish Amateur Swimming Association, Mark Nicol, at the association's head office, House of Sport in Dublin, and copied it to all the IASA's office holders.

Dear Mark,

As a result of recent insinuations in national newspapers and on radio by former national coach Mr Gibney in relation to my son Gary's performances in and out of the swimming pool, I feel obliged, on behalf of my family, to write to the Executive regarding the situation rather than have a dirt-slinging confrontation in the newspapers, which would not help the Association. Despite the fact of having been offered a tidy sum of money for our side of the story by a national newspaper, we have decided to bring it to your notice first, and if no satisfactory reply is received, we are prepared to take the matter further without hesitation.

First and foremost, for someone only recently bestowed with life membership of the IASA, and maybe still on notice from his recent position when he resorted to the gutters, he should be ashamed of himself. Apart from the damage he has inflicted on Gary's sporting aspirations, he has done irreparable damage to his academic career for one studying Medicine and hoping to be dealing with the public in future years – and I am not prepared to let this go. I have enclosed copies of the various clippings from newspapers and I have a recording of the Century Radio interview. The references made on the radio surely bring the Association into disrepute by his assertions, insinuations and his blatant poaching on air.

Gibney infers that Gary was not committed. This is nonsense. He never missed training because of socialising. The number of functions he attended in the past eighteen months was minimal. At all of the functions he attended, he promoted swimming eloquently and the functions were:

People of the Year (for which Gibney connived his own nomination, already knowing that Gary had received several by bodies outside of swimming), Olympic Council of Ireland Ball, Texaco Awards and the Jury's/Independent Sports Star Awards – at all of these he was a great ambassador for the sport.

Regarding Gary's potential being over-exaggerated by the media – this is ridiculous. The fact that he had one of six fastest times ever recorded for the 200 metres breaststroke event in Paris last February plus any of his last two best times in a 50-metre pool would have made the final in Perth. However, on the day, this was not to be; unfortunately swimmers are not machines, they are human beings. This is where Gibney falls flat on his face. Nevertheless, Gibney had his own ideas – one week in Coventry without wave breakers and leaving ten days after most of the other top countries was his solution for the perfect preparation. Or maybe Gibney thought the £40,000 spent on the camp in Australia the previous year would help them settle in quicker for the World Championships this year. Despite the obvious drawbacks of a bout of pneumonia and final exams at UCD which also lessened his condition, Gibney makes this sweeping statement even though he decided himself to cut back on training by one morning because of his over-crowded pool.

His own ability to play one swimmer against another – and the same applies to officials and coaches, as you all know well – and having experienced his interference (in the wrong) with team selections over the years, which I can prove as a selector, is a disaster for everyone, especially the ones who allow themselves to be manipulated. Gibney also commented on transfers of swimmers and clubs poaching his swimmers when they were down; this is scurrilous as his own club, over the years, has taken more swimmers than any other club. So the theory is: it's alright for Trojans, but not any other club; rough isn't it? Yet two of his swimmers went to Kings Hospital and then in the next breath he approves Derry O'Rourke as one of the top coaches. What does he want? Gibney also intimated he had decided to step aside for a few months from the national scene to allow some gombeen take over until the dust settles and then the Messiah would return for the Olympics – a lovely gesture by him. His failure to deal with swimmers as adults is obvious and his failure to communicate with them speaks for itself; like it or not, his credibility is at an all-time low now. The only ones that respond to him are the kiddies because they know no better.

The most recent embarrassment of when Gibney turned up on an invitation for the President (of the IASA) and guest at a function to honour Gary's achievements in Paris last year was appalling to say the least, after his antics. The audacity of him to turn up after his mud-slinging story the previous day was unbelievable. Thankfully, both Jury's and Independent Newspapers were most apologetic about the situation and quite rightly pointed out there was no invitation for Gibney from either party. They obviously thought it was Mr & Mrs Budd [IASA president Doreen Budd] who were attending as indicated by the table arrangements and card placings. One observant journalist attending the awards pointed out that Gibney had more titles in the last two years than Sugar Ray Leonard, but even he thought Mr Budd or Mrs Ferguson [Malcolm Ferguson was a British coach employed by the IASA] was a bit much on this occasion. Then again, some people will go to any lengths to stay in the limelight.

The one rewarding aspect of Gary's achievements is that he is much more appreciated outside the swimming fraternity, and only as recent as Tuesday the Minister for Sport, Mr Frank Fahey, singled him out in an RTE radio interview as one of the leading sportspersons in this country getting support from the Government.

Both of Gary's main sponsors are very concerned about the portrayal of the sport at the moment by Gibney and his nasty tactics. The sponsors know it is sour grapes but are still concerned about the image of swimming and the general disarray since the 1988 Olympics issue, which was initiated by him telling swimmers there were going to the Olympics. If his sponsors withdraw their commitments to Gary maybe this would give Gibney some satisfaction, because at present he doesn't know the difference between the lies and the truth.

Finally, the only thing Gibney has going for him at present is his imagination which is second to none and obviously mesmerising to the ones who are prepared to sit back and accept it. Gibney is not a man, he is a wimp, and cannot operate without his little support groups backing him. The facts of his latest assertions speak for themselves; his radio interview is full of contradictions and falsifications. By the way, the reference to the former national coach as 'Gibney' is purposely done as, in recent radio interviews, he referred to Gary as 'O'Toole', which indicates what an ignorant little man he is. Or maybe I should have allowed for his memory lapses. Gary had been going out with his girlfriend prior to his European silver medal performance. Furthermore, we have never made a secret of the fact, either to Cospóir [the State sports agency] or anyone else, that his academic career is the most important at the end of the day and if he had to sacrifice some sessions, so be it; the system doesn't allow a European Silver Medalist [to] take an Honours Degree in Biochemistry on his sporting achievements.

If necessary, we are prepared to discuss any of the contents of this letter with the Executive if you feel any points need clarification or explanation. We do not take pleasure in resorting to these measures but we were left with no other option after his outbursts.

Yours in sport,
Aidan O'Toole.

A meeting was arranged between IASA president Doreen Budd,

secretary Mark Nicol and executive member Pat Dunford on one side and Aidan and Kaye O'Toole on the other side. It took place in the Ashling Hotel near Heuston train station, the customary venue for Leinster Branch meetings. It concluded with the resolution that Derry O'Rourke would act as a go-between to seek a formal apology from Gibney for the O'Toole family. No official letter emanated from the IASA on foot of the meeting and the entire episode ultimately petered out when O'Rourke told Aidan O'Toole, upon encountering him by chance at a gala, that Gibney had refused to say sorry.

Throughout this period, Chalkie was confiding in other people, including various officials of the IASA, its Leinster Branch, and his own club, Glenalbyn. He phoned Frank McCann, 'a serious mover and shaker in swimming' as president of the Leinster Branch, and asked for a meeting. McCann, who lived in Butterfield Avenue, Rathfarnham, suggested his local pub, The Morgue in Templeogue. 'When I told him, he seemed very supportive and he said he'd get something done about it,' says Chalkie. 'I had many conversations with him about it after, but there was no progress.'

Chalkie chose his confidante more judiciously when he dialled Carole Walsh's number one Thursday night and began: 'I've something to tell you.' They had first met on a training course for coaches in Newpark and had remained friends. Now Carole was working with George Gibney in Newpark where she was responsible for the age-group squad, the next level below the elite swimmers coached by Gibney. Carole was coaching two of Gibney's three children and her own sons were members in Newpark too. She frequently went to Gibney's home in Killiney for meetings and had become friendly with his wife, Brona, a special-needs nurse. 'I thought he was God,' she says. 'He was completely obsessive about swimming. He was really powerful. All around him were Leinster and Irish swimmers.'

For nearly an hour, Carole listened to Chalkie on the phone. He wept as he told her his story. Afterwards, her husband, Michael, came into the kitchen in their north Dublin home and found her sitting at the table, 'devastated'. She told him that Chalkie had told her he had been sexually abused by George Gibney when he was a child and that he was probably doing it to other children still.

– It's strange, I know, but I believe him, she said.

– You must report it, but there are a few things you have to think about, Carole, her husband warned.

Her first priority, Michael said, had to be their two sons who were swimmers at Newpark. 'George had invited one of the boys to stay over-night in his house three different times to save him getting up early in the morning to be at the pool. The only thing that saved him was that he never liked to sleep over in anybody's house. He was a real worrier. He didn't like to be away from home,' says Carole.

'There were some amazingly handsome boys and beautiful girls in swimming and George was very manipulative. If you were in bad form on the bank, he had the ability to change your mood. Some days he would be real intense. Some days, he wouldn't talk to you. I saw him in regular contact with boys and girls. He was very good at discovering their personal weaknesses. I'd never seen him do anything improper but it all made sense to me. The manipulation, the patronage ... it all fitted.

'He always had a smell of BO. I hated that. He could have a shower and two minutes later he would be smelling again. He seldom used bad language. Only once did I ever see him drink and then it was red wine and he was utterly indiscreet about Irish swimming. It was in Italy at an EC (European Community) club championship.

'He could actually be a very funny man. On that Italian trip – it was to Turin – the Italian men's team was staying in the same hotel as us. When we went downstairs in the morning, there was no food for breakfast, but then the Italian team came down – they were all in the Italian army and they looked fantastic in their military uniforms marching down the stairs – there was no shortage of food for them. They had whatever they wanted. When we got to the pool, there was a coaches' meeting on the deck. Orjan Madsen, the German coach, who's actually from Sweden and has a huge reputation in swimming – he wrote the definitive book on age-group coaching – he asked George: "How are things?" "Well," said George, "not good. We got no breakfast in our hotel, but then the Italian team came down and were fed royally so we're going home." So Orjan goes: "You know, this has been one of the worst organised events. Let's say we're all leaving." They called over the main organiser and George says: "We just want you to know Ireland is going home." And Orjan goes: "So is Germany." And the English coach goes: "So's England." They begged us not to leave. The next thing, down through all the tiers of seating around the pool come all these waiters carrying huge platters of bread rolls, ham, cheese, boiled eggs and cases of orange juice.'

After the phone call from Chalkie, Carole and her husband made a decision to withdraw their children from Trojans.

– Why, Mam? asked the thirteen-year-old when they told the boys, – Is it because of what George has been doing with the girls?

They left the club immediately.

'After Chalkie told me, I talked to my father about it. I went to confession and asked the priest what I should do. He said, "You can't go to the police without proof."'

'I rang the ISPCC (Irish Society for the Prevention of Cruelty to Children) and they told me to contact Great Ormond Street Children's Hospital in London because they had literature about child abuse. A friend of mine was a nurse there and she got it for me. I didn't know what to do. I rang Opus Dei because there were always rumours that George was involved with them and I even tried ringing one of the bishops for advice, but I couldn't get through. Even though I absolutely believed Chalkie I thought it was strange that he'd want to work so closely with the man who abused him, but I later discussed it with psychologists who said it was typical behaviour of a victim who often ran for approval to the abuser because of personal feelings of guilt. They said that abusers often encourage those feelings of guilt in their victims. I don't think I smiled for two years after that phone call from Chalkie. It was awful. It was actually really scary. My thoughts were filled with it. Imagine, and I wasn't even one of his victims.'

Carole phoned Frank McCann, the Leinster Branch president, and asked him to meet her.

– What's it about? he asked.

– It's about George abusing kids.

He suggested lunch in a pub beside the Ashling Hotel. They met in March 1991. Carole told him about Chalkie. McCann said that stories about Gibney had been circulating for years, but nothing could be done about them because nobody was willing to make a formal accusation. Carole said she was also worried about one of her own swimmers in Newpark who was suffering from a severe eating disorder and had threatened to kill herself. She said she suspected the girl was exhibiting symptoms of sexual abuse.

– Don't get involved, he warned Carole. And I hope to fuck the story doesn't break while I'm president.

On a Leinster trip to England, Carole was seated beside a man involved in swimming on a train from Holyhead up to London.

– You're not yourself, the man remarked to the junior Leinster coach. What's the matter?

– I heard something that's really upset me, she told him, and I don't know what to do about it. I heard that George has been abusing kids.

– Who told you?

– Chalkie.

– Do you believe him? the man asked.

– Yeah.

– Have you said it to anyone else?

– Yeah, but they don't want to know.

– Well, I'd rather not get involved either, he said.

Back in Newpark, Carole repeated Chalkie's story about Gibney to a member of both the IASA and the Leinster executives and sought advice about how to pursue it.

– I'm telling you it's not true, replied the other woman. Chalkie White had a terrible accident in Switzerland. It's left him brain-damaged. He's ranting and raving.

The spin was working.

'I think George's objective in leaving Perth early had been to put the story around at home that Chalkie's gone crazy. Attack being the best form of defence,' Chalkie believes.

That spring, Chalkie arrived at the Irish Short Course Championships in Athlone. 'I walked in. The place was packed. Nobody spoke to me. Sorry, Carole Walsh was the only one who said "Hello" to me. The word was out that I wanted to get rid of George and become national coach. People I thought of as friends ignored me. I never felt so ostracised in my life. I began to hear: "Chalkie's going crazy. Ever since his accident" …'

The Barcelona Olympics concluded on 9 August 1992 with a spectacular closing ceremony. Ireland was *en fête* to welcome home two of its boxers, Michael Carruth and Wayne McCullough, bearing gold and silver medals, respectively. Their triumphs in the ring had cushioned the disappointment when the country's best medal hope, Gary O'Toole, failed to get beyond the qualifying heats in the pool. The country's top female swimmer, twenty-two-year-old Michelle Smith from King's Hospital, fared no better, under the wing of Derry O'Rourke, her club coach and Ireland's Olympic coach. Having, curiously, been denied a State sports grant in the year of the Olympics, the best Gary managed was twentieth in the race he was favoured to take a medal in, the 200-metres breast-stroke. On RTÉ television's dedicated Olympics programme, resident swimming panelist George Gibney denounced him with almost gleeful vitriol. Reiterating the slur that his former protégé was not committed to swimming, he pronounced that Gary's career had gone downhill since quitting his coaching and that he should never have been chosen to compete in the Olympics.

Gary returned to Ireland on 10 August. 'It was a sad day for me. I was in a terrible mood,' he later told his friend, the sports writer Paul Kimmage. 'The thought of having to do what I had put off since splitting with Gibney after Perth was sickening. If I had won a medal at the games, or even performed well, I'm sure it would have been easier, but for eight days I just moped about the place feeling sorry for myself. Every night I was out on the town, drinking too much and doing anything to escape reality. And then, when I did knuckle down, I just didn't know where to start.'

In fact, it suited Gary's purpose to arrive back in Ireland as an anonymous also-ran, edged out of the spotlight by the two champion boxers. Privacy was what he needed as he prepared to keep his promise to Chalkie. He began making phone calls and writing letters, cross-checking names and relevant dates and acquiring contact details for boys and girls who used to swim for Gibney.

'There was one girl who no longer lived in Dublin. I got her address from her mother. I wrote her a letter and I put another sealed letter inside it. I said I was writing about something "that might have happened to you when you were a young swimmer in Trojans. If you don't know what I'm talking about, don't open the second letter". She rang me a few months later. She'd already started the process as a result. She'd been to the guards.

'I went to the place of work of another girl. I said to her: "This isn't a social visit". She said: "OK". She knew. Another girl I went to see in her home … she was anorexic. She said: "No, no, nothing ever happened to me". I felt not everyone was able to talk about it. I approached men too. There were men I thought it could have happened to. After all, he'd tried to get into my bed when I was eleven. I met the men and asked them straight out. I said he'd abused males as well. They all shook their heads and said "no". Do I believe them? Not all of them, no.'

When he pressed the doorbell at one of the first houses he visited, he was lifting the lid on a Pandora's Box in Irish swimming. The man who opened the door to him in the neon glow that winter's night required no introductions. Nor did he wait for his visitor to ask to see his wife. 'We've been expecting you,' said the husband, standing aside to let Gary pass. 'She's in the kitchen. Come in.'

4. The Swimmers' Stories

It is common for people who have been sexually abused as children not to report the crime until they are adults, if ever. In some cases, this stems from denial, the human mind's extraordinary capacity to block out memories too distressing to recall, but it is not the only reason. The destruction of a child's faith in figures of authority is one obvious consequence of bodily invasion by an adult, usually somebody they once trusted or whom the social norms dictated they ought to respect. There are parallels, for instance, between the scandals of child sex abuse by Catholic priests around the world and the decline in orthodox, unquestioning religiosity. The crime of child sexual abuse is predicated on complex psychological weaponry. International studies show again and again that abusers exhibit a Jekyll and Hyde duality in their make up. They flatter to exploit. They lie to maximise opportunity. They promise the sun, moon and stars before reducing their victims to mere conduits for their own gratification. They employ the silent treatment to lure them into submission. They seldom have need of physical coercion as the multiplicity of emotional injuries to the child or adolescent provides safe cover. Fear of the abuser, the pain of betrayal by an adult, feelings of guilt or shame at the pleasure of sexual stimulation, the confused equating of sex with love, the acceptance of responsibility for the abuse, the damage done to family communication, the requirement to live a lie and the impulse to protect loved ones from the knowledge of what is happening all create a shield of immunity for the abuser. The more an abuser knows about his potential victim, the more he can manipulate the young person into behaviour conducive to his motives. By putting distance between his victim and his victim's family, he turns himself into the sole reliable adult in the young person's life. He is a master of emotional blackmail. These conditions collude to make it virtually impossible for the young person to confide in anyone else, thus enabling the abuse to continue for many years, even into adulthood. The effect on the abused person can be a failure to recognise the abuse as abusive. The psychological dynamics of the crime leave the victim feeling powerless while rendering the abuser omnipotent.

George Gibney had the cunning and the power to facilitate his crimes over three decades. He had daily access to an abundance of young people who believed he could make them champions, who craved his approval, who were often in a state of semi-dress and undress and whose parents trusted him to look after them. Shooting fish in a barrel could not have been simpler. The story of Swimmer One encapsulates the classic trap.

SWIMMER ONE (Abused by George Gibney from 1979 to 1986)

I started swimming at Newpark when I was eight years of age and I joined Trojans when I was thirteen. My coach was George Gibney. He had encouraged me while I was swimming for another club. When we used to leave the club after training in the mornings, which was around 7.30, I would leave either by going through the pool way or by the corridor. George always seemed to be waiting, no matter which way I went out. He would kiss me on the lips. I was very drawn to him and I was flattered with all the attention he was giving me. When we were going to competitions, I would travel with George sometimes. He would hold my hand. The kissing got more frequent. I was thirteen when it first happened.

One day, I had a training session on my own. George was coaching me. I was standing on the starting block and he said: 'I'm going to get into bed with you this weekend'. We were going abroad with the Trojan team. When we went, we stayed in a hotel. I was in a room on my own. George came into my room. He pulled back the bed-covers, having undressed down to his underpants. I knew I wasn't happy with this. I said, 'George', and he said, 'Don't worry'.

I hadn't a clue what to do. He lay on top of me and told me to come on. I still didn't know what he wanted. Eventually, I lifted my hips and he said: 'I love when you do that'. He kept thrusting on top of me. I can't remember whether he ejaculated or not as I was not aware what was supposed to happen. I remember thinking, 'When will he stop?'

The same pattern of events occurred on other trips for the next three years. They occurred either in his car or in his hotel rooms. It started happening at home, then.

George discouraged close friendships between club members and did not like members being overly friendly with people outside the club. He disliked members dating one another or even dating anyone outside the club. I used to baby-sit for him and his wife during these years. I always stayed overnight as I was in bed by 9.15 pm in order to get up at 4.50 am for training. On numerous occasions after that first trip abroad, George would come into my room during the night. He would kiss me and undo my nightdress and generally get himself all worked up. He would then leave and come back later on when himself and his wife had gone to bed. He would wake me up and undress completely in front of me. He would get in on top of me in the bed. There was never any foreplay. He would kiss me on my face, lips and neck and fondle my breasts and touch me a lot. He would grope at my vagina with his fingers and his penis. He would thrust on top of me and come on my tummy on occasions. He was always very careful not to penetrate as I would stiffen up and call his name. I often said, when he came into the room: 'George, what about Brona?' or 'No, George'. He would reply: 'It's alright, she's asleep', or 'Don't worry'. He would always smile.

The next morning, he would come into my room around 4.20 to get me up for training and say to me: 'Come down for breakfast'. I would go down in my nightdress. There was no breakfast, and when I went into the kitchen he would start kissing me and, within seconds, I was on the floor on my back. He would take off my knickers and lay down on top of me. He would do exactly the same as the night before. Sometimes when he came in to wake me he would tell me to come down without my knickers on. I would hate the thought of going down and facing what was ahead. He would often tell me that he loved me. I was afraid of him and completely controlled by him.

During this time, a similar pattern of events to these incidents happened in his office, at the pool, in the library at Newpark Comprehensive School, at night or at weekends, in the school before training commenced, in his car going to competitions or going to UCD gym. He would always drive me. He often took me out of school in the afternoon and would take me up the mountains or to his house. We had oral sex a few times a week from when I was fourteen.

One night when he collected me from my house to baby-sit for them, he drove into the car park of a hospital. It was dark. He pushed my seat back. He took off my jeans and knickers under protest. He did not seem to notice that I was protesting. He knelt in front of me and proceeded to penetrate me with his tongue. I was pushing his head away and saying no. I was very annoyed and did not speak to him on the way to his house in Killiney. His house was not far from the hospital. George and Brona went out and, after I had gone to bed, there was a knock at the door. I answered it and it was the Gardaí. Someone in the hospital had reported seeing George's car and had given the Gardaí the registration number. I can't remember what I told them. When George came home that evening, he came up to my bedroom as usual. I told him about the guards calling. He laughed and thought it was hilarious. He kissed me and went off to bed.

I did my Leaving Cert when I was sixteen, but I did not get the subject I needed for my career choice. It was George who arranged for me to repeat my Leaving in another school. He took a copy of my timetable and he knew when I had free classes. Often when I had a free class, he would arrange for his house to be free. He would bring me there and bring me up to his and Brona's bedroom. He would have the electric blanket on. We would both undress and get into bed. I did not enjoy it.

When I finished the Leaving, George helped me get my first job. It was a live-in situation for the first year there. I never went out with my work colleagues because George refused to let me. At this stage, I was seventeen. George was obsessed with me and told me always that he loved me. Since I was fourteen, he had been getting me to write love letters to him. If they weren't to his satisfaction, he would get me to re-write them. When I was sixteen, my mother found two notes: one written by me and the other written by George expressing our mutual love. My dad confronted me and kept me out of swimming. They confronted George but, afterwards, I was allowed to continue swimming again. I wrote him a note explaining why, for the sake of my family, it had to end. George read the note and came into the girls' dressing room where I was crying and started kissing and groping me. I was in my swimming togs.

About a year earlier, when I was fifteen, his wife, Brona, found a note written by me to George in his pocket. She rang me up hysterical, accusing me of breaking up her marriage. She hung up. I told George what had happened and he just laughed it off and told me he had sorted it out.

He would not let me wear make-up unless I was going out with him. George met my parents at competitions and my parents were very impressed with the attention he was giving me. Over a period of time, he got to know my parents very well; going out to dinner with them and coming to our house for dinner. My parents presented him with some silver to thank him for my swimming achievements. At the same time, he was trying to distance me from my family by discouraging me from going on family holidays with them or even nights out or just talking about them.

I remember one incident which was very early on in the relationship. He called to our house. My mother went out of the sitting room to make tea. George got up out of the armchair he was sitting on and came over to the sofa where I was sitting, stooped down and started kissing me. He scarpered when he heard noises from the kitchen. I remember another incident which occurred when I was fifteen. I was in bed sick. George came to visit me. Mum went off to make the tea. Immediately Mum left the bedroom, George started kissing me while pulling back the bed-covers. I insisted he stop. He did stop, but treated it like a joke.

At around the same age – when I was fifteen or sixteen – he met me and, as usual, was groping and kissing me. He told me he had to collect a relation of Brona's. I think it might have been her mother. I went with him, but I couldn't be seen with him so George suggested that I get into the boot of his car, which was a Renault Fuego. I got into the boot and hid there until he dropped her off. He thought this was a great achievement.

All these things – and many more – were happening until I was twenty. By then, I was settled in my job. Five of my friends were going on a sun holiday abroad. They were encouraging me to go, but George wouldn't let me. Two weeks before the date of departure, I made up my mind that I was going and nobody was going to stop me. I told George and he was absolutely furious. After a couple of days, he calmed down, but he began putting psychological pressure on me by telling me how much he loved me and that he couldn't live without me; that he would kill himself without me. He insisted on leaving me to the bus for the airport and collecting me and was full of expectation of the night we would spend together in a hotel when I returned. In his own words, he wanted 'to see my white parts and to make sure I didn't go topless'. He sent a bouquet of flowers to the apartment in Cyprus and got me to ring him every day. When we returned home, he brought me to Jury's Hotel and booked us into a room. I was determined not to cooperate with him because I had had two weeks' freedom away from him and had begun to realise that I had a life of my own and didn't have to live his life. I had also fallen in love with a man I met on holidays.

The night in Jury's was a disaster for him because I did not cooperate in any way with his sexual antics. He got very mad. I convinced him I was too tired. He dropped me near my home the next morning. After that, he was convinced there was another man. Every day, he would wait for me in the car park at my work place. He was very mad and would threaten to kill himself. He eventually found out from me about my boyfriend and he became very violent. I was afraid of what he might do to me. One day, he grabbed me roughly and I thumped him. I told him to bring me home and he did. But he still continued to follow me around for a long time after that.

* * *

The accounts below, given by Swimmer Two and her sister, dispel any doubts that other children would have been saved from predation by George Gibney if those who knew or suspected what he was doing had taken action.

Swimmer Two (Abused by George Gibney from 1973 to 1977)

I started attending Saturday morning swimming classes at Glenalbyn in 1973. George Gibney was one of the coaches there. I progressed to competitive swimming and George Gibney was our coach. Classes were early in the morning and sometimes in the evenings. I was eleven years old. George called to collect me at my house on a number of occasions where he met my mother.

I was considered George's pet. One night I was in the dressing rooms in the club, cleaning them. I was on my own as my friend was sick. George Gibney came into the dressing rooms and started kissing me. He didn't do anything else at that stage. He did not tell me not to say anything.

After that incident, a series of sexual assaults occurred. They mostly took place in his car. At other times, they took place in his house. They happened regularly. He got me to kiss his genitals and he kissed mine.

In 1975, when I was thirteen years old, my parents went on holidays in the summer. George asked my mother if I could stay in his house while they were gone. My father did not approve, but my mother agreed that I could stay. He would come up to the bedroom where I was staying to say good night. He got into the bed, but I don't think a whole lot happened. His wife Brona would be in the house and he would get me to fondle his genitals and he would fondle mine. There were also occasions when I was in his house and his wife would be in the house and he would have me on his knee and get me to fondle him. He always wore loose tracksuits so this was possible.

On some occasions, George took me back to his house during the day, when his wife was not there. Then he would take me up to his bedroom. Nearly always, he would get me to perform oral sex on him and he would do the same to me. One occasion stands out in my mind. I had spoken to a girl friend in school about what was happening and she took me up to a priest in the Marist Fathers in Milltown. I told the priest what was happening and he told me to go back to the man and tell him to stop what he was doing. After training one day in Newpark I told him what the priest had said. He slapped me across the face twice and called me a whore. There was nobody else there at the time. The abuse stopped for a while and he ignored me during training. He wouldn't even talk to me.

When I was asked out on a date for the first time, George put a stop to it. He called me into his office and told me that he heard that this boy had kissed me. He told me to stay away from him and the other boys because all they wanted was to get me into bed. So I stayed away from them because, at this stage, I was terrified of George.

On another occasion, George took me to his house in Killiney. His wife Brona was not there. He took me up to his bedroom and got me to perform oral sex on him. This was in 1975 or 1976. At this stage I knew what was expected of me. He put his hands on my head and pushed my head down to his penis. I nearly always gagged when he did this. When the oral sex was finished, he fell asleep. I got dressed and went downstairs. I was upset and, later, when he came down, he caught me crying. He asked me what was wrong. I said something about not feeling well. I was too afraid to tell him anything else. He made no comment. He was getting more repulsive to me. I hated him doing anything. I was about thirteen, going on fourteen, at this stage. On another occasion, he took me into his office and told me to strip off. He had brought some swimming togs back from Canada for me.

On numerous occasions when I was in his car (he would be dropping me home or taking me to his house or going training), he would get me to perform oral sex on him. While this was happening, he continued to drive. Nearly always, he would ejaculate in my mouth and hold my head down on him so that I would have to swallow. I remember he used a lot of talc because I always tasted it in my mouth after oral sex.

The last incident I clearly remember occurred in 1977. I think it was March, a few months before my Inter Certificate. I was nearly fifteen years of age. It happened in the evening. We were on our own in Newpark swimming pool. He was locking up and he brought me into the sauna. He tried to force his penis into my vagina. I don't know whether he actually achieved this or not. He kept telling me to help him put it in. I kept saying, 'I can't, it's hurting me'. I imagine that he did succeed in putting it in because I was extremely sore. He eventually stopped. After this, he drove me home. On the way home, he asked me was I very sore and if I had a burning feeling. I said I was and he told me not to worry and that it would go after a while. He was quite stern, as if he was annoyed with me.

The next day, there was a gala in Newpark and I avoided him as much as I possibly could. I was in the girls' dressing rooms, chatting to the girls. When his wife came to the door. She beckoned at me to come out to her. She walked on ahead of me and went straight into

George's office and I followed her in. She told me that George had told her what happened last night and that I was to go and see a priest and ask for forgiveness and not to let boys be interfering with me [it is not clear exactly what Gibney told Brona]. She opened the door and let me walk out. I didn't appear in Newpark for about a week or two. Both George and Brona phoned the house and spoke to me. They told me not to let what happened interfere with my swimming and that they would like me to continue swimming.

I went back because the club was going to Holland. I went on that trip, but I had no further bad experiences with George. Shortly after that, I left the club and I have not seen him since.

* * *

The following account by Swimmer Two's sister demonstrates the lack of public awareness in the late 1970s that child sexual abuse was a crime requiring intervention by the State's authorities. The prevailing mindset was that it was something best sorted privately. While that societal attitude has changed, the abject failure of the criminal justice system to successfully prosecute the majority of these crimes has seriously undermined public confidence in the proper channels. The consequences of doing it yourself, as George Gibney's abuse record shows, can be devastating.

Sister of Swimmer Two

Our family came to know George Gibney when my younger sister started swimming at Glenalbyn. He coached her team. Every child that swam there seemed to adore him, my sister included. He would sometimes call around to our house and ask her to baby-sit and she would do so at the drop of a hat. No one thought anything of it. Our parents weren't really close to George Gibney and I remember my father didn't particularly take to him. On one occasion George called to the house when my sister was sick and went up to her room. The two of them were alone up there for some time until my father asked my mother to call him down for a cup of tea.

I am ten years older than my sister. I first realised something was wrong about the relationship between George and her in 1977, when she was fifteen. One of my other sisters told me she had asked her about George kissing her and could she get pregnant. My older sister and I discussed it and we agreed together that we would confront George. We decided not to tell our parents. This was in or around May 1977, just before our younger sister's Inter Cert exams. We did not tell her what we were about to do.

We went to Newpark, where George was coaching, on a Tuesday at lunchtime. We asked to see him and he brought us into his office. I broached the subject first. I said: "I believe you are interfering with ————— sexually." George was sitting on the side of his desk. He was silent for a few seconds. Then he said: "It's over. It's finished." He said he was upset and disturbed and that he had been either to nuns or priests nearby about it. As he said this, he took a medal of some sort and a religious relic with a picture on it out of his pocket and held them in his hand. He seemed very sorry for what he had done to our sister. I remarked that she could get pregnant. My older sister said if our father ever found out that he would kill George. She said if he gave us his word that he would never touch our sister again we would not tell our parents. Then we left his office.

I was surprised that he did not deny the accusation. As far as I was concerned, it was over and finished. I did not realise the extent of the abuse at the time. I did not tell my sister about our meeting. She was about to do her exams. I did not realise that other children had been abused too. I only became aware of this in or around January 1993. I am annoyed with myself that I didn't do more at the time to protect my sister and the others. After she did her exams that year, she concentrated less on her swimming. Eventually she left the club.

5. 'Fatal Fire Investigated'

Experts from the Garda Technical Bureau are still examining the Dublin house in which a mother and baby girl died when it caught fire early yesterday.

They are trying to establish the cause of the fire at 39 Butterfield Avenue in Rathfarnham. The deceased were named yesterday as Mrs Esther McCann (30) and her 18-month-old daughter, Jessica. Mrs McCann's husband, Frank, is thought to have discovered the blaze when he returned from work. He was taken to the Meath Hospital after attempting to rescue his family but was discharged later.

A Bord Gáis spokeswoman said a technician had gone to the house at the request of the fire brigade but that gas had been eliminated as a cause of the fire.

(Page 4, *The Irish Times*, Saturday September 5, 1992).

If Gary O'Toole returned from the Barcelona Olympics with a mission to expose George Gibney's secret criminal life, Frank McCann too came back to Dublin driven with purpose, though his was more sinister. Double-murder was what the president of the Leinster Branch of the Irish Amateur Swimming Association had in mind. His motive was not complicated. Esther, his wife of five years, and Jessica, the little girl they were trying to adopt, had become an inconvenience. They would go to their deaths unaware that they had got in the way of his sexual proclivity for teenage girls.

Like his colleagues, George Gibney and Derry O'Rourke, McCann had cultivated a false persona. He was not at all what he seemed. Outwardly, as a non-drinker and a non-smoker with an exemplary work ethic, he lived the quintessential clean life, almost to the point of Puritanism. To those who knew him through swimming, however, he was a jovial character, with a ready answer for everything and a streak of arrogance. Tall, thin and bespectacled, his stern appearance was softened by a persuasive articulacy.

He was born in 1960, one of four sons with an adopted sister, Jeanette, the youngest. In his early years, the family home was one of the Guinness-owned cottages in Manor Estate, Fernhill Road. The house was a perk of his father Frank Senior's job as a cooper in the James' Gate brewery, where he had followed his own father before him into a livelihood of barrel-making for the famous stout. When the family traded up to Wainsfort Road in Terenure, Frank Junior attended secondary school at Templeogue College, a Holy Ghost Fathers' sister school of Rockwell College boarding school in Tipperary and St Mary's, Blackrock and St Michael's fee-paying schools in Dublin. Templeogue College, which subscribed to the motto, '*In virtute scientia*', 'Education Rooted in Values', had a reputation for excelling in sport.

After sitting his Leaving Cert in Templeogue, McCann followed his father and his grandfather into Guinness where he was the company's last apprentice cooper. Ready access to the company swimming pool, where George Gibney had started his coaching career nearly fifteen years earlier, nurtured his talent as a swimmer. He had been a member of Terenure club's 4 x 100m freestyle sprint relay team in the late 1970s. With his wiry physique, McCann was a strong swimmer and competed internationally before turning his attentions to coaching. He occasionally trained the Irish A squad as a stand-in coach. When he was let go by Guinness in the grim economic climate of 1982, he and a more experienced colleague set up their own company; Woodland Coopers Limited produced ornamental barrels designed for use as garden plant holders in a small factory in Greenhills industrial estate near the Naas Road. It was not long in business when McCann bought out his partner for £9,000, but soon after the factory was extensively damaged by a suspicious fire. Traces of an inflammable substance were found in the aftermath and a full investigation was launched. No one was ever charged with deliberately starting the fire. Nor was the insurance ever paid out. McCann eventually sold the company for IR£92,000; more than ten times what it had cost him to purchase his partner's half of it.

In November 1991, he entered into another business partnership, this time with his brother, Bert. They bought a pub called the Mary Rose in Blessington, west Wicklow; Frank drawing on the proceeds from the sale of Woodland Coopers. They renamed it The Cooperage in a genuflection to the trade of their forebears. But events were already in train to upend this new order too.

Esther O'Brien had come to live in Dublin in the mid-1970s. She was a vital, vivacious and intelligent woman. Her sister, Marian Leonard, who was older by two years, describes her as 'cherubic looking, with big brown eyes and an open, innocent face'. The sisters grew up in Talbot Place, in the centre of Tramore, County Waterford. Their father, Thomas, a native of the seaside town, was employed by CIE, the state-owned public transport company. Their mother, also named Esther but known by her second name, Brigid, hailed from a farm in Fenor, outside Tramore. She was working as the manager of a general provisions store in Tramore when she met her husband and continued to work there after the birth of her first child, Phyllis, who would grow up to be a nun, ascending to the position of director of the Marist Order in Rome. When her second child, a son, Pat, was born seven years after Phyllis, Brigid gave up her job to rear her family full-time.

It was an idyllic childhood for Marian and the baby of the family, Esther, who was born on March 29, 1956. The girls went to school at the Sisters of Charity in Tramore and spent the long summer holidays swimming in the sea and, later, joining the local surf club. In the 1960s, Tramore was a popular destination for family holidays with its long strand and fairground amusements. It was a nice place to grow up.

'Phyllis was eleven years older than me. She entered the Marist Convent in Carrick-on-Shannon when she was only seventeen years old. It meant that in those early years Esther and I could only see her on our monthly expeditions when Dad drove the family on what seemed like an endless journey across Ireland. The sad silence in the car on the journey home was unnatural for us two chatterboxes. Esther was angelic. She had big brown eyes and olive skin. She was open and innocent looking. By contrast, I was freckled with an unruly mop of hair. When there was mischief, I was the one who always got in trouble. It was always "What are you up to?" and "Mind your little sister". We spent a lot of our time causing problems for our big brother, Pat. It must have been hard for him having to contend with the two of us! Esther was great fun, absolutely cracked, so full of life and laughter. People gravitated to her. If she went to a party, she'd know everyone by the time she left. She had a great eye for people who might feel left out and she would involve them – sometimes whether they wanted to be involved or not. It wasn't something she did consciously. She just did it. She was the essence of a people person. Through school, she always had loads of friends. She was very bright and she did very well academically. There wasn't a bit of badness or malice in her. She always saw the good in people.'

In 1973, Marian moved to Dublin to join the civil service. Within two weeks, her father died. Her husband-to-be, Billy Leonard, accompanied her home and supported her through that period of loss. They married six months later, on September 8, and set up their first home in a flat in Cabra. Esther did her Leaving Cert exams and moved in with the couple while she studied psychology at UCD for two years. 'She'd bring fellow students back with her if they were in need of food, a bed or even a wash. Billy and I were saving to buy a house, but possessions came a poor second to people for Esther. That was a trait that never changed.'

After college, Esther landed a job as banqueting manager in the five-star Shelbourne Hotel on St Stephen's Green, 'Dublin's best address' according to its stationery, but she felt unfulfilled by it and signed up for a word-processing training course on Greenhills Road. She had a natural aptitude for the burgeoning computer skills sector and, at a time when serpentine dole queues were an intrinsic part of the Irish landscape, she was never without a job. She worked as a technology adviser to MJ Flood office supplies, the multinationals IBM and Nexus, and the accountant Bernard Somers, a future director of the Central Bank. She was independent, happy and popular.

Then along came Frank McCann.

Esther had been going out with a long-term boyfriend who decided in 1986, as many others of their generation did, to emigrate to Australia, lured by the promise of plentiful job prospects. He urged Esther to go with him and she considered it seriously but she felt too emotionally attached to Ireland and her family to go. She made the heart-breaking and fateful decision to stay behind. As soon as her boyfriend left, Frank McCann stepped into the gap.

'He was on the edge of a crowd Esther knew. Within a week of her boyfriend leaving, he arrived at our door with flowers for Esther and chocolates for me,' Marian recalls. 'They went to the pictures that night.'

McCann wooed Esther determinedly. 'I remember they went to a banquet in the Shelbourne one night and Esther came home and said how much she liked him. She used to like a pint of Guinness, but she said that she hadn't had a drink or a smoke that night and that he had told jokes and been charming and they had great fun. She admired his clean living and work ethic. He was solid and reliable.'

They were married in Kimmage Manor on 22 May 1987, with a reception afterwards at Stackstown Golf Club in the Dublin Mountains. The groom's prolonged absence from the celebrations prompted a rumour to circulate afterwards that he had slipped away from the party for a sexual interlude with a young female, although this was never confirmed. Marian had already noted that McCann subtly excluded her from planning the wedding and from any central involvement in the day itself. Looking back, she believes that the entire marriage was a sham; that McCann calculatedly set out to marry Esther to provide him with a front of respectability. What the happy bride did not know as she made her wedding vows was that a teenager with special needs who used to swim in Frank McCann's Terenure club was already in the third trimester of her pregnancy with his child. The newly-wed Mr and Mrs Frank McCann moved into their house at 39 Butterfield Avenue in Rathfarnham after their honeymoon. Three months later, a son was born to the teenage swimmer. Esther would go to her grave oblivious to the child's existence.

Arrangements were made to have the baby adopted directly from the hospital. The facilitator was Ireland's best-loved priest, Fr Michael Cleary, known as the Singing Priest for his role in a clerical cabaret act that toured the country. Cleary, who appeared on the altar with the former Bishop of Galway for Pope John Paul II's youth mass during his 1979 visit to Ireland, was a vocal family-values advocate and a successful late-night radio presenter. It would emerge after his death that he had lived clandestinely with his housekeeper, Phyllis Hamilton, and their child, Ross, in the priest's house in Harold's Cross while denouncing divorce and contraception from the pulpit. Cleary had some practice in the arranging of adoptions. His and Phyllis's first-born son had been privately placed with a family in south Dublin in the early 1970s. The exposure of Cleary's double life would shock the country a decade after Frank McCann's son was placed with another family.

'Michael Cleary never considered our family or Esther,' says Marian. 'Cleary arranged for Frank to pay £500 "medical expenses" to the [pregnant] girl's family and he threatened Frank that, if he didn't pay up, he would tell his new wife about the baby. Following Esther and Jessica's death, I rang Michael Cleary, when I learnt of his involvement in McCann's secret life. I told him I would have expected more from him. I asked him did he not think of contacting Esther's family, that we could have done something about it. He told me what I needed was solace and not to be looking for vengeance. He recommended I read some book he'd written. He said it would help me find peace.'

Problems first surfaced in Frank and Esther McCann's marriage in October, 1987, five months after the wedding, and two months after the birth of his secret child. Outwardly, it was a successful marriage; Esther kept Frank's business books for him and taught him and some of his swimming colleagues how to use the computer. When he ran coaching sessions at Terenure Swimming Club, she was on duty at the door, collecting the admission fees. She was socially at ease and an asset to him. Yet, almost from the start, he was cold to her.

'He lost interest in her. He put distance between them. She was very lonely. He lost interest in her sexually. Esther had no inhibitions. She wouldn't have thought twice about consulting sexologists, for instance, if that was what she thought it would take,' says Marian. 'She would have liked to have had children. She'd stopped using protection before they were married, but you need to have sex to get pregnant. Frank's father died in the autumn after their wedding and Esther was worried he wasn't grieving. She offered to get him counselling, but he wouldn't hear of it. Frank never hit her. There was never violence in the marriage. Just coldness.'

In retrospect, Marian Leonard recognises a strangeness in Frank McCann. He used to hire the Terenure pool every Friday evening for use by his extended family. All the McCanns were strong swimmers, regularly participating in the IASA-organised open sea swim in Dun Laoghaire held every August for registered members of the association. The clan called their Friday evenings at Terenure pool 'the McCann Hour'. Frank's mother and father, his siblings, their families and friends would all pile in. One evening, Marian was in the pool with her young daughter, the third-generation to carry the name Esther. As mothers of small children are wont to do for convenience sake, Marian had left the child unclothed to splash about in the pool. McCann approached her in the water and said people were objecting to little Esther's nudity. 'Frank, she's two,' replied Marian indignantly.

'Sometimes, I'd be in the changing rooms getting my daughter ready for the pool and Frank would walk through. There would be teenage girls changing in there and it didn't feel right. When I suggested he should go round the other way, he said: "I'm the only man allowed in here."'

In 1991, a new addition arrived in the McCanns' home on Butterfield Avenue. Frank's only sister, Jeanette, announced she was pregnant, to the consternation of her mother. She came to live with Esther and Frank. Esther liked the girl and was glad of her company. She wanted to bring Jeanette and the baby back to Butterfield Avenue after the birth, until the young mother settled into her new circumstances. She cautioned Jeanette to take time with any decisions about whether to have the baby adopted, warning her that, once she clapped eyes on her baby, she might find parting with the child an impossible wrench.

Jessica McCann was born at 5.05 am on Mothers' Day, Sunday 10 March 1991 in the Coombe Women's Hospital, weighing 5lbs 2ozs. Esther was present for her arrival into the world. The baby was kept in a special care unit for two days before getting a clean bill of health. Prior to Jeanette's discharge from hospital the following Thursday she asked Esther and Frank to become Jessica's parents as she did not feel she could give her little girl the life she needed. On the succeeding Friday night during the McCann Hour at Terenure pool, Frank's mother, Joan, announced that he and Esther had decided to adopt 'a baby'. That the baby was, in fact, Frank's niece was not mentioned during the back-slapping and squeals of congratulations that greeted the happy news.

From before the birth, Esther had been keeping a diary on her computer for Jessica. She gave it the title, 'Memories for Jessica'. Though the computer was destroyed in the fire, the Garda forensic team managed to salvage the hard disc and to retrieve her personal files, assisted by Marian Leonard's knowledge of her sister's passwords. On Wednesday 27 March 1991, Esther wrote:

Brought you to the clinic in Rathfarnham to be weighed. Honestly, child, you are a big pudding! Weighing in at over 7lbs – and only two and a half weeks.

Jessica was christened in St Aengus's Church, Balrothery, Tallaght on 16 June, Fathers' Day. Esther chose 'Mary' as Jessica's second name out of devotion to the mother of God.

I always said my first-born girl would be called Mary. Well, you are my first-born, best girl and always will be, Esther wrote in her computer diary.

The christening was followed by a party in Butterfield Avenue attended by various officials and coaches from McCann's swimming fraternity.

On May 20, 1991, the Adoption Board received the official application form from Esther and Frank McCann for permission to adopt Jessica Mary McCann.

'Legally, they didn't even have to do it officially,' says Marian. 'Jessica's surname was the same anyway. Formalising it wasn't necessary. But I was anxious to see it formalised, knowing the marriage wasn't going so well. Frank didn't have any real interest in Jessica. When there were other people around, he'd pick her up to display her. When the display was over, he'd hand her back. Still, if it did come to a separation, Jessica was a McCann baby.'

While they waited for the Adoption Board to reach a decision, Esther and Frank lived like strangers. He had commenced a sexual relationship with another teenage girl. In addition, he was working late hours in the bar in Blessington, and was immersed in the coaching and administrative affairs of Leinster swimming. The branch was incorporated as a limited liability company, separate from the IASA, on 20 August 1991. He flew to Brussels on 17 July for six days at the Youth Olympics. One of his proudest possessions was his gold chain of office bestowed on him as president of the Leinster Branch. His swimming buddies – Gibney, O'Rourke and the rest – seemed to be in the house perpetually.

'They were his friends. That was his circle. Esther hated Gibney being in the house. When they were there, she was treated like an intruder. They used to have swimming meetings at the table in the breakfast room and you had to pass through that room to get to or from the kitchen. If Esther needed a bottle from the kitchen for Jessica, she had to go through the room. There would be silence while she walked through. McCann swore a lot. I remember being there a couple of times when Chalkie White rang and he'd say, "Tell that bastard I'm not here".'

In the middle of her husband's frenetic activities, the hand of doom shook Esther's world. On 19 July, her adored nephew James, Marian's eldest child, was found to have a malignant tumour in his left leg. He was taken from Cappagh Hospital to the Mater Hospital for treatment. He was only sixteen. In her diary, Esther wrote:

Not a day to be forgotten for any of us, possibly the blackest day in a long time. Things will get better and James will be well again after treatment.

The countdown to the 1992 Olympics was a busy time for McCann. Not long home from a swim training camp in California, he set off for Florida in March 1992 as team manager for the Alamo Cup in Ford Lauderdale. One of Derry O'Rourke's swimmers in King's Hospital, the future Olympic triple gold medalist Michelle Smith, was a member of the Alamo Cup team. 'There were a couple of us who [were] teenagers at the time and we used to joke: "I wouldn't go near him because he'd give you the creeps",' she recalled.

'There was nothing behind it. We couldn't have known what it was. It was a total shock when we heard what happened to his wife and child.'

As Leinster's president, McCann prepared to travel to Barcelona that summer. Having none of his club's swimmers on the national team, he had to pay his own way. The trip was costing him between £2,000 and £3,000. Before his departure for Spain, he had to organise the annual Liffey Swim, which was due to take place on 18 August. Despite his workload, he had time to meticulously lay a trail of false leads as a precursor to murdering his wife and child. 'He was still continuing his job and the swimming and, on the side, planning his killing of Esther and Jessica,' says Marian.

His plan clicked into action late one night while he was at the pub in Blessington and Esther and Jessica were asleep in Butterfield Avenue. A ringing phone woke Esther to the discovery that her electric blanket was ablaze. The incident was put down to one of those freak events that happen in life. Besides, Esther had other things on her mind, as she entered in her diary for Jessica:

Your own darling James has had the most terrible news imaginable today and he doesn't even know it yet. Marian in pieces and I am not so good myself. Two tumours on the left lung to be operated on end of July – no end to the cruelty!

On July 28, McCann phoned Bord Gáis to report a leak. Esther and Jessica had again had a narrow escape. Esther had awoken to a bad smell which she described as being like the smell of onions, but which she recognised as gas. She lifted Jessica from her cot and put her in the car which she then let run down the driveway to avoid causing any spark that could trigger an explosion. Esther went to her mother's house and phoned Frank at the pub in Blessington to alert him to the gas leak. The timing of what was, at minimum, the second attempt on their lives coincided with Esther's ongoing heartache. James was undergoing surgery on his lungs, as the cancer had spread. McCann knew that Marian would not be around and was unlikely to turn up unexpectedly as she would be at her son's bedside. Esther wrote in her diary two days after the incident:

My darling daughter Jessica, you have grown and become a beautiful child. You have been walking now for a little over a week and have given up holding onto the walls in search of your own bit of independence. 'Cup of tea' and 'up a daisy' with constant talk of 'Daddy', 'O Mammy' and 'Mammy's baby' … Lots of talk and every day brings new joys … Ten teeth to show for all the months of painful teething … The hottest and driest summer in years …

A gas inspector, responding to McCann's complaint, called to the house and found 'a colossal leak' and 'an explosive level of gas' in the house.

Only with hindsight would a pattern become discernible. It certainly was not a coincidence that, in the same month, the Adoption Board had notified Esther and Frank's solicitor that it had decided to reject their application to adopt Jessica after receiving a phone call from a woman on 16 April 1991 alleging that McCann had fathered a child with her teenage daughter. The McCanns' solicitor, however, informed only Frank of the decision. Esther was never told. Time and again, she phoned the Board's office to try to find out what was causing the delay. Finally, she was invited to a meeting where everything would be explained. She was given an appointment for a meeting on Monday 7 September, the office being shut for the summer holidays in the month of August.

As she waited, her husband was getting ready to leave for

Barcelona with his swimming club. One day, while he was packing for the trip, Esther picked up her camera and captured a riveting image of Jessica. In the photograph, the child she loved as her daughter is sitting in Frank McCann's fastidiously packed suitcase atop the couple's bed, her face dominated by enormous brown laughing eyes. At the age of eighteen months, Jessica had a personality of her own and was uttering complete sentences, such as 'Thank you very much' and 'I want my bottle now'.

At lunchtime on the Thursday before her scheduled appointment with the Adoption Board, Esther called to Marian's home in Firhouse. James was to escort a friend to a debs dance in Tramore the following night and Marian was going down with him. 'Frank used the fact that we were all coping with James's impending death to get away with the attempts on Esther,' Marian believes. Esther, who was very close to James, called in to wish her nephew a good time at the dance. That night, she phoned Marian in Tramore, and talked about the problems in her marriage. 'I'm fed up with this,' she said. 'I'm going to have it out with Frank tonight when he comes in.' Marian understood she was talking about the lack of communication in their relationship and the Adoption Board's protracted deliberations about Jessica. 'She said she was going to tell him she'd move on with the adoption on her own if he wasn't interested.' Marian never found out if her sister got the opportunity to initiate that conversation. In the early hours of Friday morning, her husband, Billy, phoned her in Tramore to say that Esther and Jessica were dead. Though she remembers little of that morning, she has been told that she immediately began telling the people around her that Frank McCann was the killer.

He had arrived home from the pub in the early hours of 4 September to find a crowd on the road in front of his house and smoke billowing from the windows. He had run to a ladder being raised to a window by a fire fighter and attempted to climb it. Several neighbours ran after him and held him back. They were utterly taken in by his performance as distraught husband and father. When he fainted, the neighbours rolled him onto his side, loosened his collar, and called an ambulance. While he was being ferried away to the Meath Hospital, fire fighters entered the house and made a poignant discovery. They found Esther, with extensive burns, lying on the landing, her arm reaching towards the door of Jessica's bedroom. The child was dead in her cot, still with her soother in her mouth. Only later would it be noted that the Leinster Branch president's chain of office, which had been on the hall table hours earlier, was gone.

On being released from the Meath Hospital without need for treatment, McCann went to Tallaght Garda Station to assist with inquiries as the distraught widower. From there, he went to his mother's house in Terenure which was thronged with shocked relatives and friends calling to sympathise. One swimming acquaintance found him sitting at the table in the kitchen demonstrating tricks with a box of matches. 'Poor Frank, he's down in the kitchen showing how to do tricks with matches,' the official told a colleague on returning to the sitting room. 'God love him, he must be out of his mind on medication.'

The bodies of Esther and Jessica were brought to the Catholic church in Firhouse on Monday, 7 September; the day Esther had been due to attend the meeting about Jessica at the Adoption Board. Scattered among the congregation were officials of the IASA who had been scheduled to attend an aborted emergency meeting at the association's headquarters in House of Sport on the Longmile Road that day to discuss correspondence containing allegations of child sex abuse that had been mysteriously removed from the office. During the church service, the bookish-looking grieving widower was helped onto the altar by his sister-in-law, Phyllis. In a short eulogy, he said, 'I was not the only man Esther loved. There were other men'. After a startled silence, he went on to talk of Esther's love for her nephew, James, who was terminally ill and their friends' son, Conor, who suffered from cerebral palsy. Afterwards, he would comment that he had not left 'a dry eye in the house'.

On Tuesday, the cortege left Dublin for Tramore. It stopped at a village in County Carlow en route to allow mourners a rest. McCann got out of his car and walked back to the car carrying Marian and Billy Leonard, who were nineteen years married that day. He handed his wife's sister an envelope. Inside was a wedding anniversary card, on which he had written: 'To the best sister-in-law in the world'. For Marian, it was one of several surreal moments in the day they buried Esther. At the funeral mass, the widower delivered another brief eulogy. He thanked the people of Tramore for their support, but he seemed strangely unmoved by the occasion or his proximity to the two coffins, a pair of Jessica's tiny shoes on top of her white coffin. Then, looking out at the congregation, which included many of his friends from the swimming association, he said he would like to read a poem. It was by Thomas Burbidge and entitled 'A Mother's Love'.

Oh, what a loveliness her eyesGather in that one moment's space,
While peeping round the post she spies
Her darling's laughing face ...

Esther and Jessica were buried together in a single grave. Afterwards, in a pub where the mourners had gathered, everybody said how lovely the poem was that Frank had read out. None of Esther's family wanted to admit that it was they, not he, who had chosen the verse. When they left the pub for the home of one of Esther's cousins who had invited everyone back for food, McCann behaved in the most bizarre fashion imaginable. As his car passed by a group of young girls in the town, he leaned out the window, wolf-whistled and yelled: 'I'm a free man.' He left Tramore early and drove back to Blessington, his Leinster Branch chain of office conspicuously laid out on the back seat of the car. He was heading back to The Cooperage for a party. As they had been walking out of the graveyard earlier in the day, he had leant in towards Marian Leonard and informed her that he was due back at the pub for a surprise sixtieth birthday party that night that he had organised for his mother. Afterwards, Marian heard reports of how he had paraded into the party, holding aloft a birthday cake lit with candles and singing 'Happy birthday to you, happy birthday to you, happy birthday dear Mammy ...'

'He didn't have emotions. He didn't know what appropriate emotional behaviour was,' Marian concludes. A week after Esther and Jessica died, Garda James Murphy from Rathfarnham station was on duty preserving the scene of the fire on 10 September when McCann stopped by to chat. He told the Garda 'in a jovial way', that he had encountered some friends a few days before and that he had been telling them about plans he was making for a barbeque. The widower of one week said his friends found this very funny and they had laughed. Garda Murphy kept a note of the conversation. Two weeks after the funeral, McCann flew to California, where he had been on a swimming camp the previous year, for a fortnight's holiday. The insurance company paid him £10,000 for the fire damage to his house, but he left the undertaker's bill to be paid by his wife's family. In the following weeks and months, he filled his diary with appointments for meetings with his swimming colleagues.

There was never any other suspect. On the morning of 4 November, Garda ballistics experts conducted an experiment in the Phoenix Park to establish how the fire in Butterfield Avenue had reached such an intensity so rapidly. That afternoon, Gardaí arrived at The Cooperage and arrested McCann under the Explosive Substances Act, permitting his detention for forty-eight hours. While he spent that first night refusing to answer questions in Tallaght Garda Station, a meeting was underway in the Ashling Hotel during which he was formally re-elected president of the Leinster Branch of the IASA. To McCann, it must have felt as though it was his reward for double murder. The icing on the cake should have been his automatic elevation to presidency of the IASA in time for the next Olympic Games in Atlanta, but he had not reckoned on a dogged Garda investigation rendering that a dream too far. The next day in the station, when it was put to him that he had fathered a child with a teenager and that the Adoption Board had refused his and Esther's application to adopt Jessica for that reason, he replied: 'It was all such a horrible mess. It had to be sorted out.' He said Fr Michel Cleary had phoned him at the time the teenage girl was pregnant to discuss the baby's welfare and that he had gone to meet the priest and the girl's father at Cleary's house. He said the priest had asked him if he had a problem with young girls. McCann claimed he had stormed out of the house and had heard nothing more until the Adoption Board raised the matter. He told Gardaí he had intended killing himself in the fire too. When they asked him why he had brought petrol into his house, he said: 'I was going to finish it off. I was going to clean up the mess – me, Esther and Jessica.' He was released, pending a file being sent to the DPP.

On 22 April 1993, McCann was arrested and formally charged with the murders of Esther and Jessica. He pleaded not guilty. Just two weeks before, Marian's son, James, had died at the age of eighteen and was buried in Tramore alongside Esther and Jessica. When Gardaí went looking for McCann, equipped with the arrest warrant, they found him fitting out a mobile home, complete with pipework beneath the floor, in Stradbally, County Waterford, a neighbouring seaside town of Tramore, where Esther had grown up. He was held overnight in Tramore Garda Station, which is situated a few hundred yards from his victims' grave. After making his statement in Tallaght Garda Station the previous November, he had been voluntarily admitted to St John of God's Hospital in Dublin with a nervous breakdown. While there he had met a female patient with whom he began a relationship. He moved into her home with her after they discharged themselves. She introduced him to her son and McCann was welcomed by her unsuspecting family.

He was defiant to the end. When he was refused bail by Mr Justice Declan Budd in the Central Criminal Court, his lawyers instigated an appeal to the Supreme Court on a legal point but it was never pursued. McCann had been sent to Mountjoy Prison to be held in custody pending his trial, but he managed to get himself transferred to the Central Mental Hospital in Dundrum. There, he gave swimming lessons in the hospital pool to some of his fellow inmates, who included Brendan O'Donnell, found guilty, but insane, for the murders of Imelda Riney, her three-year-old son Liam, and Fr Joe Walsh in County Clare, and John Gallagher, who murdered Annie Gillespie and her daughter, Anne, in Sligo. After several months in Dundrum, McCann was dispatched back to Mountjoy upon the discovery of duplicate keys to his cell in his possession. His escape plan was foiled.

6. A Black Year for Irish Swimming

There is an adage that truth is stranger than fiction. It certainly applies to the macabre conjunction of circumstances that befell Irish swimming in 1993, the year of the IASA's centenary. In the month of April alone, the president of the Leinster Branch of the IASA, Frank McCann, was formally charged with double murder, the IASA's most distinguished coach, George Gibney, was charged with the rape and sexual abuse of seven children and teenagers, and his successor as national coach, Derry O'Rourke, was being investigated for the same category of crimes against eleven children. In other spheres of life, such a confluence of horrors would have come to a head, burst open and, ultimately, provided a catharsis. Organisations founded upon the celebration of individual accomplishment however do not always adhere to the normal instincts of a community, and so it was to prove in swimming. The compulsion was to drown the truth. It would take forty more months before the first of the sport's ruling criminals would go to jail. In the meantime, rank and file swimmers were given no information by the authorities in their sport about the unfolding events. Journalists whose antennae were pricked by flimsy rumours were fobbed off with a charade of business-as-usual, so effectively that one newspaper glowingly described George Gibney, shortly before he was charged, as 'a man of vision and intense commitment to swimming'. The victims themselves, as they began to find their voices and relate their stories to investigating Gardaí, were abandoned by the mothership, the IASA. Other than the arbitrary anchor of individual friendships, they were left isolated and feeling stigmatised by a governing body most concerned with keeping up appearances. Having already had their childhood desecrated by the paedophiles at the pool, they now found themselves plunged into an uncertain period with no end in sight. The tragedy for many of them was that there would, indeed, be no conclusion.

Garda investigations of allegations of child sex abuse are notoriously problematic and time-consuming, mainly because of the absence of physical evidence and eye witnesses by the time the victim can summon the courage to report the crime. For this reason, the Director of Public Prosecutions (DPP) tends to favour caution, deciding in only three of every 1,000 case files on child sex abuse to instigate a prosecution in the courts, according to a 2002 report commissioned by the Royal College of Surgeons. Compared to the neighbouring jurisdiction in Northern Ireland where the public interest is one of the considerations for initiating a prosecution, the Irish DPP pursues a policy of only bringing charges in cases that have a good chance of being proved in a courtroom, leading to minutely detailed Garda investigations. By that measure, the investigation of George Gibney was swift. From the time Gardaí were first notified in December 1992, it took three months to compile a file containing compelling accounts by seven former swimmers of the abuse he inflicted on them as children and young teenagers. The DPP gave the instruction to commence the prosecution and a warrant was issued for Gibney's arrest at Dundrum district court on 2 April 1993. He was arraigned three days later, at the age of forty-five, at Dun Laoghaire district court on two counts of the statutory rape of girls under fifteen plus fifteen counts of indecent assault on four females and one male, between January 1967 and December 1979. The incidents were alleged to have taken place at Newpark Sports Centre, Gormanston College in County Meath, at the house in Greenville Terrace and in Gibney's home in Killiney. The court was told that he had made no reply when charged. Judge William Hamill remanded him on his own bail of £2,000 with an independent surety of another £2,000. In his application for bail, Gibney's solicitor, Gerry Brady, observed that the alleged offences were 'very old'.

When he left the courthouse after being charged, Gibney was involved in a traffic accident that typified his self-importance and arrogance. A car in which he was travelling in the back seat with his head down, apparently attempting to evade newspaper photographers – despite a court ban on identifying him – drove directly onto the main road, hitting the side of a passing car. No one was hurt and Gibney was later driven home to nearby Killiney in a Garda van.

The speed of the Garda investigation of complaints about Gibney serves, by contrast, to accentuate the IASA's inertia. After nearly three months of tic-tacing with his former swimming friends – phoning them, writing letters and turning up unannounced on their doorsteps – Gary O'Toole was satisfied that what Chalkie had confided to him on the Perth flight was only a fraction of a quarter-of-a-century's crime spree in swimming by George Gibney.

'A lot of them had confided in their parents and that made it easier because they had someone to talk to on a personal level. All they wanted was to have it taken care of in a judicial way. I discreetly asked why the police couldn't go straight to the victims and I was told that they [the swimmers] would have to make the approach. I knew Chalkie was seeing a counsellor who used to work with us in Newpark and I believe that he went to the guards in Blackrock. That's what got it going.'

What caused Chalkie's biggest shock upon hearing that his allegations had been reported to Gardaí was his own unexpected reaction. 'I hadn't been to my counsellor for a few months because of the Olympics and when I went back he told me he was duty-bound to report what he'd found out to the police. I didn't object to that. What shocked me was he said they'd already got statements from six other victims and they were willing to meet me but, whether I met them or not, they were carrying on with the investigation. Why I was shocked was finding out I wasn't the only one. It was like I wanted a monopoly on the hurt and finding out it had happened to other people made me very angry.'

It was Gary who had encouraged the six other former swimmers who confirmed to him that they had been abused by Gibney to go to the Gardaí and make formal complaints. Meanwhile, he had other people he wanted to meet. In December, as the net began to close around Gibney and he knew the Gardaí had sufficient cause to investigate, Gary wrote to the Leinster Branch of the IASA on 13 December, requesting a meeting.

'There were a lot of rumours flying around at the time and I wanted them to be told the real story,' he explained in a newspaper interview four years later. 'I didn't want them turning around at a later date when it hit the papers saying they knew nothing about it. Every one of the abused swimmers had been a member of the association at the time they were being abused. Did the association do anything about it? No way.'

The meeting was arranged for Tuesday 15 December 1992 in the Ashling Hotel. Gary was accompanied to it by Chalkie White and by the husband of a female swimmer whom Gibney had abused (the man who had answered the door saying: 'We've been expecting you'). The Leinster Branch officials present were the president, Harry Kavanagh, the secretary, Mary O'Malley, and the treasurer, Eddie Eaton. Gary spoke to them alone, first. He told them that George Gibney was a paedophile, that he had been sexually abusing boy and girl swimmers since the 1960s, that Gibney had tried to get into bed with him in California, and that he had to be stopped. He recounted instances of Gibney's deviousness and said that, even as he was speaking, Gardaí were taking a statement from Gibney's wife, Brona. One of the officials asked him what he thought they should do about it. He urged them to unilaterally remove the coach from Irish swimming, starting by cancelling a swimming course for eleven to fifteen-year-olds scheduled for Newpark Sports Centre on January 2 and 3, under Gibney's supervision in conjunction with the Leinster Branch. Chalkie White and the victim's husband then joined the meeting. The second man informed the officials that his wife had been repeatedly sexually abused by Gibney when she was aged from nine to fourteen years.

Addressing Chalkie, whom he knew, Harry Kavanagh then asked: 'What are you doing here?'

'I'm here because George Gibney sexually abused me when I was a boy,' Chalkie answered.

It was a dramatic moment, but not powerful enough, it would seem, to make any real difference. Harry Kavanagh arranged to meet a Garda Inspector the next day only to be informed that the investigation was already underway. Galvanised by this knowledge, he went to meet Gibney a week later, on 23 December, and urged him to stand aside from the January coaching course at Newpark, but Gibney retaliated with a threat to sue if there was any attempt to stop him. In the end, the course for juvenile swimmers went ahead, run by Gibney. No information about the Garda investigation was conveyed to members of Trojans, Gibney's primary source of prey.

Gary O'Toole says, 'There were very good swimmers on the scene at the time with the ability to go to the 1996 and the 2000 Olympics and here was me saying "Your coach is a paedophile, not to be trusted". I was going to them on the back of a very disappointing performance in Barcelona. I could have been bitter and twisted about that and looking for revenge, for all they knew. Chalkie didn't break down at the meeting, but he found it very tough. The other man confirmed for them that his wife had been abused by Gibney. He had nothing to do with swimming and this was his first experience of that world. He wasn't impressed. They didn't say sorry to either of them.'

Nor, up to the time this book was written, had the swimming authorities ever expressed gratitude to Gary O'Toole for exposing paedophilia in the sport.

The next day, Gary wrote to the national organisation, the IASA, requesting a meeting 'to discuss some extremely disturbing information that I have come across'. By now, his father, Aidan O'Toole, had already informed the IASA president at a gala in Guinness that George Gibney was in serious trouble for molesting young swimmers and he asked him to organise a meeting at which Gardaí would attend. The president took legal advice. The meeting never happened. Now Gary wrote to Hilary Hughes, the association's honorary secretary and an active member of Chalkie White's club, Glenalbyn: 'The information that I am in possession of pertains to the serious matter of 'Child Sexual Abuse' and a swimming coach that has carried out these gross acts of indecency for many years,' Gary wrote. 'The matter takes on even greater proportions when this coach's standing within the Swimming Association is considered. You will, of course, appreciate that I am writing to you as a medical student in UCD, a mature adult and, finally, a member of your Association since 1976. Please be assured that I would never request this meeting if I thought that I would be wasting the Association's time.'

A meeting with the IASA was arranged for 20 December, again in the Ashling Hotel, but it was called off at the eleventh hour in a letter to Gary from Hilary Hughes. She said she was acting on the instructions of the president, Pat Begley, after consulting the association's legal adviser.

Recounting these events in the *Sunday Independent* five years later, Paul Kimmage, a former international cyclist and friend of Gary, wrote: 'Furious, O'Toole phoned a member of the executive and demanded an explanation. The officer informed him they had been instructed not to get involved by the association's solicitor. O'Toole flipped: "But you are involved. All of the victims have one thing in common apart from the fact that they've been abused by Gibney – they're swimmers! They're all members of your association and you don't want to get involved! Do you know how important this is?" But when the conversation grew more heated, the official hung up.'

A month later, Gary received another letter clarifying the IASA's position from Hughes, in whom Chalkie had confided around the time of the World Championships in Perth about Gibney's abuse. She wrote: 'Further to my letter to you dated 17 December 1992, I would advise that the advice we received from the IASA legal adviser is as follows: the IASA cannot act on mere rumour and innuendo and the person concerned has a basic right to his good name and reputation unless and until [a] first hand complaint is made in the first instance and thereafter justified.'

Aidan O'Toole believes: 'There were a lot of people involved at the top of swimming who were only interested in themselves and what they could get out of it; wearing the blazers and getting to the Olympics. If anyone stepped out of line, they'd put them back in their place promptly. That was the attitude all the years I was involved in swimming. Gary O'Toole was a headache for them. He wasn't an asset. He was a headache.'

Gibney was suspended on full pay by the management company at Newpark on 20 January 1993 and a year later, on 17 January 1994, his pay was terminated too. Ever defiant, he countered by threatening the company with an unfair dismissals claim at the Labour Court and on 9 August 1994 he received IR£19,000 in full and final settlement of his pay claim. The swimming association, meanwhile, continued to pursue a policy of see-no-evil, hear-no-evil throughout Gibney's sporadic court appearances. The awkward fact that he still enjoyed honorary life membership of the IASA was not mentioned.

Silence prevailed too in relation to mirror events being played out across the Irish Sea. The IASA was historically close to its British counterpart, the Amateur Swimming Association (ASA), employing some of its officials from time to time to work in Ireland as coaches. It was natural that, among the relatively small cadre of personnel travelling to the same international events, personal ties would be established between British and Irish officials. A friendship had blossomed, for instance, between George Gibney and his opposite number in Britain, Paul Hickson. The pair often met on the banks of pools around Europe and beyond and were seen to get on well together. They were the Olympic coaches for Ireland and Britain in Seoul in 1988 where Hickson's team took three gold medals. When news broke of Hickson's criminal history, also in 1993, it gave pause for thought about how endemic child sex abuse might actually be in swimming. More worryingly, some people began to wonder if it might be something other than a coincidence that these two friends and swim supremos in their respective countries now stood accused of such crimes.

In December a Press Association report was published by numerous newspapers under the headline, 'Hunt for Swimming Coach Accused of Sex Assault'. It said that former Olympic coach Paul Hickson, forty-five, from Luddon Lane, Baltonsborough, Somerset had skipped bail and disappeared three months before he was due to stand trial for sexually assaulting eight teenage girls. He had denied the charges, which were alleged to have happened in Swansea between 1985 and 1991. Hickson's passport had been confiscated before he absconded. Prosecuting lawyer, James Jenkins, explained to Swansea Crown Court: 'It was feared that with his international connections, stepping outside the jurisdiction would have been a simple thing to do.' A South Wales police spokesman was quoted, saying 'He is well known in sporting circles at home and abroad but we have not been able to trace him despite our inquiries. We are appealling to anyone with information to contact us.'

In the end, Hickson was apprehended and brought to justice. He was jailed for seventeen years in September 1995 (subsequently reduced to fifteen years on appeal) for raping two females and indecently assaulting thirteen others while coaching them at school and college. Evidence was given that he had committed a catalogue of sex offences spread over a fifteen-year period while he was in charge of swimming clubs in Norwich, England and Swansea. One woman described how he frequently raped her at his home during school lunch breaks, starting when she was thirteen. Hickson, who was married with an eight-year-old daughter, accused the thirteen women of fantasising about sex with him. Even more perturbing was the revelation that in 1988, seven years before he was convicted and shortly after his appointment as Seoul Olympics coach was announced, three senior swimmers had complained about his conduct to the ASA and asked that his appointment be cancelled. The ASA had ignored their pleas.

Back in Ireland, similarities were surfacing in the case of George Gibney. The IASA's behaviour betokened an organisation paralysed with disbelief. When the number of criminal charges against him was increased from seventeen to twenty-seven in May 1993, Aidan O'Toole lodged a formal complaint to the IASA under section 44.1 of its constitution, dealing with 'behaviour likely to bring it into disrepute', on behalf of his club, Triton in Bray. Once more, the response kicked for touch. On July 8, he wrote again.

Dear Mrs Hughes,

Further to your letter of 2 June, it does not surprise me that you are unclear regarding our club's complaint. As far as we are concerned, the Association have been blinded for a long time and hoping the problem would go away.

With regard to the Constitution, I believe our complaint is covered by 44.1, behaviour likely to bring the Association into disrepute. Mr Gibney has been charged with twenty-seven offences, which I assume would come under this category. I would also like to remind you that Mr Gibney was in charge of a course held in Newpark last December, organised by the LBIASA, which is under your jurisdiction. At this stage the officers of the IASA knew about some of the pending charges. Furthermore, an incoming President has openly stated that it was a personal vendetta by Chalkie White and my son – how naive can one be! – and I wonder why? What chance has swimming got with a mentality like that?

Your stand and handling of this situation would be laughable if it were not so serious. These are not sweeping changes; they are facts. The man has so far been charged with raping two swimmers and interfering with God only knows how many more since 1967!

Swimming is supposed to be a clean and healthy sport. I hate to see anybody undermine it. That's one of the reasons for my persistence. We can all stand back and ignore the problems, but that will only play into the hands of the type of person we are talking about – the very reason he has got away with his antics and abuse of swimmers for so long.

Those of us who think there is more to life than ego-trips have to stand up to the 'ignore it at all costs' merchants. After all, swimming belongs to everybody and we have a duty to protect it from people like Gibney. We owe it to the future generations. At the end of the day, swimming will be a better and safer sport despite the set-backs.

Stopping any person interfering with children is surely more important than any other way I can think of for the advancement of swimming. This is 1993; Gibney has been engaging in his behaviour since 1967. The Association gave him the power and he thought he was infallible. It is ironic that on the first day of your Centenary Nationals, Gibney will be facing a judge in Dun Laoghaire Court, awaiting his fate. At least, the Swimming Association should have suspended him pending police enquiries, and at the end of the day you could have said you had done your bit for the future of Irish swimming.

Interesting to see the new Code of Conduct form for swimmers. I hope you have established one for officials. Or is their conduct beyond reproach?

Regarding my credibility, I don't think you or any of the present Executive are the ones to judge under the circumstances. Also, may I remind you that this complaint is from the Triton Swimming Club and, as an affiliated club, we are entitled to our views.

Thankfully, it is the DPP who is pursuing the matter, not the IASA. Your attitude is appalling, to say the least.

Aidan O'Toole,
Head Coach.

Triton Swimming Club eventually disaffiliated from the Irish Amateur Swimming Association in protest at its inaction and unsatisfactory response to complaints.

The IASA received an allegation about yet another coach at this time. He was an Englishman, coaching at a provincial swimming club in Ireland when a respected member of the sport wrote to House of Sport warning that the coach, a member of the National College of Hypnosis and Psychotherapy in the UK, had been dismissed by a British club amid rumours of child sex abuse. The coach was about to escort a group of young Irish swimmers to Coventry for a competition. The IASA's secretary, Celia Millane, contacted two clubs in England where he had previously been employed, but they said it was so long since he left they could not assist with enquiries. When a solicitor's letter arrived on behalf of the coach threatening legal action for defamation, the matter was dropped. The following year, March 1995, the coach was charged with child sex abuse crimes in an English court.

By Christmas 1994, George Gibney's luck and, by extension, the IASA's too, had taken a fortuitous turn. After the book of evidence was served in his prosecution on 26 June 1993, his lawyers had applied for a judicial review on two grounds: the delay since the alleged offences and a lack of precision in defining the incidents alleged. Failing to persuade the High Court that it should stop the Circuit Court proceedings against him, Gibney's lawyers went to the Supreme Court in December. Patrick Gageby, senior counsel (who would also represent Derry O'Rourke), made the case that Gibney did not possess any records for Trojans from the 1970s and, therefore, had no documentation on which to rely for his defence. This assertion ran counter to club members' impressions of him having always kept detailed swimming and training records, there having been no active committee in the club Even the sport's bible, *The Swimming Times*, had been moved to extol his meticulous. record-keeping more than once. The Supreme Court, however, saw merit in his lawyers' submissions and sent the case back to the High Court for a judicial review. At the end of a one-day in-camera hearing on 21 July 1994, the High Court issued a prohibition order, forbidding the DPP from pressing ahead with the prosecution. The proceedings were formally discontinued in September 1994.

News of the termination of Gibney's prosecution was greeted by one elected swimming official that day with a telling exclamation of vindication: 'I told you there was nothing going on,' he declared, dismissing the detail that Gibney had only got off on a legal technicality. Despite media speculation that the DPP was likely to appeal the High Court's decision, no appeal was ever lodged. He was a free man with his reputation deemed worthy of legal protection. Worse, he could walk into any public place in the country where children gathered. The rank failure of the Irish criminal justice system in the case of George Gibney set a tone of such ambivalence by the establishment about crimes against children that other victims from various walks of life would suffer the consequences long after he had fled the jurisdiction. A month after the Gibney decision, the seeds of a sensational political crisis were sown when it was reported that an RUC extradition request in the name of Fr Brendan Smyth had been lying dormant in the Irish Attorney General's office for seven months. Smyth was a Roman Catholic priest wanted by police in Northern Ireland on charges of child sex abuse. The political controversy culminated in the withdrawal of the Labour Party from the coalition government in November and the resignation of Albert Reynolds as Taoiseach and leader of Fianna Fáil. Over the coming years, the system would again demonstrate its ambiguous attitude to crimes of child abuse by failing to apply for the extradition of George Gibney; the abysmally low rates of prosecution for these crimes indicate that the chances of proving them in court are regarded as a major consideration in determining whether to press charges.

When the people who were abused as children by Gibney were informed of the High Court's ruling, their reaction was described as 'palpably angry' by somebody who knew many of them. 'Some of them are barely holding onto their sanity,' he said.

The collapse of Gibney's prosecution was to provide the catalyst for one of the most intrepid acts of Irish journalism. Johnny Watterson, a sports journalist with the *Sunday Tribune* and a former student at Newpark School, had been watching Gibney's case meander through the courts. When he walked free, Watterson went to his editor, Peter Murtagh, and told him there had been a grave miscarriage of justice which had to be exposed in the public interest. The *Tribune*'s legal adviser on defamation, barrister Hugh Mohan, a future chairman of the Bar Council, was consulted. His advice was that, unless the victims' sworn statements to Gardaí could be obtained, the story was a non-runner. It would be an open and shut case of libel to accuse somebody of child rape after the courts had failed to convict him. It took the best part of twelve months to acquire sufficient documentation to satisfy the legal imperative. Mohan took the unusual precaution of interviewing the victims himself, along with Watterson. As a double safeguard, the story was sent for a second legal opinion, this time to one of the brightest and most formidable senior counsels in the country, Adrian Hardiman. He identified three potential legal traps: the libelling of Gibney; the indirect breach of the victims' anonymity, provided under the sexual offences code; contempt of court for defying the president of the High Court Mr Justice Declan Costello's prohibition on the publication of Gibney's name during his application to the High Court for judicial review.

'There is no doubt that this story is gravely defamatory,' wrote Hardiman, a future Supreme Court judge. 'In fact, with only one exception (an allegation of mass murder), it is the most serious defamation I have ever had to consider. It is calculated to destroy the subject's reputation conclusively, end his career beyond hope of redemption and probably ruin his life generally.'

On the other hand, he wrote, the legal defence of justification – 'that the words complained of are true in substance and in fact' – was governed by the ordinary civil standard of balance of probabilities. Hardiman considered the evidence available to the newspaper as capable of discharging the onus of proof on the publisher but, he warned, 'it is extremely likely that the subject will sue'. Murtagh's decision, in a display of committed journalism growing ever rarer with the spread of the commercial media, was to publish and be damned. On Sunday morning, Gibney's victims, who had exhibited extraordinary courage in agreeing to cooperate with the paper, woke up to the sound of deafening silence on the nation's airwaves. Not one broadcaster dared mention the story of Gibney's rampant sexual abuse of children, for fear of being sued. As Irish defamation law provides a Teflon protection for wrong-doers, their fear was understandable. Yet, the *Sunday Tribune*'s exposé achieved a seismic shift in Gibney's personal fortunes. He never did sue for libel, and that gave license to the rest of the media over the succeeding years to consistently brand him 'George Gibney, the child sex abuser' with impunity.

By the time the *Sunday Tribune* published the story, Gibney had fled. He left Ireland immediately after the High Court hearing, not even hanging around for the verdict. He pitched up first in Scotland in July 1994. His victims were appalled when news drifted back to Ireland that he had secured a job on a stg£10,800 salary in Edinburgh as chief coach for Warrender Baths Club, founded in 1888 and the premier club in Scotland. He sat the job interview on 22 July, the day after his judicial review hearing in the High Court. He told the interview panel that he was, at present, working as a clerical assistant in a tax office, but that he had three other job offers he was considering. He said that if the Warrender job worked out, he might move his family over to Scotland. A written record of the interview noted: 'He came over primarily as a salesman. He was polite, well-dressed. Very confident and had good eye contact.' When asked by the club doctor how he would deal with swimmers' menstrual problems, an inherent consideration in the sport, he gave the impression of being 'uncomfortable' discussing the matter. As Warrender had heard sketchy rumours of an allegation of sexual abuse by Gibney, he was asked outright at the interview to elucidate on it. He said the incident had occurred twenty-five years earlier, when he himself was a teenager. Another of the interviewers stated that the case to clear his name had been upheld in the Irish courts, with the judge implying that it should never have reached that stage. Gibney did not demur. Nor did he give a satisfactory answer when one of the interviewers asked how he had become aware of the job vacancy at the club. The same interviewer 'felt that some of Mr Gibney's answers were tailored in advance to certain questions. It all seemed too good to be true. There was an element of serendipity to this appointment but, as a person, he seemed quite pleasant.'

Gibney's four-page CV would have assuaged any doubts. It cited his appointments by the Irish swimming association to national coach (1981-1991), Olympics coach (Seoul 1988), IASA national director of swimming (1991), along with his sports manager of the year award in 1990 and his RTE television commentary for the Barcelona Olympics. The published works he listed were: 'It's All In the

Blood (Research Study into Lactate Testing Procedures)'; 'Olympic Preparation (Submission to the Olympic Council of Ireland)'; 'IASA Report on AIS Training Camp (December 1989)'; 'National Programme Review (IASA 1989-1990). His memberships included the IASA's technical committee, its educational and coaching committee and its medical committee, as well as the Irish Recreational Management Association, the Irish State's Committee of Elite Sports Persons, the National Training & Coaching Centre at Limerick University and the National Coaching & Training board. Top of his list of achievements was Gary O'Toole's 1989 European silver medal and third place world ranking that year.

Among the references he supplied was one from John W. Harris, former principal of Newpark Comprehensive School and headmaster of the prestigious Sandford Park School in Ranelagh at the time the reference was written on 28 April 1994 (a year after Gibney was charged and two months before his prosecution was abandoned).

'TO WHOM IT MAY CONCERN', [began the reference typed on Sandford Park stationery.] *'I have known George Gibney for approximately eighteen years and worked with him as a colleague when I was Principal of Newpark Comprehensive School and George was Manager of the School Sports Centre. As a manager George displayed outstanding qualities of organisation, leadership and administration. His commitment to his work was extraordinarily strong and he always impressed greatly by his willingness to work without counting the hours. He always demanded and received the highest standards from those who worked with him. His handling of the financial side of the work was always efficient and beyond reproach. He is a gifted swimming coach, having gained high qualifications and recognition of his talents in this area. I can recommend George as a man of many talents who throws himself*

wholeheartedly into all that he undertakes. I will be pleased to answer any specific questions on George's behalf.

Signed: Dr J.W. Harris,

Headmaster.

In April 1995, Gibney returned twice to Ireland, to attend a swimming gala and a children's coaching session at two clubs affiliated to the Ulster branch of the IASA. The invitation was extended to him by a former officer of the association. When the *Sunday Tribune* found out that Gibney was once again coaching young swimmers, the paper sent a photographer and an undercover reporter to attend one of his training sessions at the Warrender pool. The subsequent publicity led to Gibney's sudden departure from Scotland. Gardaí in Dublin, who were privately 'frustrated' when the prosecution was aborted, tipped off their colleagues to his presence in Edinburgh. He next surfaced as coach for the North Jeffco Swim Team in Arvada, Colorado, though how he managed to enter the US remains a mystery. One source is adamant that he had already secured a green card in a visa lottery for admission to the US. 'That's the way his mind worked. He'd obviously been anticipating he could use it if he was ever caught for abusing minors. He was a great one for covering all eventualities.'

The United States of America operates more stringent immigration procedures than nearly any other wealthy country in the world. The standard visa application form not only enquires of would-be visitors if they have ever been convicted of serious crimes, but also if they have been the subject of a police investigation or allegations of a criminal nature. The apparent ease with which he was able to flit from one country to the next, then from one US state to another US state and from one job to the next job, caused suspicion among some of those campaigning for his return that Gibney may have benefited from the assistance of somebody – or some people – with considerable influence. It could, of course, be explained by his acquisition of a green card before the accusations ever emerged, but his possession of a special US visa remains no more than an unsubstantiated rumour. He had a habit of turning up at swimming clubs offering his services just when they were about to recruit a new coach. Like his prospective employers in Edinburgh, the club officials in Colorado unearthed flimsy information about the criminal charges while checking out his references. 'George said the charges were trumped up,' recalled John Whitmore, the club's aquatics director. 'He had a very impressive resume and all the indications were that he was an excellent coach.'

He was hired by the Colorado swimming club in May 1995, but resigned the following January when his reputation followed him across the Atlantic. As he packed his belongings to head for California, Gibney was learning the true meaning of the boxing axiom that you can run, but you cannot hide.

His old rival, Derry O'Rourke, was not to be so lucky. Having since had nine years in jail to cogitate his denouement, he might even feel disposed to blame all his troubles on his predecessor as national swimming coach. In January 1993, a former senior swimmer chanced upon a cryptically-worded report about Gibney in an Irish immigrants' newspaper in her newly-adopted country. It said that an unnamed senior sports coach in Ireland was being investigated by Gardaí for sexually abusing young people during three decades of his stellar career. The woman put two and two together and concluded that the man in question must be her old swimming coach. It was the spur she needed to finally break the bond of secrecy. She picked up the phone and rang Garda Metropolitan

Headquarters in Dublin and asked to be put through to the domestic violence unit.

'Hello,' she said, to the Garda at the other end, 'I want to make a complaint about Derry O'Rourke.'

7. Derry O'Rourke & King's Hospital

As heroes go, Bart Nolan was not your classic swashbuckler. It was what made him the perfect nemesis for the swimming blazers. He was a blow-in, unimpressed by bourgeois conventions. A docker born and bred beside Dublin's quays, and proud of his heritage, he spoke bluntly and it made him enemies. Some of them resided in the upper echelons of swimming, a sport that would have passed him by entirely had it not been for the talent his son, Bart Junior, exhibited at an early age.

Bart Senior was born in 1929. He grew up, one of a family of nine, in a one-room flat on Peterson Lane, off Townsend Street. Back then, the area was part of the Joycean hinterland of early-hours public houses and workmen's braziers, a skip across the river from the infamous Nightown. The Nolan family had been in the neighbourhood since the 1700s. Home was a tenement house. At fourteen, Bart quit school at City Quay and went to work selling coal door-to-door and provisions from Montgomery's vegetable shop in Townsend Street. From there, he progressed to the Dock Mill Company in Barrow Street and laboured on the docks for a while before taking the boat to England where he stayed for eleven years. In 1964, two years after returning to Dublin, he married Mary. Their son, Bart Junior, was born in 1967. The child took to the water as a toddler, developing an effective breast-stroke with Seaspray Swimming Club on the Navan Road. In May 1980, his father took him out to King's Hospital club in Palmerstown, Derry O'Rourke's fiefdom, to have his talent honed by the best. In the years ahead, Bart Nolan Snr would become, first, a friend of O'Rourke's and, later, one of his most dogged adversaries.

O'Rourke was the Olympic swimming coach for the twenty-second games in Moscow the year the Nolans arrived in King's Hospital. Ireland's three entrants in the swimming pool came home empty-handed, as did future world champion boxer Barry McGuigan, who dropped out in the third round. Those Moscow games have gone down in sports history for the US-led boycott by sixty-five countries in protest at the Soviet invasion of Afghanistan. But in the whispering eddies of Irish swimming, that Olympiad is significant for a different reason. It culminated in the formal imposition of a lifetime ban by the IASA on Derry O'Rourke, national coach since 1976, serving as Olympic coach again. Mystery still shrouds what happened, with scant enlightenment provided by a cursory footnote in the association's records. What is known is that RTÉ's swimming commentator had to depart Moscow suddenly on being informed of his mother's death. Derry O'Rourke took his place as substitute commentator for the State-owned station, the Irish contestants having failed to go beyond their first swims of the games. When it was discovered that one of the Irish swimmers had got lost in the Olympic village during the spectacular opening ceremony, O'Rourke was admonished and served with the ban.

As it turned out, it made no dent in his reputation. He continued to run one of the most successful clubs in the country and was looked up to by officials and parents as a deity of the sport. He was even nicknamed 'God'. He was affable and not as blinkered as Gibney. Whereas Gibney, coaching the arch rivals over in Newpark, drilled the need for constant focus into his swimmers, O'Rourke had a lighter side. He emphasised the fun (though some would have described the spitting competitions he encouraged the boys to participate in at the pool as bawdy) side of swimming and his rhetoric oozed loyalty to King's Hospital swimmers. But he was two-faced. Once the young swimmers were out of earshot, he ridiculed them. In all, he coached King's Hospital Swimming Club for twenty years on a verbal contract latterly worth £10,000 a year to him. His other job was full-time manager of the pool, employed by the King's Hospital school and paid the equivalent of a teacher's salary. As club coach and school pool manager, he wielded influence over both the club members and the students.

The original terms of his employment by the school were up-dated by letter on 11 March 1977. It required him to coach school pupils, to manage the pool, to maximise its income and to ensure that there was a suitable lifeguard on duty, though he frequently left swimmers unattended while he went off for breakfast. Arrangements for handling the pool's financial transactions were to be agreed between O'Rourke and the school bursar. His conditions were further updated in a letter dated April 1, 1986. This outlined his normal hours of attendance in three tranches per working day: 6 am to 7.30 am for squad training; 3 pm to 5.45 pm primarily for the pupils' use; 6 pm to 10 pm for club and outside groups. Though a swimming association spokeswoman denied after O'Rourke was jailed that he received an additional salary from the IASA for his seven years as national coach, he indicated otherwise in an interview he gave to the *Evening Press* in May 1991. 'I'm now getting paid for doing a job that I love doing anyway,' he said, expounding on his reappointment as national coach after George Gibney's mysterious resignation in 1991. 'Swimming is a very pure sport. The more you put into it, the more you get out of it.'

Bart Nolan and Derry O'Rourke had a nodding acquaintanceship. When O'Rourke was a £2-a-week clerk in Donnelly's Coal Yard on Sir John Rogerson's Quay, Bart Nolan stood in the queue each week to collect his £3.10 wages for working on the weighbridge. O'Rourke was living in Blarney Park in Crumlin then. He had a brother, three sisters and 'nice parents'. His father was a carpenter with Dublin Port and Docks Board. His mother, a petite woman with a look of Sinead Bean de Valera, had an aura of glamour lent by one of her nephews who was known to many Dubliners as a regular performer in the Theatre Royal.

The day Bart took his son out to the King's Hospital to enroll him in the club; he met Derry O'Rourke and noted how the other man's fortunes were in the ascendant. He was thirty-four, strong and fit. His home was a substantial house standing on fifteen acres in Leixlip, County Kildare, complete with fishing rights to the river. He lived there with Julie and their six children, four of whom were members of the swimming club. Like Frank McCann, he eschewed alcohol and tobacco and lived for swimming, though he found spare time for a spot of wood-carving too. His own competitive swimming career had begun in Club Sná Colmcille based in Tara Street Baths in the city centre. He was national breast-stroke champion in the 100 metres and 200 metres in 1965 and 1967 and was international team captain in 1968 and 1969. By the age of forty-three, he could boast in that *Evening Press* interview that, with just four weeks' training and despite a middle-age paunch, he managed to swim the 100 metres breast-stroke in a faster time than he recorded in winning the last of his national titles.

O'Rourke gave the impression of being laid-back. He was nothing of the kind. He was driven, as much to accumulate wealth for himself as to create Olympic champions in his pool. He dabbled in freelance insurance sales and ran a one-man operation hawking second-hand Ford Cortinas and Escorts which he advertised in *Buy and Sell* magazine, giving his phone number at the school for customers to contact. He made a tidy sum from his IASA expenses and travelled the world. Not that he was ostentatious, apart from the sweeping trench coat and the JR-style Stetson he favoured. He drove a Volvo when the name Volvo was imbued with status, but for a long time his car was a modest yellow Mazda with a King's Hospital club sticker on the back window. It was often parked on some back road in the Phoenix Park at night, when he would be inside it raping one of his child swimmers.

'He didn't kiss me once or show any affection,' one girl he raped in the Phoenix Park later recounted in the witness box at the Circuit Criminal Court. 'It was a cold and painful act. He lay on top of me and started breathing heavily. After some time, he stopped. He told me to fix my clothes. He left me home and said I was not to tell anyone. I felt dirty and a lot of pain.'

He was a criminal steeped in luck. Getting the job with the school was his first break. The King's Hospital is one of Ireland's oldest and most venerable boarding schools, attracting the sons and daughters of the nation's burghers. Its proper name when it was founded in 1669 was The Hospital and Free School of King Charles II, though it became better known as the Blue Coat School, a nod to the uniform. After merging in the mid-twentieth century with two smaller schools – Morgan's and Mercer's – it could no longer accommodate its student population in its Georgian premises in Blackhall Place, now home to the Law Society. It relocated to an eighty-acre site beside the River Liffey in west Dublin in 1971 where it has prospered as a fee-paying co-ed day and boarding secondary school promoting a

Church of Ireland ethos and overseen by a board of governors. The swimming club, which O'Rourke founded in 1971, was closely associated with the school; the school's emblem was incorporated in the club's colours of navy blue, gold and white. Swimmers' official caps and towels all bore the school's badge and photographs of triumphs in the pool were arrayed in the school corridors, though they have long since been taken down. It was an impressive pantheon of winners. Between 1976 and 1991, King's Hospital club won more senior and junior national titles, broke more Irish records and won more team competitions than any other club in the country. It would be part of Derry O'Rourke's legacy that the King's Hospital Club was destined for extinction. When the details of his secret life finally surfaced, the school sought legal advice and ordered the club to cease using its name. The club was disbanded and a new club, named Phoenix, set up its base at a different pool in west Dublin.

Derry O'Rourke was in charge of the twenty-five-metre indoor heated pool in King's Hospital from the day it opened. For twenty-four years it gave him ready access to first-class facilities for his coaching career, and a continuous supply of scantily-clad children programmed to respect him. Unlike George Gibney, he only went after girls. Unlike Frank McCann, he liked them decidedly young; swooping when they were ten or eleven or twelve. Hypnosis was his preferred weapon of submission, or, as he called it, visualisation.

He lured Swimmer A from her old club with the promise that he would improve her performance in the pool. When he hypnotised her the first time, she swam better. 'I actually won a couple of races because, when I imagined myself winning the way he told me to visualise it, it made it seem more attainable. Because of that, no alarm bells rang to alert me.'

Swimmer B remembered leaving the boardroom – the 'Chamber

of Horrors' – when she was twelve and feeling a wetness in the palms of her hands. When she looked at them she saw the nails of her clenched fist had drawn blood. 'I'd had his visualisation treatment, supposedly to relax me,' she recalled. 'Even my toes were clenched.'

O'Rourke's second lucky break came in late 1980 or early 1981 when a fifteen-year-old boarder in The King's Hospital school told a teacher on the staff whom she trusted that she was being sexually abused by the pool manager. The teacher went to a superior in the school and relayed what the girl had told him, but no action was taken. The school has no record of the complaint. The girl has said that, when it was not mentioned to her again, she felt she had made a big mistake in talking about it and resolved to say no more. Perversely, Derry O'Rourke exploited this episode in his failed High Court application to evade the first prosecution. In his judgment of the judicial review, Mr Justice Peter Kelly recorded: 'The applicant alleges that he was never confronted with this complaint, either by the person in authority or the principal of the school or indeed anyone else in the school. Had he been confronted at that time, he said he would at least have been in a position to defend himself against allegations then rather than now, some fifteen years later.'

More importantly, had he been confronted then, countless other girls would probably have been saved from his clutches. Most of the former swimmers who swore Garda statements against him were molested and raped in the succeeding years. But he kept getting away with it. Some of the women he abused as children are astonished when they look back and see themselves – educated, articulate, ambitious daughters of predominantly middle-class parents – and they wonder how the edifice never cracked. In 1981, another swimmer complained to the club secretary that O'Rourke had been in the girls' changing rooms while they were showering. That complaint was not investigated either. Six years later, on 17 September 1987, a special club meeting was convened where parents of swimmers complained about poor pool supervision, inadequate coaching, the unacceptable condition of the pool, and the theft of property which, they discovered, was being sold on.

A different culture prevailed in the Ireland of the 1970s and 1980s. While it is fallacious to argue that people were ignorant of the phenomenon of child sex abuse, it is true that relatives of victims often preferred to dispense their own form of justice to avoid a public showdown. Whether you were a Catholic or a Protestant in that Ireland, middle-class or working class, city-dweller or country, there was an expedient method of dealing with 'dirty old men' like Derry O'Rourke. He got a thump and a warning. The inherent secrecy of this form of vigilante justice militated against a pattern of complaints emerging. Crime investigators call this 'similar pattern evidence' and it is crucial in building up a case file on a suspected child sex abuser. When O'Rourke molested a swimmer in the showers in King's Hospital in 1981, prompting the broader complaint to the club secretary about his presence in the shower area, and, unusually, the girl informed her parents, her father paid a visit to the coach the next day and delivered a message with his fists. That case never went to court with the others.

Perhaps if it had been pursued through legal channels, other unexplained events might not have occurred afterwards. One such happened during a club trip to Florida when a girl rolled up a bathroom towel, stuffed it under her hotel door and set it alight. Afterwards, it was said she did it to keep the coach from entering her room. The girl later confided in another coach that O'Rourke had made sexual advances to her. Back in Ireland, O'Rourke asked the girl during a gala if she had been complaining about him.

'Why would he approach me if there wasn't a complaint made,' she reasons. 'He was always making sexual innuendos, saying he wanted to check your pulse and putting his hand on your chest. That sort of thing. On away trips, he would walk into your bedroom without knocking or he would come to your room late at night and say: "You're having trouble sleeping, I'll do relaxation therapy on you."'

In Dublin one day a loud argument was overheard in the headquarters of the IASA between Frank McCann and Hilary Hughes. They were shouting about a letter that had gone missing. It has since been confirmed that a substantial proportion of the association's files had been wiped from the computer. After this row, in September 1990, McCann and IASA treasurer Ray Kendall (who went on to become an executive member of LENS, the European governing body for swimming, after the Gibney and O'Rourke scandals) visited Derry O'Rourke at King's Hospital. The pair had never been seen on the premises before and the visit was considered highly unusual by club members.

'Kids used to leave the club suddenly, without an explanation,' Bart Nolan recalled. 'You'd be talking to a kid one night and the next morning she wouldn't be there anymore and I'd say to Derry, "Is so-and-so sick?" and he'd say, "Ah sure, she gave up".' Asked if he would have considered O'Rourke a friend at that stage, he replied: 'Yeah, sure. As a matter of fact, I liked the bastard.'

King's Hospital's most famous swimmer was Michelle Smith, later to become the controversial winner of three gold medals and a bronze at the 1996 Atlanta Olympics. While she was swimming into the history books with golds in the 200 metre individual medley and both the 400 metre individual medley and freestyle, the murder trial of Frank McCann was underway in the Central Criminal Court in Dublin. The irony being that, had his murderous arson plot gone undetected, McCann would have been the one sharing the glory at the Atlanta poolside, as president of the IASA.

In April 1994, she too upped and left King's Hospital Club, but for reasons different to those that drove away girls who had swum in the lanes around her. 'I was more or less pushed out of the club,' she said in an interview with the author after her coach was jailed. O'Rourke had been coaching her since she was twelve, but she said she was never sexually abused or approached in a sexual way by him. Because of the solitary nature of her training, she said, she had been unaware until late in the day of the unspecific rumours circulating in the club that O'Rourke was being investigated by Gardaí for some crime or other. (Most of the initial speculation was that he was suspected of theft). Regarded as somewhat stand-offish by other club swimmers, she tended not to linger and chat after training and was, therefore, less likely to hear the rumours. A record of a club meeting in the Spa Hotel in Lucan shows her concern when O'Rourke became unavailable for coaching. She inquired if he could conduct her coaching sessions in an alternative pool. After O'Rourke disappeared from the poolside at King's Hospital, her husband-to-be took over as her new coach, much to the chagrin of her old one.

Two years after these events, when she returned from Atlanta with her historic medal haul and before she was found by FINA in 1998 to have interfered with a urine test for performance-enhancing drugs (but not stripped of her medals), Michelle Smith – or, Smith de Bruin, as she was by then – declined the IASA's offer of honorary life membership because she believed someone in the organisation was leaking confidential documents about her to the media. Her failure to even partly attribute her success in Atlanta to her old coach and her club seemed a glaring omission. So too was O'Rourke's silence amid the cacophony of congratulations. Later, when she unsuccessfully appealed FINA's four-year competition ban on her at the Court of Arbitration for Sport in Lausanne, Switzerland, the IASA's absence from her shrinking band of supporters was notable.

Michelle Smith had met her future husband, Erik de Bruin, a Dutch discus-thrower and shot-putter, at the Barcelona Olympics in 1992, the last of the three consecutive games in which he competed. The following year, the IAAF, the International Athletics Federation, banned him for four years for having illegal levels of testosterone in his body. De Bruin moved to Ireland and began coaching his girl-friend at King's Hospital at the end of 1993 – the year Gardaí began investigating O'Rourke. The next year, she finished fifth in the 200 metres butterfly at the European Championships. In 1995, she became the first Irish woman to take the European titles for the 200 metres butterfly and the 400 metres individual medley. An entry in IASA records dated June 1994 indicates that the relationship had soured between the sport's golden girl and the authorities in the IASA. It 'noted that Michelle Smith has not supplied an address at which she can be contacted in Holland and all communication must be done through her parents' home in Rathcoole'.

She recalled: 'Derry wasn't happy when Erik started coaching me. Erik started to have a look at my training and what he saw didn't really make sense. I'd done most of my training by myself, without any guidance. I would have welcomed it and I asked for guidance, but I didn't get it. There could be ten or fifteen people standing around the pool in the morning when I would come in because he used to write up a session on the board and then go off for tea. He once told me, when I was about twelve, that a parent had come up to him at the side of the pool and said, "Michelle's a great little worker," and he'd said: "She'll never make it as a swimmer because she's too small". He didn't really mind if other swimmers didn't train but, when we had to swim relays, I felt it was unfair to compromise my own performance. I had a mind of my own and I tended to be stubborn at times. We would have clashed.'

Other former King's Hospital swimmers agree that O'Rourke lacked the sort of discipline in himself as a coach that he demanded of them in the pool. Yet he produced record-beating results. He was fortunate that the club's reputation attracted some of the country's best talent, which he actively sought out by visiting and writing to parents of swimmers from other clubs who showed championship potential. He was also a natural motivator, despite a tendency to be grumpy. While over in Trojans, Gibney ordered his charges not to mix with members of other clubs, O'Rourke actively communicated with other clubs. He organised more away trips that most other coaches, set regular targets for his relay teams and individual swimmers and ran competitions. For some time, he acted as a sales representative for the international Speedo swimwear company and he used this as an incentive in King's Hospital. When swimmers met their targets, he would present them with a pair of Speedo togs, which were highly desirable in Ireland's pre-Celtic Tiger era. It was typical of him to distribute written pep-talks to his charges. In one such circular, having drummed home the necessity to refine technique, increase endurance and give total dedication, he finished with a characteristic flourish. 'Swimming is something I want you to take seriously, but above all, I want it to be great fun for you. It is fun at KH. We enjoy swimming fast. We enjoy winning. We are different at The King's Hospital.'

Shortly before Christmas in 1993, after Erik de Bruin's arrival on the scene, O'Rourke invited Michelle to a meeting alone with him to discuss why she was not training under a substitute coach brought in by the club to replace him in his absence. By this time, he had been banished from the grounds of King's Hospital, but continued to teach younger swimmers in another west Dublin pool in the mornings and turned up in King's Hospital from time to time to put up schedules of training times on the notice board. Erik de Bruin intervened when he saw O'Rourke approach the swimmer and warned: 'As long as there are rumours about you, you will not be alone with Michelle,' according to de Bruin. Bart Nolan recalls that day. 'My son, Bart, and Michelle Smith were both doing their own training sessions at this stage. Bart had won six senior medley titles. O'Rourke went up to de Bruin and challenged him. An argument developed between the two of them. I still didn't know what Derry had been suspended for. I heard de Bruin saying to him, "You stay away from my girlfriend". Alarm bells rang with me. Until then I thought he might have been suspended over money. Everything was very hush-hush in the club. After that day neither Michelle nor Bart ever returned there.'

The couple packed up and made their base in de Bruin's native Netherlands, though the IASA continued to be her registration body. Her relationship with the association came under the microscope in Atlanta when her application to compete in the 400 metres was initially rejected because it was not received by FINA until after the 15 July deadline. Irish officials, who were responsible for lodging the application in compliance with the rules, insisted they had handed over all the required documentation to the Olympic Council of Ireland on July 9. The refusal to allow her compete was overturned at 11 o'clock on the night before the event.

'It was a relief to be away from the IASA,' she said. 'There was always hassle. I couldn't see it at the time, but I could feel it lifting from me when I went to Holland.'

Unknown to her, in November 1992, two years before Michelle Smith left the club, another swimmer went home to her parents and told them that Derry O'Rourke had sexually assaulted her at the pool. The seventeen-year-old girl, who had only joined the club eight days earlier, said that when she had arrived late for training, O'Rourke got her to press against a bench while he felt her arm, as if to check her muscle. He then took her by the hand and led her into the storeroom where he put his hands inside her swimsuit and cupped her breasts. (Garda evidence at his sentencing hearing six years later would attest that this was his *modus operandi* for launching serious sexual assaults on his victims). At the end of the swimming session, he offered her a lift home and asked: 'Will you be nice to me?' The girl told her parents that when she had asked him what he meant, he replied: 'We could go up into the Park on the way home.'

The parents did not procrastinate. They requested an urgent meeting with the committee of King's Hospital club. It was attended by the president, Michael McCann, the secretary, Barbara Claxton, and the treasurer, Penny Statham, as well as the swimmer. The parents repeated what their daughter had told them. This was the first formal complaint the club committee as an entity had received in relation to Derry O'Rourke, and the committee members said that they would investigate it. The remedy they proposed at the end of the process was that the coach would no longer be permitted into the girls' changing rooms. The committee members said that when they challenged O'Rourke about the incident he claimed it was standard practice to measure swimmers, that the girl was 'well developed' and that he had used the inside of her tight-fitting swimsuit to locate her pectoral muscle. The committee wrote to the swimmer and her parents on 18 November 1992 stating that the parents had behaved impeccably in their handling of the matter. They thanked the swimmer for telling them directly about the incident.

According to the Murphy Report in 1998, Michael McCann asked the swimmer to make a further written statement to justify any action they had taken and 'which might prevent any further alleged incident occurring'. The following day, the committee wrote to O'Rourke, accepting the latter's explanation for the incident. 'The committee believes that you have behaved correctly in your handling to date of the matter and particularly wishes to thank you for telling us directly your version of the alleged incident,' went the letter to O'Rourke. 'The quality of your coaching and the training programme supervised by you ... must go hand in hand with increased prudence and caution when dealing with swimmers who are often at fragile stages of their personal development. This ... committee in no way wishes to place you in any form of straight [sic] jacket or to modify that natural exuberance of swimming and coaching leadership which communicates so well to our young swimmers ... but we do urge great caution that you do not place yourself in any situation which might be misinterpreted or misconstrued by others.'

The parents were not happy with the committee's response. They went to their solicitor and to Gardaí about the incident, but they were advised that there was insufficient evidence to pursue a case. At that point, they took the precaution of getting their daughter to write a full account of what had transpired. Showing remarkable prescience, they lodged the document in a bank, pending future complaints about O'Rourke by other swimmers.

The Murphy Inquiry found that the complaint was taken seriously and formally by the club and was fully documented. 'The President of the committee stated that the coaches were instructed that measurement of female swimmers, from November 1992 onwards, was to be done by females and, that, on away trips, the practice of having a female chaperone was obligatory. A change in the structure of the dressing rooms was agreed with the school to avoid common male and female shower areas.' But, Murphy added: 'this was not minuted, or written up at the time.'

In January 1993, Gardaí commenced their inquiries, prompted by the complaint made by the woman living abroad who had read a newspaper report about the investigation of Gibney and assumed the story was about O'Rourke. She was the same swimmer who had got lost during the opening of the Moscow Olympics in 1980, after which O'Rourke was banned by the IASA. She has confirmed to the author her belief that the real reason for the ban was that somebody in authority had seen O'Rourke leaving her bedroom in Moscow. 'That was the last time he had sex with me,' she said.

There were soon a dozen females, aged from seventeen to forty-plus, who were prepared to testify in court that Derry O'Rourke had sexually abused them. A former student at King's Hospital told how he had regularly raped her in his car while it was parked at the back of the sports centre and in his house at weekends or on school half-days. A second woman recalled how he had shown her how to use tampons when she was thirteen. A third woman said he had called her into the storeroom to be measured soon after she joined the club, that he put his hand on her chest, she hit him and he fell down. Later, when he summoned her younger sister to the storeroom to be measured, the witness accompanied her, to O'Rourke's displeasure. He raged at her that she was a useless swimmer and she was wasting everybody's time.

In August 1993, a parent in the school went to see the principal, Harald Meyer, and told him there was a rumour going round that the swimming coach was being investigated by the Gardaí. Meyer made his own inquiries and was interviewed by Gardaí on 7 September, eight months after the first complaint was made by the woman in America. Following that interview, he contacted a past-pupil who had left the school in 1983. She confirmed that O'Rourke had sexually assaulted and raped her when she was twelve years old; this was

Above: Well-known swimming coach Derry O'Rourke in 2005, after being sentenced to ten years in prison; he pleaded guilty to two charges of rape and four sample indecent assault charges on dates between 1975 and 1978. He was first jailed in January 1998 with sentences totalling 107 years.

Right: Former Olympic and national swim coach, George Gibney.

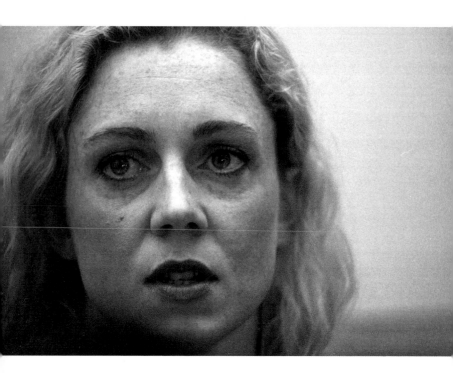

Michelle Smith De Bruin (above) controversially won three gold medals at the Atlanta Olympics in 1996 after quitting King's Hospital Swimming Club and its coach Derry O'Rourke who, she claimed, isolated and belittled her, though he did not sexually abuse her. A complaint she made about the presence of former KHSC committee members at a coaching session she gave following O'Rourke's imprisonment led to the temporary resignations of two Leinster branch officials. Her denunciations of the sport's authorities, who also included George Gibney and Frank McCann, during her career, intensified political pressure to establish the Murphy Inquiry.

When Chalkie White (above) was a promising young swimmer, he was sexually abused by George Gibney. As an adult, he worked as a swimming coach alongside Gibney, which prompted him to confront Gibney about the abuse and confide in Gary O'Toole, among others.

Right: Gary O'Toole as a young swimmer.

Below: Gary O'Toole & his father, Aidan O'Toole.

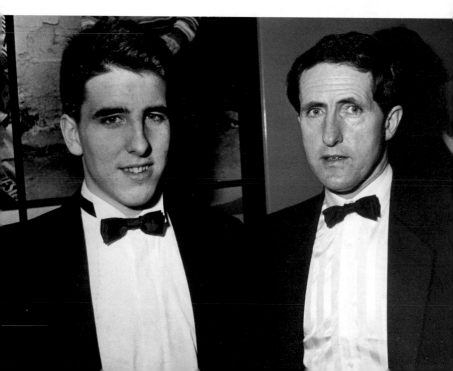

Frank McCann with his wife Esther and baby Jessica, pictured at the First Holy Communion of Esther's niece, also named Esther.

Above: Baby Jessica McCann, aged eighteen months, sits in Frank McCann's suitcase as he packs for the Barcelona Olympics in 1992.

Left: Esther McCann, 'There wasn't a bit of badness or malice in her. She always saw the good in people.'

Above: Frank McCann being led from the courts after his conviction for murder.

Above: Judge Roderick Murphy, who chaired the state-appointed inquiry into the abuses in Irish swimming.

Below: Father Ronald Bennett, former sports master at Gormanston College, being led from the courts after pleading guilty to five sample charges of indecent assault on dates from 1974 to 1981.

the same girl who had confided in the teacher in 1980 or 1981. The school said it had no record of her complaint. The woman said she had never told her parents for fear of being blamed for what had happened.

O'Rourke's victims emerged one by one. 'I was in a gym in Malahide one day and this girl came up to me and asked me was I the woman who coached in Trojans,' recalls Carole Walsh, George Gibney's former assistant in Newpark. 'She said she had heard about the guards investigating Gibney and she was surprised because she thought King's Hospital was the only place things like that happened. I said: 'Did this happen in King's Hospital?' She said: 'Yeah'. I said: 'Did it happen to you?' She said: 'Yeah'. She was badly abused. I asked her to contact the guards in Harcourt Street. This girl had been a drug addict. She was an alcoholic. She'd made several attempts at suicide. She said she remembered swimming in the Leinster Championships in the Guinness pool. Derry told her parents she needed a rest and he brought her to a room off the pool. She went in and the next thing she was waking up, feeling sore between her legs. She went back out and swam, but not well. Another day, I was driving a girl who I was coaching to Edenderry. She was gorgeous; a little chocolate box beauty. She started telling me she was abused by Derry. She said she never told anybody because Derry had been kind to her family and she was afraid of jeopardising that. She was crying in the car telling me. Her case never went to court. Her boyfriend wouldn't allow it.'

On Friday, September 10, 1993, The King's Hospital principal, Harald Meyer, served written notice on the pool manager that his employment was being immediately suspended and he was, herewith, barred from the building. 'I have been made aware of certain complaints about your behaviour in the pool/changing room area in the past,' he wrote. 'Investigations are in progress. If these investigations prove to be of a serious nature, there could be serious consequences for the school. Pending the outcome of these investigations, it is my duty to tell you that you are suspended from work on full pay until further notice. You are not to enter the school premises as coach, lifeguard or parent until further notice from me. Deliver keys to Bursar at 1 pm today. The Board of Governors and the school's solicitors have been fully briefed and have advised me to act in this manner.' Meyer told the author after O'Rourke was jailed that he verbally notified two officials of the swimming club within forty-eight hours of serving the barring notice on O'Rourke.

'I was out at King's Hospital one day in September and I saw one of Derry's children. He looked like he was crying and I asked him was his father sick [because he was not at the pool]. He said he was and I said "I hope he'll be alright,"' recalls Bart Nolan. 'The pool was closed for the afternoon session, and for the next three days. The club president came in but he didn't tell us what was wrong. I demanded a meeting but he said he couldn't tell what was going on at a general meeting. Up to that day, I'd never heard the word "abuse" mentioned about Derry. Anyway, there was a meeting at the Spa Hotel in Lucan, chaired by the president, Michael McCann, with a solicitor present. We still weren't told why Derry was being suspended. I remember the committee secretary yelling out: "Tell the people the truth!"'

Michael McCann, a Trinity College graduate with a successful debt-recovery business in Celbridge and electoral aspirations with the Progressive Democrats, was the president of King's Hospital Swimming Club. He wrote to the headmaster on Saturday, 11 September saying that O'Rourke had shown him the statement suspending him. McCann continued: 'I am instructed by the committee of our club to advise you that the club regards the action of the school as interference of contract between ourselves and Derry O'Rourke ... that should Derry O'Rourke be reinstated or not by the school after any charges against him are shown to be baseless and his national reputation or stature within the IASA or personal standing within the club be in any way damaged so that he is no longer employable by the club in his present capacity, the swimming club will seek appropriate financial recompense from the King's Hospital School.'

A week later, on Friday 17 September, Michael McCann wrote an extraordinary epistle to the Garda Commissioner, Patrick Culligan, addressed to Garda Headquarters in the Phoenix Park. Contrary to assertions he made elsewhere that the committee had not been informed of the nature of the complaints being investigated or even what agency was doing the investigating, the letter is clearly concerned with allegations of child sex abuse and Garda activity. It could also be read as showing a lack of concern for the welfare of the club's children, flagging the committee's intention to repatriate O'Rourke to his place beside the pool in under three weeks from the date of the letter, in defiance of the school ban.

Dear Commissioner,

I am writing to you as President of the King's Hospital Swimming Club which is affiliated to the Irish Amateur Swimming Association and which is based at the King's Hospital pool, Palmerstown, Dublin 20. Our club is the primary renter of pool time from The King's Hospital, a day and boarding secondary school. Our club is run by a Committee between General Meetings. Our head coach is Mr Derry O'Rourke. We are some 22 years in existence and comprise of some six coaches, some 120 families and some 300 swimmers aged from four to twenty-six years. The Club is among the top five in the country.

Deep Deception

Our Head Coach, Derry O'Rourke (aged mid-forties, happily married with six children), is an employee proper of the school with a title of Pool Manager. He is responsible for the management of the pool area, the renting of pool time, and the teaching of swimming to pupils at the school itself. He is also retained by our Club for coaching to national and international level.

I was apprised of a situation last Friday 10th September 1993, when the Head Coach Mr Derry O'Rourke, asked for a meeting with me. He produced a letter from Mr Harald Meyer MA, Headmaster of The King's Hospital, in which the Headmaster informed him (and I paraphrase from memory as the letter was couched definitely in legal terms): that the investigation was linked into a current case before the Courts; that the current case/investigation was in the Dublin area. [Author's note: Meyer's notice of suspension to O'Rourke had made neither of these references.]

This, Commissioner, is the background to our present problem.

I state at this point that Derry O'Rourke has been at The King's Hospital for the past twenty-four years or so as Pool Manager;

that he has been Head Coach at our Club for the past twenty-two years;

that I am personally aware in the past ten years of the quality and calibre of persons who have served on the Committee of the Club who would never allow misconduct to occur;

that complaints to the Committee against Derry O'Rourke have been the usual cut and thrust ones to be found in any swimming Club (and usually by parents) regarding training, procedures, selections, etc;

that there was only one instance in the past twenty-two years of coaching to this Committee's knowledge of a complaint by a family regarding their daughter which might have been construed as sexual, which was investigated by three Committee members who gave unanimous agreement that the complaint was mistaken and the incident without foundation;

that the swimmer in question continues to swim happily with the club;

that swimmers have consistently over the years transferred to our Club because of the quality of his coaching;

that because of the very disciplined nature and tight focus of swim and gym training in our coaching system, we do not have what might be termed 'problem' children or teenagers, as such are very soon weeded out by the discipline of the sport;

that trained swimmers in their sport are highly tensed persons in whom it is very easy to notice any lack of concentration or personal problems.

I further state that to (my) knowledge the only case currently before the Courts is one of the DPP-v-George Gibney former National Coach, Olympic Coach in 1984 and 1988, an official of the Irish Amateur Swimming Association and former coach to Trojan Swimming Club, which is being handled by Blackrock Garda Station;

that a past President of the Leinster Branch of the IASA, Mr Frank McCann (no relation of the undersigned), was before the Courts earlier this year on charges of murdering his wife and child in Rathfarnham;

that on Saturday 27th November evening President Mary Robinson is due to officially open our KH International Winter Gala at the Guinness Pool, Watling Street, Dublin 8;

that this being our Centenary year, President Robinson is also due to attend a banquet of the IASA the same night at the Royal Hospital Kilmainham, Dublin 8.

Deep Deception

The Committee is of the opinion that if publicity occurs based on any hint of scandal attaching to the suspension from duties of Mr Derry O'Rourke at The King's Hospital or linking him with the Gibney case or similar, then not only Derry O'Rourke, but also the Club, the IASA, the Olympic Committee and the King's Hospital School itself (are) in for a very rough time, which could lead to the cancellation of the mentioned invitations to say the least.

While I can accept the sheer coincidence of two sets of unrelated criminal proceedings referring to high ranking officials in the Irish Amateur Swimming Association in the space of one year, it would stretch my credulity and that of the public at large, were a third incident to arise in this our Centenary Year.

Specifically, the Committee of this Club wishes to know where possible and as soon as possible:

1. If an official/authorised Garda interview took place on Tuesday 7th September with Mr Harald Meyer at The King's Hospital.

2. If this investigation is linked to the DPP-v-George Gibney case.

3. If official, what the likely time span of the investigation will be, i.e. will it be over before Monday 4th October, when Mr Derry O'Rourke is due to resume him (sic) duties with the Club.

4. If the investigation proves baseless or is never proceeded with or prosecuted by the DPP (i.e. due to lack of credible evidence), as the Committee has a moral responsibility in the correct running of the Club, can the Committee find out in some way the nature of the investigation so as not to place the members of the Club in any future moral danger and so itself be accused by parents/members of negligence in the performance of duties.

I remain,
Yours faithfully,
Michael JC McCann PhB, MA
President 1993

The committee of King's Hospital Swimming Club gathered in the West County Hotel in Lucan for a special meeting on 1 October. The treasurer, Penny Statham, and Derry O'Rourke were the only absentees from the officer board. The club's solicitor, Paddy Nelligan, addressed the meeting, which was also attended by some senior swimmers and some parents, including Michelle Smith and Bart Nolan Snr. The solicitor said Derry O'Rourke's solicitor had written to the school demanding his reinstatement and, if the school refused, O'Rourke would pursue his claim formally. Michael McCann read out a prepared statement recounting that the headmaster had notified him in a meeting on Friday 10 September of O'Rourke's suspension. He claimed Harald Meyer had not told him the nature of the complaints being investigated. McCann said that the next day, Saturday 11 September, Meyer would not confirm who was investigating the complaints. He concluded, on behalf of the committee, that it was their collective opinion the events surrounding the matter had been orchestrated. However, the Murphy Report, published five years later recorded that, having requested the club president's diary for the period, it found an entry about a phone call between McCann and Meyer at 4pm on 15 September 1993, with the comment: 'Yes, Garda Inv.' Both Statham and Claxton denied to the Murphy

Inquiry that they were aware of the reason for O'Rourke's suspension from the school. Murphy found that there was 'a failure to communicate to the executive committee by individual officers who had knowledge of allegations'. It adjudged [in the case of both O'Rourke and Gibney] that: 'The supervision of the two named coaches by their club committees fell short of an adequate standard.'

At a general club meeting on October 14, a parent asked if O'Rourke would resign in the interests of the club. The coach was present at that meeting, but he was restrained from answering by Michael McCann who stated, wrongly, that there had been no official or unofficial contact with the school about the suspension. It was at this meeting, convened a month after O'Rourke was banished by the school from the premises, that the club secretary, a married woman with children and a successful career, resigned from the committee. She issued the following written statement to the elected and the ordinary members.

'As secretary of the club, I wish to make my feelings known. As this committee is elected by the members of the club, I feel all committee members should have the same knowledge and trust to work together on the committee.

'I do NOT feel the committee is being totally honest with its club parents and members. I realise, of course, that they are constrained in some instances by the law. However, I feel as the elected secretary to this committee, that I cannot continue to sit on a committee that is making decisions that I totally disagree with. Because of legal problems the committee is unable to tell everything they know and, as the parents and swimmers do not know the full story, they are in this case, therefore, dependent on the committee to do the right thing. I cannot morally support the line the committee is taking in this case. I feel we should take our lead from The King's Hospital School. Derry O'Rourke, an employee of the school for

many years, has been forbidden to enter school grounds. I would expect that the school would NOT have taken this very strong action against him without good reason. Remember also they are being advised by one of the best firms of solicitors in the country.

'When I took on the job of secretary I did so with the best intentions. I did the job to the best of my ability under the circumstances and have attended every committee meeting held. I was not invited as secretary to attend any of the meetings at the school. Michael [McCann, club president] *said he felt I was too inexperienced and excitable to attend. I would advise any would-be secretaries amongst you to remember those words, and I would ask Michael how does one gain experience if not through learning on the job? Please also note that, although I have gone back to school, this only happened since the last week in September and did not interfere in any way with my duties with the swimming club.*

'Thank you to the parents and swimmers with whom I have had dealings as Secretary. I hand in my resignation as from now.'

The decision to suspend O'Rourke was ratified by a special meeting of the school's general committee on 20 October 1993. A resolution was passed at the same meeting to sack him. He resigned from the staff of the school on 12 November, receiving two months' salary for November and December. He had already tendered his resignation as national coach to the IASA three days earlier and, in return, had been offered a place on the committee of the Leinster Branch. He declined. And still the club stood firm in its support of him.

More than two months after Meyer had briefed the two club officials about the ban on O'Rourke, it came to the headmaster's notice that the coach had been seen in the vicinity of the pool. Meyer wrote to the club president on 29 November informing him that O'Rourke's presence there contravened the ban. He would be required to write to the club again, the following 21 April, saying that Gardaí had alerted him that O'Rourke had been coaching at the pool. He expressed concern in his letter to Michael McCann that O'Rourke at been coaching at the pool during the Easter holidays and that he had previously substituted for another coach. McCann replied four days later that the Leinster Branch of the IASA had rented the pool for a training course for club coaches. He said he understood that the Leinster Branch had invited O'Rourke to assess the course participants. Other than that, McCann wrote, O'Rourke had only been present at the poolside in his capacity as the parent of club swimmers.

Despite Michael McCann's dire warnings of something akin to a constitutional crisis in his September letter to the Garda Commissioner, King's Hospital's centenary winter gala did go ahead as scheduled at the Guinness pool. The official opening was performed by local Fianna Fáil TD Liam Lawlor on Friday night, November 26. The race starter was Derry O'Rourke. The club president was an avowed believer in O'Rourke and trenchantly defended his 'good name'. Even after O'Rourke was jailed, Michael McCann told an inquiry appointed by the government to investigate child abuse in swimming that he still believed the complaint made by the seventeen-year-old swimmer in November 1992 'lacked substance'.

The prevailing atmosphere during this period was one of incredulity. The committee believed it was not at liberty to broadcast to the ordinary club members what was going on behind the scenes and, beside any legal constraints on them, it must have been hard for them to believe that O'Rourke had been leading such a sick double life. He was, after all, the founder and the public face of their club and, unlike Gibney, he had a more likeable personality. In February 1997, Michael McCann wrote to the *Sunday Times* newspaper, threatening to sue it for libel over a story it ran about the seventeen-year-old girl's complaint to the club committee in November 1992. 'This matter was immediately investigated by myself and two other lady members of the Committee,' he wrote. 'The matter was seen unanimously by us to be without foundation – the female swimmer was going through a difficult period at the time. The family wrote to the Committee to thank us for our efforts and our quick attention.' Ten months later, a solicitor wrote to the *Sunday Times* about the same article. He was acting on behalf of Penny Statham who, along with Barbara Claxton and Michael McCann, had conducted the investigation of the allegation. The letter demanded 'reasonable compensation to our client for the most serious damage to her good name' by implying that the committee had not properly investigated the complaint, along with a submitted four-paragraph apology and retraction to be prominently published in the newspaper within seven days.

As the committee persisted with its obfuscation, Bart Nolan's patience ran out. Along with Swimmer A and three sets of parents (including the mother and father of the girl whom O'Rourke assaulted in November 1992), he formed an *ad hoc* protest lobby. 'Parents for Change in Irish Swimming' was convinced that if standards were to improve in the protection of children in swimming, it was up to responsible parents to force change to come about. The group started meeting informally under Nolan's chairmanship two or three times a week in a room in the West County Hotel. They founded their own club, the Grattan Swimming Club, and registered it with the IASA. The club, which continued to exist after O'Rourke was freed from jail on 1 March 2007, paid 8euro per member to the association in recent years (plus, in a twist of irony, levies imposed by the IASA to foot the legal bills incurred in defending O'Rourke's victims' damages claims). The existence of the club gave them to right to speak at meetings, and they used it – much to the ire of other delegates. Over the years, Nolan staged a one-man picket, complete with placard, outside the association's annual general meetings. He was arrested (briefly) in May 1998 in Salthill, Galway after Gardaí received a complaint from a swimming official attending the AGM. His crime had been to hand out leaflets entitled, 'Is Your Child Safe in Swimming?' which posed the question: 'If mandatory reporting is not required, is MORAL COURAGE optional?' On another occasion, Nolan was banned from a King's Hospital gala in Ringsend. When he defied the ban and turned up anyway, staff at the Sportsco venue applauded him. 'I was the only docker in swimming and what I've seen there isn't exactly a great advertisement for the sport,' he says. 'Judge Roy Bean, the hanging judge, said he could never hang a man for asking questions but he could for answering them. I always quote that to them. They don't like it.' Whenever Nolan and other members of Grattan Swimming Club raised questions at meetings about the sport's failure to respond satisfactorily to complaints of child abuse, they were referred to as 'the sex people'.

Three months after the ban was imposed on Derry O'Rourke by the King's Hospital school, the oddest thing happened. On December 7, 1993, the King's Hospital club committee issued a statement to its swimmers and their parents announcing – not that the coach was being investigated by Gardaí and had been barred from the school premises – but that he had been promoted by the club four days earlier to the newly-created position of Development Director on a one-year contract. An intrinsic element of this bespoke role was to develop juvenile swimming and, for this, he would be paid IR£15,800 for the twelve months – more than half as much again as he was getting as coach. The statement implied that O'Rourke had actually resigned as coach in order to take up this more important task in steering the club towards fulfilling its potential. No minute exists to indicate that O'Rourke's unprecedented appointment was put to a vote by the members.

'To this end, Derry O'Rourke, our Head Coach for the past twenty years, has tendered his resignation as Head Coach to the Committee, which the Committee has accepted,' the statement announced. It added that the committee also proposed to develop swimming for minors (thirteen and fourteen year olds) in another named Dublin pool, 'again under the direction of Derry O'Rourke'. This was the same committee whose President was aware of O'Rourke being investigated by Gardaí and whose other two members had been made aware a year previously of an allegation that O'Rourke had sexually assaulted a swimmer in the showers.

O'Rourke delivered a pep-talk to club members upon taking up his new appointment, which he liberally sprinkled with invocations for divine favour. 'My fervent hope is that God's good grace will continue to guide us and that His will can keep our King's Hospital traditions intact,' he wrote. 'There can be no place in King's Hospital for disharmony or argument.' He specified a target of IR£50,000 annual income for the club. He said he would drum up sponsorship working by phone and fax machine from outside King's Hospital, but that 'I can be in attendance on the bank' to train coaches. 'The potential for our club is limited only by our imagination,' he enthused. 'Personally I am burning with enthusiasm to develop the whole thing. By a tragic accident of circumstances, we have been given an opportunity to develop our club on the lines beyond any club before in Ireland. We could be the future of Irish swimming.'

In order to sanction the new job for O'Rourke, the club's constitution had to be amended. The new clause required that the development director be appointed by the committee for twelve months at a time and that he 'shall be overall responsible for the teaching and coaching of swimming with the club'. It stipulated that all other coaches be appointed in consultation with him and that he would ultimately have the say in selecting swimmers for galas and competitions. One of the objectives of the new post, as defined by Michael McCann in a letter to O'Rourke dated December 3, 1993, was to develop an alternative pool site.

'When things blew up in terms of Derry and the school we weren't told what had happened,' Michelle Smith de Bruin recalled. 'We were told he was unwell. Why did the committee tell us he was sick? ... Why did they hide the truth? We were told that he wasn't allowed on the pool deck by the school but the committee of the club said they didn't know why. I, in effect, had no coach. At the same time, Erik stepped in, but Derry still had an involvement in the club. Derry wasn't happy when Erik started coaching me. There was another coach brought in when Derry stopped coaching. The club told me I could do my own training session with Erik in the mornings but, in the afternoons, I'd have to do the same as everyone else. I said to Derry: 'You were national and Olympic coach. You know this won't work as a programme'. He said: 'Yes, I know, you're right'. He said he'd speak to the committee. But they didn't change their minds. I had to row in with everyone else's training session in the afternoons. There were three coaches coming to sessions and the whole senior group was turned upside-down. I was being coached by four different people.'

A row erupted between Michelle and Erik de Bruin on one side and the Leinster Branch after the couple agreed to run a series of training sessions for swimmers aged twelve and upwards under the auspices of the Leinster Branch in the winter of 1997. In October of that year, the IASA had asked the Leinster Branch to investigate the conduct of the 1993 officers of King's Hospital club in the handling of complaints about O'Rourke, but the investigation never went ahead. 'On the first day, when I arrived at the pool, I was shocked to see one of the members of the [King's Hospital] club committee there,' said Smith, who received a letter from O'Rourke while he was being investigated urging her to turn to God. 'I didn't think it was appropriate that these people be involved in my training days because I was under the impression that the Leinster Branch was going to have an investigation of its own into the events surrounding Derry's suspension.'

Her solicitor, Peter Lennon, wrote to the vice-president of the IASA, Mary O'Malley, outlining his client's concerns and expressing Smith de Bruin's resolve to have nothing to do with members of the King's Hospital committee. A tumultuous branch executive meeting was convened the following Tuesday night at which Statham and Claxton were asked to stand aside. According to reports afterwards, accusations and counter-accusations ripped through the room about the bizarre way the King's Hospital committee had responded to the Garda investigation of O'Rourke, culminating in his promotion with a 50 per cent pay increase. A delegate asked if the committee had taken legal advice before promoting him to Development Director. The answer was 'yes'. Someone else asked if the club president had tried to find out why Gardaí were investigating the coach. The reply came back: 'We were told there was no investigation.' By the conclusion of the meeting, the club secretary Barbara Claxton and its treasurer Penny Statham – both long-serving members of the Leinster Branch executive – had resigned in protest at what they regarded as unwarranted criticism of their actions. At the ensuing annual general meeting of the Leinster Branch in a Kilkenny hotel on 22 November, a motion was passed to discuss Claxton's and Statham's resignations. Standing orders were suspended to allow a debate on the role of the

King's Hospital committee and a vote was taken to bar members of the media from the debate. It was carried by thirty-three votes to two. Some delegates complained that Claxton and Statham had been 'treated shabbily'. Demands were made that critics of the pair either justify their comments or apologise to the women. The outcome was that they were reinstated at the AGM with a formal statement being issued by president, Harry Kavanagh, in which he regretted the embarrassment the episode had caused the two women. 'The president apologised for the fact that, in an earlier statement, their names had been mentioned,' the press release stated. 'That, understandably, caused concern and embarrassment to both people.'

In July 1995, Barbara Claxton, who had been King's Hospital Club secretary at the time of the November 1992 complaint and was now club president, issued the following statement to the members. 'On Monday 10 July, I understand Derry O'Rourke was arrested and charged with alleged sexual offences ... to my knowledge there has only been one incident which had been reported to the committee in 1992. Other than that one complaint, I personally am unaware of any other complaint either during my seven years on the committee or beforehand.

'When Derry O'Rourke was suspended from King's Hospital School the club was given to understand by the school that the reason related to something which happened within the school and had nothing to do with the swimming club. At no time have the club been told differently. As the club operates on school property and they did not allow Derry O'Rourke to coach at the pool but as he was permitted on the bank and on school premises we, the club, employed him as Development Officer. At all times we acted with legal advice. Had we dismissed him then without any cause we could have been involved in legal action which the club could not afford.

'If any member of the club or of this committee knows of any incident and had not reported to the committee, they have failed in their duty to the club, their position as a member of the committee and more importantly to all the swimmers in the club.'

The Murphy Inquiry accepted Claxton's evidence that she did not know that the investigation related to O'Rourke's conduct at the pool and in the changing area.

The day after Derry O'Rourke was sentenced to jail in 1998, an IASA official was quoted in the press. 'I wish they [the victims] had come to us about it,' she lamented. But more than fourteen years after he was banished from the grounds of The King's Hospital, leading to the circumstances in which the Leinster Branch formally apologised to two club committee members, the coach's victims would still be waiting to hear the word 'sorry' addressed to them by the swimming association. During a week of intense negotiations between lawyers to settle the compensation claims of twelve victims in February 2008, one of the plaintiffs' requests was that the swimming authorities and the school formally acknowledge, once and for all, the suffering they had endured. They did not demand any acknowledgement of failure on the part of the swimming authorities in the knowledge that such an admission could amount to an acceptance of liability and two more of O'Rourke's victims were still negotiating a settlement through a separate legal team. (These were finally concluded in July 2008). The defendants, for their part, attempted unsuccessfully to bind the women into signing a confidentiality clause to keep the terms of the agreement secret. Unlike the swimmers who were abused by O'Rourke, they seemed not to have grasped the lesson that there could be no more secrets.

8. 'The Most Devious

Psychopath'

The passing of 1993 brought no relief from Irish swimming's *annus horribillis*. The repercussions of the events it had set in train were going to be felt for many years to come; for so long, indeed, that one commentator wondered if someone high up in the sport had accidentally smashed a large mirror; or two.

The New Year began with news of the death from cancer of Fr Michael Cleary. 'His loss will be felt by many,' mourned the leader of the Opposition in the Dáil, John Bruton, in tributes published in the first newspapers of the year 'Fr Cleary used simple day-to-day words to pass on values that have endured for generations.'

A week after the funeral, a man whose child the priest had fatefully arranged to be adopted was ushered into the Central Criminal Court in the Four Courts by prison officers for the commencement of his trial on charges of double murder. Frank McCann pleaded not guilty. Kenneth Mills, senior counsel for the DPP set out the State's case that he murdered Esther McCann and Jessica McCann in order to avoid having to tell his wife their application to formally adopt Jessica had been rejected by the Adoption Board on the grounds that he was an unfit adoptive father, thereby saving his reputation from certain ruin.

In the first week of the trial, Detective Garda Brendan Gallagher was shown an exhibit by a prosecution lawyer. It was a mass card addressed to Frank McCann. Inside was written the message: 'At the request of Ha, Ha, the Holy Scripture of the Mass will be offered for Francis McCann, at the request of the Rev. Burn.' Evidence was given that the words, 'Burn You Bastard', had been daubed on the rear wall of the Cooperage bar in Blessington on September 3, 1992, mere hours before Esther and Jessica died. During his detention for questioning in Tallaght Garda Station, it was testified; McCann had claimed that he was the victim of a campaign of intimidation by a mystery man. He claimed that someone with 'a clear, well-spoken accent' had phoned him and threatened: 'Pay up'. Otherwise, the voice had said, he would be 'burned out'.

On day seven of the trial, a gas fitter, Norman Fitzgerald, told Mr Justice Rory O'Hanlon that he had responded to a complaint from the defendant of a gas leak at his house on July 28, 1992. He said he found that a joint connecting gas pipes in number 39 Butterfield Avenue had come apart only a week after being installed in the course of up-grading a gas meter on July 20. Somebody must have 'pulled it apart', the witness opined. On day eight, the fourth witness from Bord Gáis, Thomas Kennedy, the quality control manager for the eastern region, recalled visiting the house in Rathfarnham on September 3, 1992, less than twenty-four hours before the fire, after McCann had called him to see about having work done on his mother's house. Thomas Kennedy remembered seeing a blow lamp on the hall table in Frank McCann's house. On day nine, Patrick Walsh, a customer services manager with Bord Gáis, said there was no doubt that there had been a substantial gas leak in the house on July 28. He concluded that the original joint had been correctly fitted but that it had later been disassembled. Day eleven of the trial was adjourned. On day twelve – Thursday 27 January – the jury was sent home for the weekend by the judge.

The following Monday, January 31, having listened to ten days of evidence and a queue of witnesses, the twelve jurors returned to the Four Courts only to be told that they were being discharged. Announcing the abandonment of the trial, Judge O'Hanlon explained that there was a question over the accused man's fitness to plead. He said doubt had arisen over McCann's competence to follow the proceedings and to properly instruct his lawyers and that medical evidence had been called in the jury's absence which supported the proposition that he was unfit to go on. McCann was held in continuing custody pending the fixing of a new trial date. It was impermissible in law for either the jury that was discharged that day or the new jury empanelled twenty-nine months later to be apprised of the events that had caused the sudden collapse of the first trial. What happened was that McCann had been found in his prison cell attempting to set himself on fire with a match and an aerosol can of deodorant.

McCann's second trial began on the day before Michelle Smith's first gold medal swim at the Barcelona Olympics. While the Irish nation was transfixed by television pictures of her triumphs, Frank McCann too was about to make history as the subject of the State's longest-running murder trial, though it would, in time, be superceded by the trials of Catherine Nevin for conspiring to murder her husband, Tom, and of Brendan O'Donnell, whom McCann had taught to swim in the Central Mental Hospital. The trial opened on June 10, 1996 and finished on August 15, after the jury had deliberated for eight hours and ten minutes before returning a guilty verdict. More than three weeks of the hearing were consumed with legal argument in the jury's absence about the admissibility of McCann's interviews in Tallaght Garda Station in November 1992.

Esther's mother, Brigid, and her siblings – Marian Leonard, Phyllis O'Brien and Pat O'Brien – attended court throughout the trial. So too did Jeanette McCann, Jessica's biological mother. They heard Detective Garda Seamus Quinn explain to the judge that the fire was probably ignited by somebody pouring a large quantity of accelerant, such as petrol, in the hallway and a gas blow torch being trained on a gas canister, also placed in the hall. The fire, he said, was likely to have been started by a person standing in the front doorway and throwing in a match. They also heard Garda James Murphy from Rathfarnham station testify that McCann had tried to have Esther's life insured for £50,000 two weeks before she perished in the fire.

On August 1, the trial had to be adjourned when McCann began trembling violently in the witness box. The State had completed presenting its case that morning and he had been in the witness box for half an hour. He was recalling his arrival home in the early hours of 4 September 1992 to find his house on fire; how he had run, distraught, into the garden, and how he was put on a stretcher and taken to hospital in an ambulance. His lips began to tremble.

'Did you see Detective Inspector Tony Sourke the next day?' asked the cross-examiner.

At this point, McCann started hyperventilating. The jury was led away to the jury room while medical evidence was given about his fitness to continue. There was a strong sense of déja vu. This time, however, the learned opinion was that there was no impediment to the defendant carrying on with his testimony.

Occasional forays were made to the courtroom throughout the trial by some of McCann's erstwhile colleagues in the swimming world, who had been visiting him in the Central Mental Hospital and Mountjoy Prison since he was charged. They heard the State pathologist, Professor John Harbison, give factual evidence about the condition of the victims' bodies; how the woman and the child had died from inhaling smoke and fumes when 'a raging inferno engulfed their home' and about the 'extensive burns' on Esther's body. A couple of swimming people returned to court for the closing speeches in August. They heard the State reiterate its theory that McCann had opted for double-murder as preferable to the curtailment of his ascent through the swimming ranks in the event of his secret life being divulged if Esther had found out about the other child.

He showed no emotion as Mr Justice Paul Carney sentenced him to two concurrent terms of life imprisonment for the murder of his wife and the child she used to call 'my darling daughter'.

In his retirement, Detective Inspector Tony Sourke, who had interviewed him in Tallaght Garda Station over those two days in November 1992, said of Frank McCann: 'He was the most devious psychopath I ever dealt with.'

9. 'He's Always There'

On July 7, 1994, in the lacuna between Frank McCann's two murder trials, Derry O'Rourke's unprecedented contract of employment as Director of Development was terminated by King's Hospital Swimming Club, on the instructions of the committee. He was given three months' notice. In his president's report at the club's annual general meeting on 31 January 1995, Michael McCann explained that the new position had not worked out 'for administrative and financial reasons'. He thanked O'Rourke for his 'outstanding contribution' and added: 'We parted on amicable terms.'

By the time of the AGM, the Garda file on the investigation of Derry O'Rourke had been with the Director of Public Prosecutions for almost two months, having been forwarded to his office before Christmas 1994. Yet the president's statement continued cryptically: 'There is no place in Irish amateur swimming for unfounded criticism, nor is there a place in King's Hospital Swimming Club for private agendas.' The club secretary also paid tribute to O'Rourke in her report to the AGM.

He was formally charged in Kilmainham district court in July 1995 with ninety counts of child sex abuse. On July 10, 1995, the book of evidence was served. Having watched his counterpart, George Gibney, walk free from a battery of similar charges, O'Rourke was not fazed, for he was about to embark on the same course of action. In the High Court, his lawyers argued during a judicial review that the alleged crimes were said to have happened too long ago for him to defend himself properly and that the allegations were so unspecific as to prejudice his position. He was innocent, the court was told, and if he had to face prosecution, he would plead his innocence to the bitter end. In a chance encounter with Bart Nolan in Henry Street in the centre of Dublin one day, the bailed coach enquired of the retired docker if he would be able to acquire some materials for him for his wood carving hobby.

– When's the case coming up? Nolan ventured, feeling awkward at suddenly coming face to face with the coach whom he had only seen from a distance in court in recent times.

– My lawyers have told me it'll never come to court, O'Rourke replied, betraying none of the discomfiture Bart Nolan was feeling. – I was doing nothing wrong, only putting my arm around them.

His optimism proved ill founded.

On 27 February 1997, the High Court refused to restrain the Director of Public Prosecutions from proceeding with the charges against (Derry O'Rourke). The earlier charges were alleged to have been committed between the years 1976 and 1984, while the remainder of the charges related to offences alleged to have been committed between 1991 and 1992. Thus, with regard to the delay between the first alleged offence and the date on which the coach was charged, there was a period of more than nineteen years, which the Court regarded as a significant period of time. However, the Court accepted the uncontroverted evidence of a psychologist explaining the delay, and took in to account also the relationship between the coach and the complainants. All of the complainants were, at the time of the alleged offences, girls of tender years, whereas the coach was an adult of about thirty years of age. The court was satisfied on the evidence that the relationship between the coach and the complainants was not merely one between adult and children. It was a great deal more than that, by virtue of the position held by the coach, his status as a swimming coach of some note, and the position of the complainants at that time.

Further, the Court was satisfied that the charges were sufficiently specific so that the coach was in no way prejudiced by them. Indeed, rather than alleging an offence at a date unknown in a particular calendar year, each year was broken down into four quarters and each allegation was made in respect of a particular quarter. Accordingly the Judge could find no basis upon which to prohibit proceeding with the prosecution. (Report of the Independent Inquiry into Matters Relating to Child Sexual Abuse in Swimming).

'We made legal history,' said Swimmer A afterwards. 'It took five years from making my initial Garda statement to the day he was convicted. One of the hardest moments for me in court was meeting a girl who had been an absolutely fantastic swimmer in King's Hospital. She would have been one of my heroes. She was the one who made the first complaint to the Gardaí. She turned to me during one of the court recesses and said how she remembered me joining King's Hospital and that she knew I would be next on his hit list. She said she felt the guilt of knowing it but not being able to do anything about it. She was crying, and I was crying. Hers were tears of guilt. My tears were because she'd had to carry that awful burden all those years.'

Twenty-three months after he was sent to jail, Derry O'Rourke made his first public appearance when he returned to Kilmainham district court to face dozens of new charges of child abuse. The fifty-nine new counts of indecent assault brought his running total of charges to 149. These fresh charges pertained to six female swimmers and paedophile crimes he committed against them between 1970 and 1992. All six women had contacted Gardaí after their former coach was jailed in January 1998.

* * *

K was in the kitchen of her family home that day in January 1998 after O'Rourke was taken in the prison van to the old Curragh jail. The radio was chattering in the background. Suddenly, she stopped doing whatever she was doing. She thought she knew the voice coming from the radio. It was Swimmer A, talking anonymously. She was telling Pat Kenny about Derry O'Rourke's relaxation and visualisation stratagems and his appetite for measuring girls' muscles in the Chamber of Horrors. When Kenny accidentally addressed the woman by her authentic first name, K sat frozen in her kitchen. The woman had been one of her cohort of swimmers. The realisation seeped into her like dread. There could be no more denial. No more running from her childhood.

'I picked up the phone and rang a girl I knew and I said: "Oh my God, it's true. I'm one of them." After that, my skin erupted in lumps. These lumps came out all over my head and my body. I had pains, aches, headaches, exhaustion. I couldn't sleep. I was all over the place. When I went to see the guards and they took my statement, they said they'd have to go to see him in the Curragh Prison. I panicked. I was like a scared child. I said: "Are you going to tell him I told you? Forget it, just forget it. You can't tell him what I said." It took them another hour to calm me down.'

O'Rourke had strolled into her family's happy-go-lucky life when she was ten years old. Fate struck at the national swimming championships when he approached her parents after seeing her swim and offered to take her on as one of his elite troupe of swimmers. They were proud that their first-born child and only daughter was being head-hunted by the sport's supremo and signed her up with King's

Hospital Swimming Club.

'I don't remember the first time [he sexually abused her]. I don't remember a time when it wasn't happening. Can you understand that?' she asks. 'It wasn't only about touching you. It was the way he looked at you. During competitions you would hear his voice above all the other voices. When you were getting out of the pool and he was sitting on the far bank you could feel his eyes on your neck. He was in your neck. It was fear. The girls' changing rooms were at the far end of the pool. He would be sitting at the top. You had to walk the whole length of the bank in your togs to get to your lane. He would look at you the whole time.

'I wouldn't be there in my head when it was happening. You had to go away, to shut it off. I loved swimming. I wanted to swim but I didn't want to be there. I was suffering from depression while I was swimming, as a young child. I can see that now. At that time it was expensive to be a member of King's Hospital. My brothers all played rugby but their sport was put to one side for my swimming. At weekends, there were medals coming home, there were trophies coming home. For me, swimming was the best thing in my life. I was so happy when I was in the water. And yet the worst thing in my life happened to me when I was swimming. There were trips abroad for competitions. I remember one trip to Germany. He didn't tell me until shortly before it that I'd been picked to go. He did things like that to have control over you. He told my dad that I was going on the trip and Dad was thrilled, but he said: "You don't have to come. I'll take good care of her". Dad used to get up at 5.10 every morning to drive me to the pool. He'd sleep in the car in a sleeping bag with a hot water bottle Mam made for him. Sleet, snow, whatever. Mam would have breakfast ready when we got home and Dad would drive me to school. Then Mam would collect me at 4.30 and drive me to the pool and I'd be there until 6 pm. My dream was to swim for Ireland.'

K is telling her story in the same kitchen where she first acknowledged to herself that she was one of O'Rourke's victims. The silverware of her roseate progress in the swimming pool is nowhere to be seen. She still has the shoulders of a swimmer though. They are strongly defined as she reaches for another cigarette. The butterfly used to be her best stroke; the one that lifts the swimmer like a dolphin out of the water in thrashing cascades. It should have carried her to exhilarating heights. Instead, she sits and smokes and says: 'My new year resolutions every year are: one, I'm not going back into hospital and, two, I'm not going to kill myself this year.'

She knew what O'Rourke was doing to her was 'wrong'. At seventeen, she packed her bags and left Ireland. 'I kept moving – to other jobs, to other countries.' She banished every memory of O'Rourke from her mind, without knowing she was doing it. 'And I became a hateful person. I have only made one good friend in all the years since I was seventeen. I never had a real relationship with a guy, the way other girls did. I'd be drunk. I wasn't comfortable with people. If a male put a hand on my shoulder, I'd jump. I was physically sick. I was a horrible person. I was angry. I dug myself deep into my work. My life was work, sleep, eat, drink. Alcohol became my best friend. I used to go to bed at night and say, "God, what did I do so bad that made me like this?" Trying to live with myself was horrible.

'I was the regional manager of a big food company with two hundred people working for me. I was working a hundred hours a week. I had a four-bedroom house and I was paying the mortgage on my own. I knew when I got home at night, when I drove up my car and the lights of the alarm would flicker when I'd press the button, I knew I had to be me and I couldn't be me. I lived abroad for ten years. I was in London in 1995 when I got a phone call one night from someone at home saying he'd been arrested and wondering what it might be about. I said I didn't know but I remember thinking when I put the phone down: "I know what it's about". It started to grow inside me, but I kept pushing it down.

'I came home for a break and I was drunk and I said something. It must have been in the papers about him around then. The next morning Mam asked me about it, but I wouldn't say anything. That morning, I got on a plane and said I'm never going back there. Mam was starting to put two and two together. She used to go to Mass every morning and she would see him and his wife in the front pew. While the file was with the DPP, my mam had to sit in the same church as him. She and Dad told me: "No matter what happens in your life, you can always come home". I remember watching Andrew Madden [a former altar boy sexually abused by the Catholic priest, Fr Ivan Payne] on the *Late Late Show* and thinking "How can he tell the whole country what was done to him – I couldn't do that".'

K's complaint, and those of five other females, came to court in July 2000. O'Rourke pleaded guilty to all charges and was sentenced to seven years imprisonment in 2001, to run concurrently with the sentences he was already serving. (A third prosecution of rape charges against him, relating to a student in King's Hospital school from 1975 to 1978, ended on 24 January 2005 with the imposition of another ten-year sentence. It was back-dated to the year 2000, to run concurrently with the twelve years he had received at the outset, in January 1998. In effect, he would not serve a day extra for all the subsequent rape and assault convictions he collected after the first trial). In all, he would serve nine years in jail out of 130 years handed down by the courts.

'Even in court, even with him in handcuffs, my brothers had to hold me,' K continues. 'I went downstairs to the toilets and I couldn't come out. I was too scared. I'd never been in a courtroom in my life. I'd never spoken to a guard. I walked out of court that day and I'm sure the file went into a cabinet and a key was turned in it and that was the end of it, as far as the system was concerned but it was far from over for me. I left court with one of the other girls and we were like two children. I was that little girl who used to go swimming: frightened. That was in July. In November, I took an overdose and threw myself down the stairs. I had a total breakdown. The times I've done it [attempted suicide], I wanted death. I didn't want to be talking to anybody the next day. I didn't thank anybody for helping me. I hated my family for saving me. When I got home from hospital, Mam was at the door. She put her arms around me. I said: "Mam, I'm going to be OK". She said: "K, all I want is for you to be OK".'

It was a bright summer's day when K picked up a voice message left by a Garda on her phone to call him back at the station. She tapped out the number.

– You left a message for me to call you, she said.

– Yes, he said, I'm afraid we've pulled a middle-aged woman out of the canal and your phone number is on the body.

– What colour is her hair? asked K.

– Light brown. It looks as if she's just had it done.

(I knew in my heart then. Mam had got her hair done on Saturday.)

– Is there a red car?

– No—

Oh, thank God, she thought.

– ... but there has been one seen in the area.

Her father and one of her brothers went down to the canal to identify her fifty-eight-year-old mother's body. She was wrapped in a body bag. Her skin was still warm, despite having been in the water. She cannot have been long dead when a passerby had spotted her from the bridge overhead and raised the alarm. Four days before taking her life, she had told her only daughter how much she loved her and how sorry she was for failing to look after her.

'He killed her,' says K. 'I can't even think of my mam's death without him being there. He's always there. He might as well have stood behind her and pushed her into the canal. It never goes away. It's what I am as a person now. Everything that has happened in my life is a result of what he did to me. Mam is dead. It's ironic that all my parents ever wanted was for us to be able to swim. And Mam drowned.

'I was back in hospital in June and I remember seeing Colm O'Gorman [who was sexually abused by Fr Sean Fortune in the Catholic diocese of Ferns] on television talking about what happened to him. I thought to myself: "How can he sit there and talk about it? My God, he must be better." It gave me hope that one day I could get better and maybe I could talk about it and it would help somebody else. There's probably somebody now starting to acknowledge what happened to them and when that starts your world starts to collapse.

'They let me out in September and I ended up in casualty in London. I'd taken an overdose. In February I ended up in the secure unit, the lock-up unit, in John of God's in Dublin. The light bulb over the bed was removed. They took away my deodorant and the belt of my pyjamas. There were no chairs, no locks in the doors. The picture I had of Mam, they took the glass out of the frame. I had my cigarettes, but I had no lighter. I asked Dad to bring in a lighter, but they must have checked him before he came in and they confiscated it. I was mad. I'd wanted the lighter to set my dressing gown on fire. You know the way an oak tree grows for a hundred years and when it's cut down its roots are so deep in the ground that they'll never be gone? Well, when someone touches a child it hurts so deep, like the roots of that oak tree. You can't just cut it out, can you?

'Jim McDaid was the Minister for Sport and he was in charge of swimming when all this was going on. He said [during the general election in May 2002] that people who committed suicide were selfish. He doesn't realise how much he hurt people. I've spent most of my life trying to kill myself. I know what it's like to want to do it. It's the only way to get some freedom and peace. My Mam was the most fantastic, wonderful mother. … She was the most kind-hearted person you could meet. She wasn't selfish.'

***

That January day in 1998 when Swimmer A walked from the Four Courts to her family business after watching Derry O'Rourke go to prison, she triggered a series of national events when she picked up the phone and rang the Department of Arts, Sport & Recreation. She had been part of Bart Nolan's group meeting regularly since the news began spreading in King's Hospital about the Garda investigation of O'Rourke and she had learned valuable lessons about the need for persistence.

'How did I arrive at this point?' she asks. 'I was an only child, born into a middle-class background. My parents were self-employed. They worked very hard and I benefited from it with private schools and ballet classes. My father was an amazing man. He was fanatical about hurling and Gaelic football and he was incredibly kind. I knew from a young age that his love was unconditional. He doted on my mother. When things were tight, he always ensured she got her hair done or bought a new dress for herself. My mother and I share what I can only describe as a precarious relationship, which was exacerbated by the fact that at fifteen I told her Derry was doing things and she said there were always dirty old men, even in her day. End of conversation. The utter feeling of isolation was overwhelming at that point. Alcohol became my crutch. It was easy. On away trips for swimming, it was easy to get loaded under the supposed supervision that we should have had. At home, my parents didn't drink. I drank vodka or whiskey or brandy that could be topped out without too much bother. I thought I had it hidden well. I'd have a couple before school in the morning. I never drank enough to be intoxicated, just enough to take the edge off the day and get me through it.

'My redemption came when I was twenty-five. Outwardly, I was successful. I had my own business and I was engaged – mismatched, but still engaged. Nobody realised the struggle I had passing a pub. I could smell the alcohol from the door. I longed for the security I used to feel in smoky dark corners, just me and my best friends – Bacardi and coke, vodka and bitter lemon, Canadian Club and slimline. One evening, I got chatting to this lovely fellow about the Dublin social scene and some of the people we both knew. Then he said the most extraordinary thing. He said, "You drink much". I didn't know whether it was a statement or a question. It turned out this guy was – is – an alcoholic. At that time he was on the dry for ten years and he was a sponsor in the AA. He told me afterwards he'd recognised similar personality traits in me that made him ask the question. I knew my time was up. I had to start looking at things sober.'

Having quit drinking at a time when she was aware that Gardaí were investigating George Gibney for crimes against children, Swimmer A found herself inexplicably troubled.

'I threw myself into my work but still I was waking at night deeply upset but not knowing what exactly was wrong. Eventually, one day in work a client, who does a bit of part-time swim coaching, said in conversation, "Oh, by the way, I believe your old coach is under investigation." The walls came tumbling down. This was it, my Armageddon.'

After what Swimmer A had gone through in her life, she was not going to be easily put off by the elusiveness of a government minister. When Jim McDaid's secretary told her the minister was in Donegal and unavailable, she insisted that he would want to talk to her. An appointment for a meeting the following week was offered and accepted.

'The day I walked out of court … my life was never going to be the same again,' she recalls. 'I can't actually say that I felt elated. There was – and is – so much that needs to be changed to make it safer for kids to go swimming. Once I got the appointment to meet the minister I needed to get the facts and figures and a group of people around me so that we could give him a representative flavour of what had been going on. I was keen to have Chalkie White there to highlight the incredible miscarriage of justice in the George Gibney case. I arranged to meet Bart Nolan at his house on the Saturday. We pored over documents and, basically, I put together a structured presentation to bring to McDaid.

'We met the following week – Bart, myself and [she names a fellow victim and four parents from the club]. Annmarie McCrystal, the solicitor who'd come to court with one of the other girls, was there too. I distinctly remember, as we stood outside the Dáil before going in to meet the minister, someone asked me what Chalkie White was doing there [because he hadn't much to do with Derry]. I said we had to draw attention to the total ineffectiveness of the swimming authorities in their response to children's welfare and safety and that we especially needed to highlight the George Gibney case as his victims were still in limbo with no sign of closure. So off we went, this band of warriors with one common purpose – to make things safer. We were an inconvenience to a lot of people. We were branded trouble-makers. We were all so green. We thought we'd been brought up in a system that worked for us. The amount of political machinations that went on was an eye-opener. As the saying goes, fools rush in where angels fear to tread.'

10. On the Run

The jubilation that greeted the jailing of Derry O'Rourke in January 1998 amplified the denial of justice to the victims of George Gibney. Though he was effectively sentenced to a life on the run, he was still a free man. His erstwhile colleagues and swimmers in Ireland were left behind to deal with his legacy. He would haunt them for as long as a conclusion was denied them. Those who campaigned to secure justice for O'Rourke's victims fought relentlessly to have Gibney brought back to face trial, but the State decided not to appeal the High Court's order in 1994 to stop his prosecution and the DPP never sought his extradition back to Ireland to face fresh charges. When the one-time celebrity chef, Donegal-born Conrad Gallagher, was extradited from New York on charges (of which he was subsequently acquitted) relating to the theft of paintings from the Fitzwilliam Hotel in Dublin, a five-star establishment on St Stephen's Green, Bart Nolan wrote to the Minister for Justice, Michael McDowell. 'If you can extradite Conrad Gallagher for three paintings, why can't you extradite George Gibney for seven rapes?' he demanded.

By this time, Gibney was pursuing an enforced nomadic lifestyle in the US, wandering from city to city and from state to state whenever his past life caught up with him. Back in Ireland, while his wife set about acquiring a legal divorce from him, the swimming authorities were slower to sever their attachment to their one-time kingpin. He remained an honorary life member of the swimming association for a number of years after he fled. His membership was only finally withdrawn in the spring of 1997 when questions were asked about it in the media after motions to annul it had been voted down at two successive AGMs of the IASA. The reason given for removing the membership was that he had failed to reply to letters sent to various addresses abroad where he might have been, requesting him to explain why the honour should not be withdrawn. His talent for coating himself in a veneer of respectability accompanied him to the US where he was a registered coach and a member of USA Swimming until 1998.

'I was devastated when he got off on the technicality in the High Court,' says Aidan O'Toole. 'It was typical of the way he could manipulate things to suit himself. But when he was gone out of Ireland I felt he had actually got the worst sentence of all because he can never come back now. He could have done eight or ten years in jail and he'd be out by now. He can never come back to this country because he knows he'll go to jail if he does. He's getting run out of everywhere in America once people there find out what he did.'

Gibney has never been long without a job or a place to live in his adopted country. In February 1998, he was found working in stock control for a food company in Denver, Colorado, where he was living with a single mother. Ominously, the woman had a teenage daughter. Gibney bought the house where the three were living for $250,000. Once his cover was blown at the food company, he went job-hunting again. Next, he turned up as the head of fund-raising administration for the Disabled American Veterans' Centre in Denver. On being challenged by a reporter as he was leaving at the end of a day's work about a new Garda investigation into fresh allegations against him that was underway in Ireland, he laughed: 'I've no reason to come home. That was all sorted out before.'

After that he got a job with a Colorado aviation company, Frontier

Airlines. He fled that position when a crime reporter from the *Irish Star* tracked him down. The story the reporter filed quoted a warning from a local businessman: 'East Denver is not a good place for somebody like that. People are not going to be one bit happy he's here. It's time for him to go.' He surfaced next when RTÉ television's *Prime Time* door-stepped him in Calistoga, California where he was employed at a five-star ranch-style hotel. In March 2007, the *Sunday Tribune* hired Intercoastal Investigations, the same private detective agency in San Francisco that *Prime Time* had used to find him. It took the agency under 24 hours to locate him in Orange City, Florida – population 7,000 – where he had a job in a hotel in nearby Lake Mary. His home was a newly-built condominium, close to a communal swimming pool, which he had purchased with a $150,000 dollar loan from Bank of America. On the doorstep outside his condo was a sculpture of two children kissing. His neighbours in the gated Enterprise Cove community said he had introduced himself to them as John Gibney. One of them described him as 'the nicest, sweetest guy'. A child welfare police officer in Florida confirmed that Gibney was being watched because of his history in Ireland, but that no complaints had been filed against him in the US.

A spokeswoman for the US embassy in Dublin explained that its standard visa application form specifically asks: 'Have you ever been arrested or convicted for any offence or crime, even though subject of pardon, amnesty or other similar legal action?' The child protection police officer in Florida agreed it was unlikely that any barrier would be raised if Ireland sought Gibney's return to face trial. For the men and women who were routinely raped and abused by him when they were children, the cold reality is that journalists seem to be the only people from Ireland searching for George Gibney in the US.

Gardaí expected that they too would have cause to seek him out when the new complaints from other victims started to trickle in, but that was not to be. Eleven months after Gibney fled Ireland for Scotland; the day before escaping prosecution in his High Court judicial review, another one of his former swimming protégés came forward and alleged that she had been raped by George Gibney. Her delay in reporting the crime was caused by an attempt she had made to end her life in 1994, as Gibney's case had been unfolding in the courts. When she recovered sufficiently, she disclosed to a doctor that her old coach had raped her in a Florida hotel room when she was seventeen years old and had held her captive in the locked room for several hours. The swimmer's mother and father went to meet three officials of the IASA at the Ashling Hotel by appointment on Sunday May 21, 1995 and informed them of the crime committed against their daughter on the overseas training camp in 1991. A month later, on 13 June, the parents met two officials of the Leinster Branch and apprised them of the crime.

The history of sexual crimes committed against this girl are particularly disturbing. She was targeted by two abusers at different stages in her early life, a phenomenon which is by no means rare. When she was five years old, her mother was hospitalised for six months with a life-threatening illness. While her father would visit his wife at the hospital, the child would be sent to the house three doors down, where other little girls about her own age were minded by their live-in grandfather.

– If you tell anybody, your mother will die and it'll be all your fault, the grandfather threatened her after the first time he sexually abused her.

She was five and a half.

The abuse was a regular occurrence, becoming increasingly severe and rough. Once, when she was seven, she came home with scrapes and bruises and had to make excuses to her parents to explain her physical injuries. When she was nine, her parents, worried about her psychological withdrawal, brought her to Temple Street children's hospital. It was concluded that her symptoms were a natural reaction to her mother's prolonged absence from home. Her parents hired a private tutor to come to the house because she had fallen behind academically. All the while, the abuse was continuing. It did not stop until she was eleven, when the other family moved away from the locality and took the grandfather with them.

When a swimming pool opened in her neighbourhood and the girl went there for the first time, she discovered an avenue of escape. Swimming became her life. 'It felt like I was flying,' she remembers. 'Like I'd been freed. I put everything into it. I really focused. It happened so quickly. One year, I wasn't able to swim. Within a year, I was breaking Irish records. People were wondering who I was.'

One day, swim coach Carole Walsh, having watched the girl in her local pool, phoned her parents and told them their daughter had the potential to be a great champion. Carole recommended Trojans Swimming Club in Blackrock where she was still contentedly coaching side by side with George Gibney, mere months before the events which would unmask him. The girl joined Trojans in 1990, Gibney's last full year as the IASA's national coach; the year Chalkie White confided in Gary O'Toole on the flight to Perth. 'I've felt guilty ever since for advising her to move to Trojans,' says Carole, who remained unaware of Gibney's secret life until she received the phone call from Chalkie after Christmas that year. Newpark pool was eighteen miles from the girl's home. Every morning at four o'clock, her alarm clock would go off and her father would drive her to Blackrock, arriving for the stipulated 5.15 am kick-off. While her father slept outside in the car, she was swimming her heart out in the pool. 'I was so driven. All I wanted to do was to go to the Olympics at any cost. That was my dream.'

'She was a great swimmer; one of the best,' Carole Walsh recalls. 'I remember her coming for her assessment in a black leotard. She couldn't do the breaststroke. I was going along beside her with a pole as she swam up the pool. Two years later, she was beating the best in Ireland. Three years later, when she was on a double dose of antibiotics for a sore throat, she broke several Irish records. Without doubt, George Gibney robbed her of the Olympics.'

Gibney showered the girl with attention. He promised her he would make her a star. He gave her gifts of swimming togs and tracksuits and hats and goggles. He hugged her every time she swam well. At the national championships, she streaked home first in four races. She was sixteen years old and poised to be selected for the Olympic Games in Barcelona in 1992.

Then the sun went in. It happened when she was competing in Holland with Trojans. After one of the swim meets, she returned to her hotel room to dress for a disco that was part of the swimmers' official itinerary. 'Gibney came to the room and started saying how bad I was and that I was never going to get anywhere. Then suddenly, he jumped on me. He pushed me down onto the bed. That was all. Then he left the room. After that, he completely ignored me for a couple of weeks. I was wondering what I did wrong. Back home, at training, he'd act as if I wasn't there. I felt all this guilt. I was swimming my hardest, training extra hard to get his attention.'

In 1991, Trojans had a training camp in Tampa, Florida to prepare for the upcoming national championships in Belfast where swimmers would be selected for the Olympics. The swimmers were assigned to host American families, returning to their houses for a daily siesta after morning training and before going back to the pool for the afternoon session. One day, the girl's host family was away and she lingered at the poolside with another girl after everyone else had dispersed. Out of nowhere, Gibney appeared. 'Come on,' he said to the two girls, 'we'll go for breakfast.' She picks up the story. 'The three of us went for breakfast. Then he drove us to a hotel that I didn't know. He brought me to a room and said: 'You, get in there', and he went off with the other girl. I don't know where he brought her. He came back to my room after a while and he said he wanted to talk to me about my swimming. He started ranting and raving that I was so bad at swimming and how disappointed he was in me. I was sitting on a double bed. He jumped on me and raped me, there on the bed. He threatened that if I told anybody, he'd sue. He said nobody would believe me and my family would have to sell our home and our car and we would be out on the streets. He said it would be his word against mine. Then he left.

'When he was gone, I just sat on the floor in the room. I couldn't leave because I didn't know where I was. I didn't know where the hotel was. He came back about three hours later with his wife and loads of kids and said: "Come on you, we're going swimming now". People saw me crying, but nobody came near me. My host family asked me what was wrong and I said I was home-sick. I rang home and I told my mother that he'd locked me in a room, but I didn't tell her he raped me.'

At the national championships in Belfast that year, the girl's legs shook so badly when she was standing on the starting block waiting for the off that she could not swim. 'Even then I kept crying all the time. I couldn't stop.'

Finally, in 1994, the year the High Court released Gibney from the criminal charges and he fled to Scotland, her trauma reached crisis point. She feigned an injury to get out of swimming in a competition. It was the beginning of the end of her glittering swimming career. Her new world of hope and purpose and promise was disintegrating, unknown to those who loved her. The trauma of keeping her secrets was literally threatening to kill her. On Halloween night, she was rescued from the sea by a friend after her first suicide attempt. In the days that followed, she grew more and more distressed. 'She was beside herself,' her mother remembers. On the advice of a friend she went to see Professor Moira O'Brien, the IASA's honorary medical officer whom she had been attending for physical treatment as an elite swimmer and whom Chalkie White had previously told about his abuse by George Gibney. The dam within the girl burst. She told the doctor about the six years of abuse she had suffered from the grandfather until she was eleven and about being raped by George Gibney when she was seventeen. The doctor had the girl transferred to the Mater Hospital for psychiatric care. She was placed on twenty-four-hour suicide watch. With the girl's permission, Moira O'Brien phoned her mother and told her that her daughter had been repeatedly sexually abused as a child and that she had been raped by George Gibney.

'She had fallen down the stairs about two months before all this happened. Odd things were happening to her then. I know now she was doing dreadful things to herself. She was screaming out for help. Dr O'Brien told me on the phone that my daughter had been abused by the neighbour when she was little and then raped by George Gibney. I can't even tell you what I thought when I heard it. It was the first I'd heard about any of it. We had other children. They were all living at home and going to school. We were working all God's hours to pay for the swimming because she was so talented. You feel so guilty, you know. We protected them, as we thought. I was like a mother hen. I never went out socialising or anything. I was always at home. My husband loved the swimming and he was with her all the time. Yet, he was able to get at her.'

When the girl rallied sufficiently after her failed attempt to drown herself, she made a sworn statement to Gardaí about the abuse inflicted on her by the grandfather. Two other females came forward and alleged that they too had been abused by the man when they were small children, in another part of Ireland. He fought the case through the courts, following George Gibney's trajectory of escape, but his judicial review failed, like Derry O'Rourke's. He finally pleaded guilty and was sentenced to five years in jail on conviction of seven charges of child sexual abuse of the three girls. The man is dead now. She heard he died of natural causes in prison. In passing sentence, the judge remarked that it was probably no coincidence that one of the girls was later abused by her swimming coach.

'I felt I got a bit of justice. It wasn't my imagination. It wasn't me going mad. It wasn't all in my head.'

That experience of the criminal justice system emboldened her to make a statement against Gibney. He had eluded the earlier charges on the technicality that they were too old to defend himself against, even though most of them had related to the same years (or post-dated them) as the charges against the convicted grandfather. In September 1995, when she made her statement against Gibney, it was only four years since he had raped her. It seemed just the case to nail him and, besides, three other former swimmers had also sworn allegations against him. The investigating Gardaí thought they had a sure-fire case this time. They were talking about having him extradited from the US. The girl's counselling sessions were concentrating on getting her psychologically strong for the ordeal of being cross-examined in the Central Criminal Court.

An aura of defeat radiated from the detectives who arrived at her door in November 2004 to break the news that the DPP had decided, once and for all, that there was going to be no prosecution. One of the main reasons for the decision, they said, was the expectation that Gibney would insist on an individual trial in each of the complainants' cases, as was his legal right. It would be a divide and conquer strategy, made to measure for child abuse cases where the corroboration of victims is often the most persuasive evidence in the absence of witnesses and physical evidence.

After the detectives left, she walked the short distance to a field belonging to a religious order and hung herself from a tree with her scarf. Inside, she felt dead already. The prospect of seeing the man who raped her being jailed by a court of law had been the only thing keeping her engaged in living. At first, when the guards told her, she had felt relief. She would not have to go to court after all, she thought. She would not have to see his face ever again. But the relief did not last long.

'The fact that he was never brought back from America has had a terrible effect on her,' says her mother. 'She did dreadful things to herself for months and months and months after. She has the life of a tortured person now. She can't live with the feelings she has.'

It was a priest who cut her down from the tree. Her parents got the call from the Mater Hospital. They were well drilled in the procedure by then. The hospital calls had become part of their lives over the years. Often, she would get up and leave the house in the middle of the night and wander aimlessly. Sometimes, she was brought to A&E bleeding profusely after cutting her body indiscriminately with a knife or blades. Other times, it would be an overdose of pills. But she had never tried to hang herself before.

'It was the anger,' she explained the rage that supplanted the initial relief. She felt like flotsam left to drift after some catastrophe at sea. She who was once a future Olympic star. The girl who cut through the water so fast that bystanders on the bank turned to one another and asked what her name was. A name to watch out for in future, they all agreed. That name lost to her now as she reluctantly chooses anonymity to protect herself.

'The guards were brilliant. They couldn't have done more,' she says. At the time of writing, seventeen years after that fateful training camp in Florida with George Gibney, she still takes six pills to quell her anxieties every night, she visits a psychiatrist every week, attends a cognitive therapist twice a week and, occasionally, is admitted to a hospital A&E unit after harming herself. The financial cost alone has been enormous. She does not socialise, cannot work full-time and has never had a proper romantic relationship. She has suffered from anorexia, her weight dropping to under five-and-a-half stone at one stage, though she stands 5'10" tall. She has also been diagnosed with bulimia, causing bursts of weight gain, and she is addicted to over-the-counter cough medicine. She drinks a couple of bottles of Benalyn every day. She is too ashamed of the slash marks on her body to ever put on a swimsuit and streak through the water again.

While the girl testified to the Murphy Inquiry that she was assaulted and raped by Gibney, the report did not deal with it at any length for fear of prejudicing a prosecution potentially arising from the ongoing Garda investigation. Similarly, if Moira O'Brien gave evidence to the Inquiry about her dealings with the girl, it has not been publicly recorded due to these legal constraints that existed at the time. When asked by the author to recount her memory of these events, O'Brien declined.

The girl has received no help from the swimming association. Nobody in charge has picked up the phone or rung the doorbell to sympathise with her and her parents. When she instructed a solicitor to initiate a civil action for personal injuries in the High Court against George Gibney, the Irish Amateur Swimming Association and the Olympic Council of Ireland (OCI) in 1997, she was given short shrift. Both the IASA and the OCI questioned the validity of the plenary summons on the grounds that the two organisations were limited liability companies. A solicitor acting on behalf of the OCI wrote to the girl's solicitor that it intended fully defending itself against her legal action. At the time of writing, she has not received a single cent from either the swimming association or the Olympic Council, two organisations that would have greatly benefited had her potential to be a world-beater in the pool been realised.

'Her mother rang me when she was admitted to the Mater after the first suicide attempt,' says Carole Walsh. 'I went to see her in the psychiatric unit and she told me what George had done to her. After that, I used to collect her from the Mater, sign her out and bring her to the Guinness pool for a training session, as part of her treatment. One weekend, I was driving her home for a short stay out from the hospital. She asked me if we could go to a shop because she needed to buy something. I gave her twenty quid and asked her if she wanted me to go with her. She said: "No, I'm grand". I didn't know that when she got back into the car, she had a month's supply of sleeping tablets that the hospital had given her a prescription for. She had them in the overnight bag she'd brought from the Mater for the weekend. I dropped her home. Two hours after I watched her go in her front door her mother rang me looking for her. I said I dropped her home. Then she [the girl] rang me from Madigan's pub in Moore Street. She collapsed while she was talking to me on the phone. I rang an ambulance. They found her there, on the floor. She had taken a naggin of vodka with the sleeping pills. Looking back, it was like bringing somebody with a beacon on her head to George because she had already been abused.'

The girl agrees in a leaden voice. 'I think he saw a vulnerability in me,' she says. Her mother is sitting beside her thirty-four-year-old daughter on the couch in the family sitting room, holding her hand. 'I'm sorry to say this,' says her mother, searching the girl's blank eyes, 'but sometimes she's like the living dead.'

11. 'Who Knew?'

On the morning Derry O'Rourke was jailed, Michelle Smith de Bruin called for a public inquiry into the Irish Amateur Swimming Association. She was the country's most accomplished sports person at the time, her star not yet tarnished by the controversy over her tampered drug test. When she spoke about swimming, people listened. In an interview in the *Irish Independent* on 30 January 1998, she called on the Minister for Sport, Dr Jim McDaid, and the Irish Sports Council, headed by former Olympic athlete John Treacy, to examine the roles of the IASA, the committee of King's Hospital Swimming Club and the officials of both in the events surrounding Derry O'Rourke.

'Why did the committee tell us he was sick?' she wanted to know. 'If they knew the gravity of the charges, why did they keep him in the club? Why did they hide the truth? … If they did that, they have some responsibility to bear and I don't think they should be holding positions at club level or at IASA level. There are things you learn even now which I would never have known about at the time. Certain things you find out bit by bit. It seems there were people involved and who knew about Derry's case and they didn't take any action. They should not be on the committee. I think the failure of the club and the Leinster Branch of the IASA to act potentially endangered young people. I would like to see everything opened up in the club and the IASA. Who was involved? Who knew and at what stage did they know? What did they know about it? If they were in positions of authority I think they should be asked to resign, and I don't think they should be allowed to occupy positions of authority again. I think it's something that has to be done by the Sports Council and the Minister. The whole thing has to be opened up and cleared up.'

Smith de Bruin's call for an inquiry was endorsed by retired international swimmer and then newly-qualified doctor Gary O'Toole. He pointed out that the people involved in swimming throughout the O'Rourke and the Gibney controversies in the early and mid-1990s were still running the sport. Nobody had admitted they were wrong and nobody had resigned. 'You just can't imagine the kind of people that were and still are involved in officiating in Irish swimming. They seem to be a law unto themselves. They don't seem to take anything seriously,' he said on RTÉ's radio programme, *Liveline*. 'Parents need to be assured none of this is going on anymore and that officials who knew about this going on in the past will no longer be in charge of their children.'

The accusations of torpor against the authorities were rejected by the IASA's honorary secretary, Celia Millane, who said she had no doubt the families and the victims were angry and she sympathised with them. At no stage was the IASA notified or told of any allegations about Derry O'Rourke, she stated. There were no records of complaints from the period either before or during her term of office and, even to this day, nobody had come forward to say they were a victim. She did not accept that there should be new faces in charge of administering the sport in order to restore public confidence.

Writing in the *Irish Independent* the next day, Saturday, 31 January 1998, Michelle Smith de Bruin revealed that O'Rourke had whittled away her confidence in her swimming ability while he was her coach. 'I really did think at the time that he thought the other girls were better than me and that was why he had so much time for them. This drove a wedge between many of us which I thought was a result of sheer competitiveness. However, now, when I look back, I realise what was going on through all of this, while I was almost hating them for the attention and praise he was lavishing on them,' she wrote. 'He never got any further than the fat test or hypnosis trick with me. Why did no one question if he should be allowed to take young girls on their own into the gym in the dark to hypnotise them, or to the pool for special attention? Why did no one question when he made lewd comments about the young girls?'

The Minister for Sport, Jim McDaid, speaking in his Donegal North-East constituency, expressed his horror at the disclosures in court of O'Rourke's paedophile career and said he was seeking an urgent meeting with the IASA. On Monday, he was back in Dublin for the meeting in his department on Kildare Street which Swimmer A had arranged and which was attended by a cross-section of former swimmers and parents caught up in both Gibney's and O'Rourke's criminality. Swimmer A made an opening statement, outlining the known information about O'Rourke, Gibney and the authorities' responses to the two cases.

'It was tense. You could feel the nervousness,' she recalls. 'It was bound to be. We had just come out of this traumatic court case and here we were in a government minister's office. Most of us would never have even been in the Dáil, except maybe on a school trip. Part of me was very naive. I was sitting there thinking, "We're here with the highest authority in Irish sport, surely he'll do something".'

There were mixed emotions at the meeting. Coming in the immediate aftermath of O'Rourke's jailing, those he had abused felt encouraged by their recent experience of the administration of justice. They were full of hope, unlike the people abused by George Gibney. Their continuing suffering over the unfinished business of Gibney's criminality tempered the optimism of the others as they challenged the political establishment to rid their sport of the conditions that allowed men like Gibney and O'Rourke prosper. The group made five specific demands of the minister:

1. That an inquiry be established to fully investigate what had happened;
2. That free-of-charge and independent counselling be made available to the victims without further delay;
3. That there would be full disclosure of all the documentation in the possession of the Department of Sport and that a direction be given to the IASA by the minister to do likewise;
4. That any swim officials who were involved in the controversies should resign;
5. That State-funding of the IASA be frozen.

At the end of the meeting, which lasted almost two and a half hours, McDaid promised he would come back to them, via Lavelle Coleman, the firm of solicitors brought in by one of the victims. When they emerged from the Department into the nighttime on Kildare Street, the father of one swimmer let out a long sigh and said: 'I feel it's the first time in five years that someone has listened to us properly.' There were tears in Swimmer A's eyes.

Jim McDaid then met with representatives of the IASA and told them he was considering disbanding the association. Judging by what happened over the next twenty-four hours, the IASA's top brass managed to talk the minister down from his do-or-die position. On Tuesday, he issued a statement to the media without reverting to Swimmer A's group. At first glance, he seemed to be delivering what they had sought. He was, he announced, setting up an independent inquiry. Its chairperson would be chosen and its terms of reference defined in consultation with the victims. Costs incurred by the inquiry would be borne by the IASA. He invited individuals in the administration of swimming to consider their positions, a euphemism for resignation. The statement promised that the inquiry would be an open and transparent process. But antennae started to twitch in the swimmers' lobby when they read that the nature of the inquiry had already been agreed in consultation with the IASA, the organisation that was to be a substantial focus of its investigation. Nowhere did the minister's statement say that the inquiry would have the powers of a judicial tribunal to call witnesses and to order the discovery of documents. Before the week was out, the swimmers' group had rejected the proposal. On Friday, February 6, 1998, Lavelle Coleman sent a letter to the minister's office in Kildare Street informing him that his mooted inquiry was unacceptable. The fear in political circles was that, if the victims decided not to cooperate with the inquiry, it would collapse before it could even begin. High-level political maneouverings got underway behind closed doors.

The Department of Tourism, Sport & Recreation was still in its infancy when this, the most divisive controversy ever to hit Irish swimming, erupted. Up to the summer of 1997, when Bertie Ahern became Taoiseach for the first of his history-making three consecutive terms of offices, the government sports portfolio had operated under the auspices of the Department of Education, in the care of a junior minister, but Fianna Fáil had promised in its election manifesto to dedicate a full ministry to the brief. Ahern was a sports fan with a dream of building a state-of-the-art stadium as one of the great legacies of his tenure in power, though the 'Bertie Bowl', as it came to be derisively known, turned out to be no more than a contentious pipe dream. The fledgling Department of Tourism, Sport & Recreation had teething problems about its remit and tensions surfaced almost immediately between the inaugural minister, Jim McDaid, and the general secretary of the department, Margaret Hayes. There was a suspicion in political circles that McDaid was floundering and that any definitive decision about an inquiry would ultimately be made higher up the political food chain.

The tic-tacing went on throughout that second weekend as lawyers and the group representing many of the people who had been abused used whatever political connections they could muster. By Monday they were confident that they were going to get a judicial inquiry with full powers of compellability and that it was going to be announced the next day. Tuesday dawned with widespread speculation in the newspapers that, 'despite unease by some parents' about its scope of investigation, the government was about to concede to demands for a full-scale inquiry. The common thread that there was dissent in the victims' ranks indicated that some deft spinning had been conducted by unnamed government sources. Attributing anxieties to unidentified 'parents' – many with genuine concerns about protecting their children's and their families' privacy – was a clever ploy, most likely used by spin doctors who were aware that some of these 'parents' were also officials in the sport.

'While one group of parents and relations have been strongly pushing for the setting up of a judicial tribunal to try to open up the whole affair, others have expressed reluctance about the desirability of going so far,' reported Liam O'Neill, political editor of the *Irish Examiner*. 'However, all the signs last night pointed to the government taking a decision to hold a judicial inquiry although other options, including a probe by a Dáil committee, will be looked at by ministers at today's cabinet meeting ... There was a flurry of government activity at the weekend involving the minister, the Taoiseach, Tánaiste and Attorney General and yesterday Mary Harney [the

Tánaiste] said it appeared they were heading in the direction of a judicial inquiry, however reluctantly. "I'm very reluctant to go down the road of another judicial inquiry – after all we have a number at the moment – but certainly I believe that we have to get the facts in relation to what happened", she said. "The government is anxious to ensure that any inquiry will be sensitive to the concerns of parents and it is likely, according to some sources, that much of the evidence will be taken without revealing names, as was done with the Hepatitis C tribunal, or in private."

Tuesday came and went without an announcement of a change of heart by the government. Instead, David Coleman received a phone call from the Attorney General, David Byrne, requesting a meeting for the next day. Coleman agreed, on condition that the meeting was not to discuss the toothless inquiry that McDaid had announced and which his clients had rejected. Before Byrne and Coleman could get together however, the Department of Tourism, Sport & Recreation issued a press release on Tuesday evening announcing that the minister was appointing Dr Roderick Murphy, a lawyer and a well-known swimmer, to chair his inquiry, thereby reneging on the promise he had made in his earlier announcement that a chairperson would be selected in consultation with the swimmers. The news was greeted with dismay by the swimmers' group. Many of them already knew the senior counsel from his involvement in swimming and though they universally respected him they believed his appointment augured ill for an independent investigation of the small and intimate world of Irish swimming. 'There was consternation when Roderick Murphy's name was fished out of the bowl,' recalls Swimmer A.

A government spokesman confirmed that the minister had been aware of Roderick Murphy's membership of Glenalbyn Swimming Club – from which Gibney had been sacked and where, the inquiry would hear, he had sexually abused at least one child – before he announced Murphy's appointment on February 10. In fact, the spokesman said, the minister had chosen him because of his involvement in swimming, believing that his understanding of the structures of the sport would facilitate his conduct of the inquiry. Not only was Roderick Murphy a member of Glenalbyn, but he also sat on a committee in the club that had previously dismissed Chalkie White as its coach, in 1991. The sacking came three months after Chalkie had told two officers that Gibney had sexually abused him. Signs of conflict over the issue of a complaints procedure between the coach and certain officers are evident in the minutes of a Glenalbyn committee meeting of 10 July 1991. It records Chalkie White's recommendation that the club's constitution be amended to restructure the committee and it paraphrases the chairman taking 'issue with Chalkie stating that some committee members do not work.' It adds: 'Hilary [Hughes] informed Chalkie that the Committee has full authority regarding personnel in the pool, and Committee insists that Chalkie informs one member of Committee if a non-club member requests a club swim. Chalkie refused to accept this.' The reason given by the club for the termination of his employment was his 'management style'. The episode caused internal divisions. When some ordinary members attempted to secure an urgent meeting to debate it they were informed that there was no provision in Glenalbyn's constitution to call an emergency general meeting.

While Roderick Murphy had not been elected to the committee at the time of Chalkie's sacking, the record of a later committee meeting notes a suggestion by him that Chalkie re-apply for his position as coach, this time on the committee's terms. It is obvious from this note that Murphy was *au fait* with the dismissal of Chalkie, the nemesis of George Gibney and one of the primary witnesses for the inquiry. There is no evidence whatsoever that Murphy knew about the complaint Chalkie had made to his fellow committee members (it is thought unlikely that he did). Yet many of the swimmers who had been abused believed that his involvement in club decision-making and whatever friendships he had forged with officers at club, Leinster and national level would compromise his objectivity in the inquiry.

After graduating from UCD with an economics degree in 1969, Roderick Murphy travelled to Spain for a post-graduate degree in law at the Opus Dei-owned University of Navarre in Pamplona. On returning to Dublin with a doctorate, he joined the Irish bar in the autumn of 1971 and became a senior counsel in 1991. Fluent in French and Spanish, he specialised in complex and expanding areas of law, such as income tax, arbitration and commercial and property law. He was chairman of the Chartered Institute of Arbitrators, an organisation of about 450 members, largely comprising lawyers, engineers, teachers, accountants and doctors. When he married Patricia Murphy, a consultant paediatrician and former competitive swimmer, he became a late convert to swimming. It is a measure of his prowess in the water that, at the age of fifty-one, he broke a half-century-old Irish masters' record for the 200 metres breaststroke and went on to break his own record in Wales in October 1996. Four of his seven children were also keen swimmers; two in Glenalbyn and two in Trojans, where they were coached by Carole Walsh, another important witness to the inquiry. His wife's sister, Nuala Curley, a former breaststroke champion, was on the committee that drew up the national guidelines on preventing sexual abuse in sport, the 'Code of Ethics and Good Practice for Children's Sport in Ireland'. She was appointed by Fine Gael minister Bernard Allen in February 1995. From the day his appointment was announced until after the inquiry was completed, Roderick Murphy was not seen in Glenalbyn pool where he had been in the habit of a 7.30 swim every Tuesday and Saturday morning.

His appointment, recommended by the Attorney General, was met with surprise in the Law Library where Murphy had a lucrative but low-profile practice. His colleagues said he was well-liked and respected and that it was general knowledge he had 'a gentle association' with the Fianna Fáil party. 'He's a very nice man. Calm, quiet and self-effacing,' one said. Another said he would be seen as very humanitarian, but conservative on social issues, despite being related to Trinity College's Reid Professor of Law and future Labour Party senator, Ivana Bacik. He was described as an assiduous worker who lectured in commercial law at the King's Inns and on arbitration at the Irish Management Institute, a good conversationalist and a gentleman who appeared to be better known in the world of swimming than in the legal sphere. When his name was announced as the chairman of the inquiry, some swimmers said they would find it more difficult to discuss the sexual abuse they had suffered with somebody they already knew, even slightly, than with a complete stranger.

In a memo to Minister McDaid dated 16 February 1998 and entitled 'Statement of Independence', Roderick Murphy formally accepted the invitation to chair the inquiry.

'I declare that I accept to serve as Chairman of the above mentioned inquiry. In so declaring I confirm that I am independent of the Irish Amateur Swimming Association, its Leinster Branch, of the affiliated Clubs and of the two named coaches and intend to remain so.

I wish to call attention to the following circumstances.

I, my wife and children have been family members of Glenalbyn

Swimming Club since the late 1980s.

I was elected to the committee of that swimming club by the parents in autumn 1992 and again in autumn 1993 after which I resigned because of pressure of work. I was never Chairman, nor an officer of the committee.

During those two years no allegation of sexual abuse was referred to the Committee nor have I become aware of any such allegation having being [sic] made since then.

I was elected a Trustee of Glenalbyn Social and Athletic Federation in autumn 1993.

I have not at any time advised the Irish Amateur Swimming Association, the Leinster Branch and its affiliated Clubs or either of the two named coaches in relation to the matters which are the subject matter of this inquiry or in relation to any other matter.'

Murphy's appointment led to sharp exchanges in the Dáil as Opposition TDs questioned his suitability to investigate a sport in which he was actively involved. Acknowledging that he knew some of the people in swimming, he issued a public invitation: 'I hope they will come to me and, hopefully, we will be able to agree terms of reference.' Eventually, when the swimmers' alarm showed no sign of being assuaged, the government parachuted in another senior counsel, Fidelma Macken, to assist him, ten days before the inquiry began. In spite of this concession, the main bloc of swimmers reasserted their intention to boycott it.

The planned meeting between the Attorney General, David Byrne, and David Coleman, representing the victims, had gone ahead on Wednesday, 11 February. They discussed the powers to compel witnesses to attend the inquiry and to order the discovery of documents, but nothing was decided. The pair had parted with an appointment to meet again two days later.

That Wednesday evening, the Taoiseach phoned the offices of Lavelle Coleman. The call was taken by David Coleman, who put it on loudspeaker for the benefit of one of O'Rourke's victims who was in the office. Afterwards, both Coleman and the swimmer believed they had wrung a commitment from Bertie Ahern that he and the Attorney General would review the situation if the proposed inquiry proved unworkable.

On Monday, 16 February, Coleman wrote to David Byrne following a second inconclusive meeting the previous Friday, informing him that his clients were adamant in their decision to boycott the inquiry. He had been furious to discover that advertisements announcing the terms of the inquiry had been issued to national newspaper offices by six o'clock on the previous Friday evening, the day of their second meeting. 'On behalf of the Victims represented by us, we wish to place on the record their disgust at the arrogance and insensitivity displayed by the Government in their handling of this issue which, it must be remembered, involved the systematic sexual abuse of children and young adults and the possible failures of others to protect these vulnerable children. Our Clients' position remains the same in that they will not be co-operating with this Inquiry.' Coleman invited a response from the Attorney General by close of business on Wednesday February 18. He never got an answer.

The swimmers' sense of unfairness increased when the government decided at a cabinet meeting on Tuesday, February 24 to impose a cap of IR£500 on the costs the State would pay for each individual cooperating with the Murphy Inquiry. The conditions of payment were outlined in a letter from the Department of Sport to Roderick Murphy. It ordered that claims for payment of legal costs were to be made to the inquiry chairman who would verify the name and duration of any attendance by legal advisers at the inquiry. The letter's undertone of grandstanding between the government and the victims' lawyers was reflected in off-the-record briefings of journalists by political sources who spoke pejoratively of 'ambulance-chasing solicitors'. While egos clashed in a power struggle over the prize of a judicial tribunal, the needs of the injured swimmers no longer seemed to be the government's priority. Rather, the imperative was to deny a coterie of lawyers access to yet another ATM-style tribunal of inquiry.

McDaid did, however, concede to one of the swimmers' demands when he withdrew funding from the IASA. 'The future of swimming rests with the swimming fraternity,' he said in reply to a Dáil question about his decision to freeze the money. 'It is up to them to convince me and others that there is a safe environment for swimmers and that the happenings of the past cannot be repeated.' Hostilities that had been simmering within the swimming community now broke the surface. As a sport that fostered competition between individuals, solidarity was never its foremost trait but, in the accusatory climate in the lead up to the inquiry any attempt to present a united front was abandoned. Recriminations abounded. Swimmers who were abused by Gibney and O'Rourke felt they were being blamed for the cancellation of galas due to lack of finances and for elite swimmers missing important international competitions. When the media reported dire predictions by unidentified sources in swimming that Irish swimmers would be unable to compete in the Olympics because of the freezing of funds, some of those who had been abused were deeply upset at being depicted as national spoilsports. Throughout it all, still no provision was made to provide independent psychological counselling for those people who had been abused as children.

'I doubt we'll be cooperating with the inquiry now,' Swimmer A told the *Irish Independent*, anonymously. 'They didn't listen to us as children and they're not listening to us now as adults. I think it's evident they're trying to break our spirit.' Bizarrely, the Taoiseach informed Dáil Eireann the day before the cabinet decision on legal costs that all relevant parties had finally agreed to cooperate with the inquiry.

The swimmers advocacy group met that night in the splendid boardroom of Lavelle Coleman's offices in Fitzwilliam Square. They were addressed by Mary Irvine, one of the Law Library's most illustrious senior counsel with a leading practice in medical negligence. The mood among the gathering was anxious and pessimistic but unswerving. Many talked about feeling betrayed all over again, this time by the State. They argued that anybody in swimming who had anything to hide would not voluntarily testify to the Murphy Inquiry. Why, they asked, would officials possessing information that might incriminate them go and talk to a government-appointed senior counsel when there was no legal obligation on them? The group remained determined not to give the inquiry credibility by cooperating with it.

Their collective boycott lasted four weeks, until four parents finally agreed to meet Murphy at the inquiry offices in Church Street on March 9. About seventy people in all spoke to the inquiry behind its closed doors in the Distillery Building, but many of those were either on the periphery of what had gone on, or outside it altogether. Others who swore from the start that they would go nowhere near the inquiry never faltered in their resolve. Among them was a key IASA official who had supported Derry O'Rourke, Frank McCann and George Gibney. Significantly, the father and son, Aidan and Gary O'Toole, who had prised open the can of worms, stayed away.

One key figure who voluntarily contacted the Inquiry was Frank McCann. Solicitors acting for the Arbour Hill prisoner requested in writing that the Inquiry explicitly acknowledge the (un-named) double-murderer's repudiation of allegations that he tried to obstruct complaints made against George Gibney.

'As far as I can see, it was a waste of time,' said Aidan O'Toole. 'Gary and I and Triton Swimming Club didn't cooperate. For some people, it was like going to confession to get relief for their consciences. The whole thing was a failure. The hierarchy was still going to be there and they were the people we wanted to leave the sport, all of them. To illustrate how bad it was, I at one stage reported Gibney to the officers of the swimming association. The laughable part was that when I went in to speak to them Derry O'Rourke was part of the panel that was going to decide what to do about my complaints about Gibney. It was scarcely believable.'

The Murphy Report was a white-wash; it threw scant new light on how two paedophiles had prospered for nearly thirty years in the sport. Nobody was named and blamed. It did not identify George Gibney, Derry O'Rourke or Frank McCann by name, nor Newpark School or club, nor King's Hospital school or club. This despite two of the coaches already having been jailed – O'Rourke publicly identified at the explicit request of his victims – and Gibney having adopted the life of a fugitive outside the jurisdiction. Michael McCann, the president of King's Hospital Swimming Club made a written statement to the inquiry, through his solicitor. The club's honorary secretary read a prepared statement.

The inquiry suffered from the absence of key witnesses, such as the O'Tooles who, like many others, had long before cooperated with journalists to expose what had gone on. Most of the report's narrative of events had already been extensively reported in the press. Because it had no powers to summon witnesses or to order the discovery of documents, it added little to what was already public knowledge other than pieces of the jigsaw gleaned from insubstantial documents it acquired by consent. The extent to which the inquiry was emasculated by its voluntary composition was evidenced by its failure to locate the former King's Hospital school teacher who had been told by a student in the 1970s that O'Rourke abused her until she was thirteen. Even though Lavelle Coleman was able to find and interview this teacher in preparation for the High Court compensation cases, the Murphy Inquiry never made contact with him.

'The inquiry was a farce,' Swimmer A believes.

The publication of the 165-page Murphy Report in June 1998 won widespread acclaim. Plentiful sound-bites were extrapolated to make big headlines and colourful newspaper copy. On the eve of its publication, the Minister for Sport flagged disclosures made to the inquiry of yet more instances of children who were abused, without mentioning that Gardaí were already embarked on two fresh investigations into both O'Rourke and Gibney without any clarion call from the inquiry. A media salivating for more details simply regurgitated the findings without asking fundamental questions about the value of the process. Politicians, already battered by a series of expensive, establishment-rocking judicial inquiries into corruption throughout the 1990s, were relieved at Murphy's speedy completion and its relatively small budget of IR£400,000. The report contained 100 recommendations, many of them practical and useful, but its findings were, in the most part, innocuous and that was music to the ears of the body politic. It meant that the thorny matter of abuse in swimming could now be laid to rest with a political closure.

Murphy reached some astonishing conclusions. One such, at 3.13 in Chapter 7 – 'The Second Named Coach' – the chairman records the inquiry's formal finding that the complaint made by the seventeen-year-old swimmer to King's Hospital Club committee in November 1992 (one of the charges on which O'Rourke was convicted in December 1997) was 'taken seriously and formally by the club'. This was the complaint which had culminated in the committee writing to O'Rourke and accepting that he had done nothing wrong when he fondled the swimmer under her togs. Murphy also found no evidence that the secretary, Barbara Claxton, and the treasurer, Penny Statham, knew the reason for O'Rourke's suspension until after he had left though he found that Michael McCann, the club president, was aware on September 10, 1993 of the Garda investigation, contrary to McCann's protests that he was not informed by the school. In the chapter relating to complaints made about Gibney, entitled 'The First Named Coach', a specific finding was made in relation to only one of the numerous officials whom Chalkie White had told about the abuse. As with everyone else in the report, Professor Moira O'Brien was not named. Referring to her as the Honorary Medical Officer of the IASA and the Leinster Branch, Murphy records her testimony that what Chalkie had told her about Gibney was governed by a doctor-client relationship, that she disputed the geographical location in which their conversation took place, and recorded her memory of Chalkie as having been 'confused and emotionally unstable as a result of a head injury and that (Chalkie) did not want her to repeat the story'. At 43.3, the Inquiry found: 'There is no conflict of evidence in relation to the conversation' between Chalkie and the professor. 'The officer was told and, for professional reasons of doctor-patient confidentiality, did not report the abuse alleged.' In his general findings, Murphy concluded that the supervision of Gibney and O'Rourke by their respective clubs was not good enough. 'In a sport dominated by standard times, there were inadequate standards for behaviour,' he concluded. 'No one seemed to question the merits of imposing objectives which met high standards for children in competition without having regard to their overall development. ... Where the joy of the swimmer is replaced by the gratification of an adult, it ceases to be a sport. ... Complaints procedures were focused on swimmer's behaviour and not on coaches' or officials' behaviour. Swimmers who had been abused were not aware of a complaints' procedure. When they did so become aware they found the formality of Rule 33 as a procedure for complaints discouraged complaints being made. In any event, the complaints procedures were wholly inadequate to deal with complaints of child abuse and, in the case of the second named coach's club [O'Rourke's King's Hospital], became more formal in that from 1993 it was necessary to make such complaints IN WRITING (not previously required).'

Only the swimmers and their relatives who had fought for the inquiry articulated disappointment with the Murphy Report. They felt aggrieved that people who, they believed, had been involved in covering up what was going on had got away without censure. Their regrets went unexplored. The Murphy Inquiry would have a ripple effect for the whole of Ireland for years to come. As the national debate about the costliness of tribunals gained momentum, it would be upheld as a template for how to swiftly and thriftily inquire into matters of grave public interest. The innate weaknesses of a model without powers to compel evidence or to make legally binding recommendations would be exposed eight years later when Judge Frank Murphy investigated the failure of the Catholic diocese of Ferns to act on complaints that various priests were sexually abusing children. The Ferns Report was a powerful, hard-hitting document. The time scale covered by its terms of reference, including the years after

Roderick Murphy's report, showed that its predecessor inquiry into swimming had essentially changed nothing in the standards of child protection operated in the wider community. Guidelines and the reporting of complaints had, in the main, remained optional.

Roderick Murphy would be appointed a judge of the High Court two years after shutting up shop on his inquiry in the Distillery Building behind the Four Courts. What nearly everybody overlooked was that, at the end of it, still nobody had been apportioned blame, nobody had resigned and nobody had said sorry. The exercise bequeathed an oblique, comforting acceptance that all these children had been exposed to child sexual abuse because of an inherent systems failure and, in large part, it was nobody's fault.

'You get angry at it,' the Minister for Sport said after reading the report. 'It shows people were confused and hurt. There are indications these two coaches were not the only ones involved.'

Among Murphy's long list of welcome but non-compulsory recommendations were provisions for the proper investigation of complaints of abuse and the disbarment of coaches from membership of club committees and from attending branch meetings as delegates. He advised that at least one person be present at the poolside at all times in addition to the coach, and that coaches, officials and officers attend child protection seminars. He urged that victims be provided with counselling and therapy and that the swimming association appoint a full time chief executive, a measure that, when it was adopted six years later, ended up in the High Court. He called on the government to institute mandatory reporting as part of its overall childcare strategy. He said that the swimming association needed to appoint a child protection officer 'as a matter of urgency'. (Nine years later, in January 2007, the first full-time national children's officer for swimming would finally be appointed). Recommending that any law suits resulting from the criminal convictions be dealt with quickly, he wrote: 'Action needs to be prompt both in terms of criminal prosecution and civil remedies.' Perhaps it was because the report's recommendations were optional and there was no obligation to implement them that thirteen High Court cases for compensation against the swimming association and King's Hospital School were not settled until February 8, 2008 – exactly a decade after most of them were initiated. Two more cases were settled the following summer.

The most tangible change effected by the Murphy Inquiry was the restructuring of the Irish Amateur Swimming Association in the immediate aftermath of the publication of the report, 105 years after it was formed by the merger of councils in Leinster and Ulster (Munster was affiliated in 1905, but Connaught did not follow until 1952. The IASA was registered as a limited liability company with no share capital in 1985). 'Despite the best efforts of its paid employees and its voluntary officers the IASA lacks the resources and the professional administrative backing that an amateur organisation necessarily needs,' Murphy wrote. 'While the IASA has a modest premises and a small staff since 1989, the Leinster Branch operates, as the IASA used to operate, out of its officers' homes.' He said that State funding of the IASA (85 per cent of its income in 1997) was inadequate to provide the necessary administrative structure. He pointed out too that the 6,000 licensed swimmer members and 10,000 general members (almost 70 per cent aged eighteen or under) were not allowed to participate in electing the association's or branch's officers, voting being confined to a council of about fifty people, including past presidents, honorary life members and delegates from the Irish Water Polo Association and the Schools' Swimming Association. Murphy was concerned that the association's constitutional jurisdiction dealt primarily with competition rules and lacked reference to the overall development of swimmers. FINA, its international overseer, did not have provisions relating to issues of child sexual abuse.

The name chosen for the IASA's new incarnation was Swim Ireland. It came into being when a new memorandum and articles of association were adopted at an eight-hour long extraordinary general meeting of the IASA at the Ashling Hotel on Sunday, January 24, 1999. The meeting, attended by 100 delegates, was financed by a one-off grant of IR£30,000 from the Department of Sport. An interim board was appointed to oversee the transition from the IASA to Swim Ireland, with the intention of adopting the recommendations of the Murphy Report. Accusations were made during the meeting that the change of identity was nothing more than 'a cosmetic exercise' when several members of the outgoing IASA committee were re-elected to the new body. Outgoing IASA president Mary O'Malley did not inspire confidence when she said: 'I have seen a lot over the years, including manipulation of power and blatant croneyism, and I don't feel that any of these issues are adequately addressed in the new structures which have only been accepted by the IASA council – just a small proportion of the swimming community ... I believe that the new structure, as it stands now, will undoubtedly leave Irish swimming more open to manipulation than the IASA ever was.'

Forecasts by various delegates during the highly-charged meeting that nothing was really going to change gained credence in succeeding years as reform proved tortuously slow. One of Murphy's main recommendations – that the swimming body appoint a chief executive – would take six years to implement. The catalyst for the appointment was the publication of another report in the autumn of 2003, this one ordered by the Sports Council and prepared by

Deloitte & Touche business consultants. It was savagely critical of the way Swim Ireland was being run. Once again, the Irish Sports Council suspended the organisation's funding, causing the postponement of the Leisureland International competition in Galway. Deloitte & Touche revealed that Swim Ireland was at risk of being declared insolvent, that 34,000 earmarked for a 'Learn to Swim' programme had seemingly disappeared into some other programme, and that the costs for discovery alone in defending the child abuse compensation claims were estimated at 125,000. Most damning, Deloitte & Touche stated that Swim Ireland 'does not proactively operate a transparent tracking process and reporting mechanism whereby it monitors the implementation of recommendations contained in the Murphy Report'. Solicitor and former international swimmer Sarah Keane (not to be confused with the detective of the same name who investigated Derry O'Rourke) became the first holder of the position of chief executive after having to resort to the High Court to assert her right to the job. She had argued that, having been offered the position of chief executive and having accepted it, the organisation was attempting to renege on the agreement. By insisting that it did not have the money to pay a chief executive's salary, Swim Ireland ran up yet another substantial legal bill in its High Court wrangling over the chief executive's appointment. Keane secured an injunction in the High Court to prevent Swim Ireland offering the job to anyone else and, eventually, the case was settled out of court, confirming her appointment.

Maybe it was Roderick Murphy's final paragraph in his report that ultimately succeeded in concentrating minds, albeit it very, very slowly. 'Structures do not determine behaviour,' he wrote. 'Structures can only provide support for acceptable standards and can help achieve objectives. The overall tone of the evidence given to the Inquiry was one of an organisation in disharmony where the energies of well meaning volunteers were diverted, and continue to some extent to be diverted, towards recrimination and away from the goals of enthusiastic and promising young swimmers.'

While many good policies have been adopted by Swim Ireland and the structural reorganisation recommended by Murphy has given it an autonomy its predecessor did not have, it did not readily embrace the whole reform package. In contrast to its counterpart organisation in Britain which actively encouraged abuse victims to make complaints after a number of its coaches were jailed, the Irish organisation has pursued a legalistic and corporate-appearances approach. (In 2006, for example, it spent 34,178on PR services, compared to the 18,185listed under child welfare in its annual report). Its reluctance to engage in open debate (it refused to cooperate with a retrospective television documentary about O'Rourke and Gibney) and to reach out to swimmers who have been abused speaks of an enduring siege mentality. The name and structures may have changed, but the cultural inclination to deny, deny, deny is a familiar old one.

Back in 1999, after the Minister for Sport reactivated funding for the national swimming organisation, the windows had been opened on Irish swimming to let in an air of tentative optimism. It was the cusp of the millennium and a year after the inception of Swim Ireland. The original group of swimmers who had met Jim McDaid that Monday after O'Rourke went to jail remained unconsoled, however.

'Dear Dr McDaid,

Our group representing victims, parents and swimmers who vigorously campaigned for change in Irish Swimming would like to present you with a summary of events since Swim Ireland's

AGM on April 25, 1999,' they wrote to him.

The letter claimed that people who were deemed ineligible at the meeting to vote on the restructuring had improperly cast votes and that only two minutes were allocated to each delegate to speak on the proposals.

'It was exactly the same approach as that of the old IASA to issues raised: that is, never discuss them, leave them in limbo, in the hope they will be forgotten.'

There was, as it turned out, no hope of forgetting. It would take the best part of a decade to bring about significant reforms in the administration of swimming. At times, the sport itself seemed to buckle under the strain of frozen and delayed state funding and cancelled competitions but, in November 2006, chief executive Sarah Keane led a delegation from Swim Ireland to Leinster House for a presentation to the Oireachtas Committee on Arts, Tourism and Sport. In an address which politicians later lauded she informed them that her organisation had finally implemented all the recommendations of the Murphy Report (although the civil cases by O'Rourke's victims were still being contested by Swim Ireland's lawyers). She said that a robust set of child welfare guidelines was in place throughout the organisation and she briefed the parliamentarians on the progress of fifteen sets of High Court civil proceedings related to O'Rourke's criminality. What went unmentioned was a news report that had appeared in *The Irish Times* fourteen months earlier, revealing that Gardaí in County Wexford were investigating allegations of sexual abuse connected with the Kennedy Memorial Swimming Pool in New Ross. Some of the incidents were alleged to have happened up to twenty years previously. The amnesia decried by Swimmer A's group in its letter to the Minister for Sport a year after the Murphy Report was proving to be a luxury too far as yet more scandals queued up to combust in the criminal courts.

12. Fr Ronald Bennett

In June 2006, fifteen years after Gary O'Toole learned that his Olympic swimming coach, George Gibney, was a child predator, he tuned into RTE's *Nine O'Clock News* on the internet in his New York apartment at the end of a day's training in specialist orthopaedic medicine and came face-to-face with another old figure of authority from his swimming days. Fr Ronald Bennett, a septuagenarian by this time, had been filmed leaving the Four Courts in Dublin that day. He was wearing a businessman's suit and tie instead of his usual brown robe and his face, bespectacled and grey at the temples, was grim. Gary recognised him straightaway from the training camps in Gormanston College and the Catholic student games. 'I was surprised when I saw the report,' he recalls. 'I said to myself: "Jesus, there's the guy who brought us to Spain".'

'A priest has been given a suspended sentence for the sexual abuse of school boys,' the newscast reported. It said that that Fr Ronald Bennett, the former spiritual director and sports master at Gormanston College, a Catholic fee-paying school in County Meath, had been convicted in the Dublin Circuit Criminal Court of sexually abusing four students in the school. The seventy-one-year-old Franciscan friar had pleaded guilty to six sample charges of indecent assault from 1974 to 1981. Judge Desmond Hogan sentenced him to a suspended five-year prison term on Bennett's bond of 100 euro to keep the peace. The judge said the priest had perpetrated a serious betrayal of the injured men and their families and on the Franciscan order but that his early guilty plea had saved the State a lengthy trial and his victims the ordeal of giving evidence. Furthermore, he had committed the offences twenty years before and there had been no recurrence, he said. The judge pointed to evidence from the Granada Institute in Shankill, County Dublin, a controversial private assessment and treatment centre run by the Catholic brothers of St John of God where Bennett had been receiving treatment since Gardaí started investigating him in 1999, that he was deemed at low risk of re-offending.

Gary's thoughts drifted back to his own childhood. He must have been about eleven when the priest escorted him and four other Irish schoolboy swimmers in a twenty-five-member contingent to Huelva in the south-west of Spain for the FISEC (*Federation Internationale Sportive De L'Enseignement Catholique*) games. The annual competition, including track-and-field and tennis, attracts Catholic schoolboys and girls aged under seventeen from traditionally Catholic countries in Europe. It is formally recognised by the Olympic Committee. The event was inaugurated in 1948 as a forum for fostering good relations between children of different countries 'through the medium of sport carried out in an educational, disciplined and Christian manner'. Every year, the games commence with a holy mass for all the participants and officials. 'Ronald Bennett was the *chef de mission*,' Gary recalls. 'I was the youngest from Ireland that year. The other four swimmers in the Irish team were like children in the proverbial sweet-shop with all the girls around. I didn't know about Ronald Bennett so I was surprised to find out about his conviction all those years later when I was in New York.'

Bennett was an only child born to a solicitor's clerk and his wife in Tipperary town on 23 January 1935 and raised 'in a sheltered atmosphere'; according to his psychologist's court evidence. His given name was James Anthony Bennett. He was educated by the Christian Brothers in Carrick-on-Suir, going on to study for an arts degree at University College Galway and entering a seminary in Rome. Following his ordination on 25 February 1961, he returned to Ireland and was based in Drogheda where he became immersed in the Leinster league football club that became known as Drogheda FC. He was elected president of the Drogheda Supporters' Club.

Meanwhile, the Order of Friars Minor, more commonly known as the Franciscans, having transferred to Gormanston from Multyfarnham in 1956, had opened their new school in a once privately-owned country estate in east Meath, twenty miles from Dublin. Its ethos of mutual respect, social awareness and reverence for gospel values is encapsulated in its motto, *Dei Gloriae, Hiberniae Honori* ('To the glory of God and the honour of Ireland'). Bennett was appointed spiritual adviser and sports master to the day and boarding school in 1963. He organised Gormanston College's first sports day in 1964 and every year thereafter until 1993. He was president of Leinster Athletics for six years and was soon elected chairman of the Irish Schools Athletics organisation, simultaneously serving as president of the North Leinster branch from the time the region was instituted. People who remember him in his heyday say he was an advocate of the philosophy that sport provides a healthy outlet for energetic children, echoing Eamonn de Valera's vision of a happy Celtic nation. 'Fr Ronald believes firmly that the involvement of young people in sport is most beneficial not only to themselves but to their school and to society,' his curriculum vitae espoused. 'Adults who give a commitment to serving young people by organising or by coaching or by encouragement in various sports are helping the schoolboys and schoolgirls of the country to a healthier lifestyle and to fulfillment of many sporting dreams.'

A nine-hole golf course and a 25-metre heated indoor swimming pool were among the burgeoning amenities under the governance of the sports master when he took on the role at the age of twenty-nine. As spiritual director, he was responsible for nurturing the boys' piety while his more prosaic duties included organising teams of altar boys. He added the job of bursar to his multifarious titles in 1969. His office, located beside the main assembly hall, was the biggest in the school. He summoned his prey to it by announcing their names on a public address system and by operating a set of signal lights positioned outside his door. They worked like traffic lights. Green meant come in. Red meant Fr Bennett was not to be disturbed. The men he abused as schoolboys told investigating Gardaí that the green light filled them with dread.

What never came out in the court proceedings was that Ronald Bennett was a lynchpin in the world of swimming. He had his pick of victims when they were very young, beholden to his authority and massed together for schools swimming. Having been elected secretary of the Leinster Schoolboys Swimming Association in 1963, he co-founded the Irish Schools Swimming Association (ISSA), an all-Ireland organisation affiliated with the Irish Amateur Swimming Association, in February 1969. The ISSA receives substantial State grants, equal to about one-fifth of the IASA's annual allocation. It runs the minors' and secondary schools' competitions around the country every year. It is also in charge of the annual schools' international swimming gala between Ireland, England, Scotland and Wales. The ISSA was affiliated from early on to the Irish Amateur Swimming Association (subsequently to Swim Ireland) and Bennett was its honorary treasurer from 1971 onwards. He was elected ISSA president for two terms of office in 1974 and in 1990. When the Leinster Schoolboys and Schoolgirls Associations merged in 1978, he became secretary of the Leinster Branch of the ISSA too from 1978.

In addition to all that, he was invariably the Irish team manager for the FISEC games, travelling to Madrid (1971), Rome (1972), Malta (1974), Bruges (1976), Cholet, western France (1977), Burgos, northern Spain (1979), Milan (1980), Vienna (1981), Huelva, southern Spain (1982), Dublin (1983), Paris (1984 and 1989) and Andorra (1990). Despite an allegation of child sexual abuse having been made against him to the principal of Gormanston College in 1973, he continued to be the swimming supervisor on behalf of the FISEC international technical committee.

George Gibney was a close associate of Bennett's. In the early years of Gibney's coaching career, he was the senior coach for schools' training and Bennett, upon becoming secretary of FISEC, picked him in 1977 to take charge of swimmers competing in the Catholic games abroad. Gibney ran residential training camps in Gormanston College during school holiday times in the 1970s and 1980s, as did Derry O'Rourke. In the first Garda investigation of Gibney, Chalkie White said one of the assaults Gibney had committed against him happened in a dormitory in Gormanston. 'Gibney and Bennett were great buddies,' Bart Nolan confirms.

Swimmer A, who was abused by O'Rourke, recalls frequently attending training camps in Gormanston College. 'The pool was nothing to write home about and I used to wonder why we went there so often. We had training camps there at least once a year. They were always overnights. They were supposed to be bonding training camps.'

Her memory is corroborated by Gary O'Toole's. 'I remember once being on a training camp in Gormanston run by George Gibney. We were all supposed to bond down there.'

In early 1998, as Derry O'Rourke was being bundled into a prison van outside the Four Courts, a former student at Gormanston College was struggling to come to terms with years of frequent sexual abuse he had suffered from Fr Ronald Bennett in the 1970s. A married man with a good job, he was trying to summon the courage to make a formal complaint to Gardaí. He followed media reports about the setting up of the Murphy Inquiry into swimming and decided to furnish it with a voluntary testimony about Bennett, the boss of Irish schoolboys' swimming.

'The Murphy Inquiry was a very important time for me personally. I was finding it increasingly difficult to say nothing about it and let it just drift on,' he explains. 'I really felt I had to go and do something about it. My wife was against it because she felt that once the criminal process started what happened to me would become known. I was worried myself that if I started the process it would become too much for me and I wouldn't be able to cope. Putting in the submission to the Murphy Inquiry was the first thing I did about trying to expose what Ronald Bennett had done. Over time, I had written up an absolutely enormous tome about my time in Gormanston. It was three hundred or four hundred pages long. Out of that, I wrote a two-page summary. Then I rang the Law Library and asked how I could make a submission to the Murphy Inquiry. I spoke to Roderick Murphy himself. He said to write it up and send it to him care of the Law Library.

'I sent it in, and I never heard another thing. I never got an acknowledgement. After that, I awaited the publication of his report. When it came out, I read it and there was nothing in it about what I sent him except a line about something not being in the remit of the Inquiry, but I didn't think that related to Bennett. Shortly after I'd sent it into the Murphy Inquiry, I'd instituted civil and criminal proceedings. I included in my statement to the Gardaí and in what I told my solicitor that I had sent the synopsis to the Inquiry. Even though I wasn't a swimmer and it was as a student that Bennett had targeted me, it really began to dawn on me how central he was to the whole thing that had happened in swimming. He had all these strings to his bow – FISEC, the Leinster Branch, and especially George Gibney. The swimmers were coached in Gormanston. Gibney seemed to prowl there. He was a regular visitor to the school. Anyway, after the Murphy Report came out, I rang Nora Owen because she had been the Minister for Justice and I thought she might be able to find out what had happened. I got a phone call from Roderick Murphy who was then a judge. He told me he hadn't included it in the inquiry because, while Bennett had a role in swimming, my allegation had nothing to do with swimming, and he was right. But I feel Ronald Bennett was a very important person in swimming. I'm sure he operated among swimmers. His recruitment process was through everything he did in the school – running sports or the shop or being involved in athletics or swimming, whatever. Roderick Murphy also said that because I had undertaken criminal and civil proceedings it was another reason why my case wasn't included.'

This man, who made his complaint in the 1990s, was the first of Bennett's victims to contact Gardaí. He had been a day pupil in Gormanston and was aged twelve when the priest started abusing him on the pretext that he was teaching the child the facts of life, helping him to overcome his shyness, and assisting his body to mature. The précis the man sent to Roderick Murphy recounted how Fr Ronald frequently got him to make up stories about sexual acts with imaginary girlfriends while the priest masturbated both of them. In the first weeks after the boy arrived in the school, Fr Ronald brought him and another child to his office, made the children undress each other and engage in masturbation with each other and with the priest. This happened on at least three occasions. On one occasion, Fr Ronald brought the boy and about six other boys to the showers. There, naked and in pairs, he got them to masturbate each other while the rest of the group watched and the priest took photographs. He used to tell the boys he preyed on that it was 'good' and 'healthy' for them to feel 'open and free'. Often he rewarded them with crisps and sweets and minerals from the sports shop, which he ran in the basement. When other priests enquired where the boy had been after visiting Fr Ronald, he always told the truth, but they never asked supplementary questions about the purpose of his visits. 'My frequent visits to Fr Ronald's room quickly became common knowledge amongst my year-group peers and I was frequently assaulted, intimidated and slagged publicly as a result,' he recalled. 'Frequently, these assaults and barrages of name-calling were witnessed by the supervising priests, but nothing was ever done about it. These public incidents were a daily occurrence.' Bennett went on abusing this boy for three years. Sometimes, the priest brought him to the swimming pool supposedly to perfect his breaststroke and would fondle him. Other times, he brought groups of boys and encouraged them to take communal showers, while he stood watching.

In another account of Bennett's *modus operandi*, a boy he abused recalled the priest stripping off his Franciscan robe and underwear and joining him while the boy was taking a shower after training. He told the boy it was to teach him to overcome his fear of women. Whenever it happened in the shower, the man related to Gardaí twenty years later, the school was empty, usually during holiday time. The mother of a school boy abused by Bennett wrote to one of his Franciscan colleagues in 1998 expressing her outrage at the violation of her child many years before. She recalled how she and her husband had made a point of thanking Fr Ronald in person for assisting the boy in settling into his new school. When their son had eventually described what had gone on 'quite explicitly' to his parents, the mother had written to the college but nothing happened. 'I felt Fr— did not take me seriously as I heard no more and Fr Ronald remained on so I came to the conclusion that I was not really believed,' she wrote. 'I know the difficulties but, dear God, anybody in charge of young children should know where their first duty lies. I myself had to cope with my utter detestation and disgust of Fr Ronald and when I saw him on the altar at ———'s mother's funeral I was almost physically ill. But he obviously has a disorder of some kind and it does me more harm if I cannot let go and let God take care of it.' The woman and her husband made the complaint to a member of the school management in 1973 and they were assured that Fr Ronald would no longer be allowed to be alone with boys. Yet, when, at last, his case came to court it included charges relating to incidents of abuse in 1981, eight years later.

The trial judge pronounced that Ronald Bennett entered an early guilty plea to the charges in the Circuit Criminal Court whereas, in fact, he fought the prosecution right through the system, prolonging the ordeal for his victims until he stopped running virtually at the door of the Supreme Court. He won leave for a judicial review in the High Court, arguing that he could not defend himself properly because of the time that had elapsed since the alleged incidents. He also cited his age and a two-year delay in the DPP's decision to press charges as evidence that he was being treated unfairly. The High Court rejected his application but he won leave to appeal it to the Supreme Court. Only days before it was scheduled to be heard in the Supreme Court, he withdrew the appeal. He changed his not-guilty plea to guilty a week before his appearance in the Dublin Circuit Criminal Court on 29 June 2006. At his trial the following month, he faced just six of the original forty charges against him. Niall Muldoon, senior clinical psychologist at the Granada Institute, told the judge that Bennett had undergone 'considerable therapy' and was categorised at the lowest level of risk of offending. He said the priest was sexually immature when he entered a seminary and that, when he arrived in Gormanston, he was ill-equipped for the position of spiritual director and dealing with sex education matters because he could not distinguish the boundaries in relation to his own sexuality. But he would have considered himself 'a very upright man' and did not see any consequences arising from the abuse of his victims. When he read in the 1980s of the damage done by his activity, he became 'very much aware' of the harm he had done and was very remorseful, the psychologist said.

Sergeant Margaret Murrell told the judge that Bennett was arrested in 1999 and accepted there was 'substance' in the allegations made by one of the victims, but said he could not recall all the details in relation to this man. He remembered another one of the four men (three former boarders and a day pupil at Gormanston College), but could not remember abusing him. 'I presume I did these things with him,' he said. 'I regret having abused these people and I'm trying to work out with the help of counselling why it happened.' He told Gardaí he could not explain why he did what he did and he said he had feelings of 'deep shame'. The sergeant said that one of the complainants had described thinking at the time that the activity might be 'ok' because Bennett was a person in authority and it concerned sex education. She agreed with defence counsel that 'significant compensation' had been paid to the men.

Fr Padraig Loman MacAodha, director of the Franciscan house in Killiney, County Dublin, where Bennett had been living since the accusations were levelled, said he resided there under 'very stringent' conditions. He confirmed that Bennett had no contact with children and that his duties had been confined to secretarial and administrative work for the previous eight years. His faculties for hearing confession and saying mass publicly had been withdrawn and he had to ask permission to leave the house. When Bennett himself took the stand, he promised to adhere to the code of practice laid down for him by his order and to comply with the conditions designated by the Granada Institute. In directing that his five-year sentence be fully suspended, Judge Desmond Hogan stipulated that Gardaí enquire from time to time if he was abiding by the conditions of his bond. He praised the Franciscan order for 'behaving most responsibly in the circumstances' and declared: 'He is practically under open house arrest as it is and I don't wish to interfere with that.'

The sentence cried out to be challenged, and it was eight months later. The appeal brought by the DPP against its undue leniency was heard one week after Derry O'Rourke was released from the Midlands Prison, having served nine years. The DPP contended that the trial judge's decision to suspend the entire sentence did not reflect the seriousness of the offences. Victim impact reports showed that the abuse had badly affected the four boys while they were at school and afterwards. Complaints had been made to the school authorities at the time, pointed out Judge Daniel Herbert of the Court of Criminal Appeal, but the boys had been dismissed as liars. Announcing the court's decision to make two and half years of Bennett's sentence custodial, Judge Joseph Finnegan pointed out that the boys had suffered 'almost catastrophic consequences' from the abuse.

Among the evidence compiled by investigating Gardaí were letters written by two of the boys in adulthood to their abuser. Both wrote frankly about the devastating psychological effects Bennett had on their lives and how, even though now men, they were still struggling to shake off the inbred respect for the sort of authority he represented when they were children.

'I need to know from yourself why you carried out the above systematic perverted abuse on myself and why did you or how could you abuse your position in such a way that you could carry out such disgusting abuse,' agonised one of the letters. 'I have gone through all the emotions of shame, guilt, disgust, anger, repulsion and confidence battering in the past because of your abuse. At the time I did not realise the consequence of your actions, but it did not take very long for me to understand how you would affect me physically and mentally by your disgusting actions. It has taken me a long time to stop blaming myself and questioning my own integrity for your systematic manipulation and abuse and now I want some answers and explanations from yourself as to why you manipulated me in such a manner. Was I your only victim or have there been others? I await your response and explanations which, no doubt, will never arrive and thus lead me to feel further anger against you and force me to approach this abuse from a different perspective and forum. I would hope that I never physically meet you again as my feelings of abhorrence towards you are so great I would fear for my actions against you. I imagine these are the same feelings anybody would harbour against an evil, manipulating person such as yourself.'

Another letter to Bennett, from a second man whom he had abused in Gormanston College, was written two years before the Garda investigation got underway. It reveals the tortured mind of someone trying to live with his memories. 'Dear Fr Ronald,' it begins, 'Many years ago I attended Gormanston Franciscan College at which you were the Bursar ...You showed me photocopies of men showering ... I believed you ... Some of the things you told me that convinced me to act out with you, like "It'll help your self-image". I believed the lies.

However, they did the opposite. Acting out killed my self-image ... I was resentful and angry at you. This was killing me. I read about forgiveness and decided I must pray for you. So every morning and night when I say my prayers for people, I send my love and forgiveness ... At first I just cried when I said the words because I didn't really want to forgive you. But I must if I am to live in recovery. Otherwise, I will die ...'

13. 'Why Did Victims Not Complain?'

Chapter 8 of the Murphy Inquiry Report poses a fundamental question in its title, 'Why Did Victims Not Complain?' Herein lies the first fallacy that has to be debunked in examining the conditions within which the sexual abuse of children can flourish. The fact is that children did complain, but nobody did anything to stop the abusers abusing them. In the case of virtually every child sexual abuser who has been unmasked after years and decades of secrecy it has emerged that some child, at some stage, had sought intercession from an adult in authority, to no avail. The same story of children's unanswered appeals for help surfaces again and again in the Kilkenny Incest Report, the Ferns Report, the Murphy Report, the Sophia McColgan book [about her years of abuse at the hands of her father in the west of Ireland] , the personal accounts heard by the Child Abuse Commission, the experiences of Andrew Madden and Colm O'Gorman in their respective Catholic dioceses and media interviews with an endless flow of witnesses. Yet the mantra goes on: Why did nobody complain? Its popularity can be ascribed more to the soothing ointment it offers grown-ups' consciences than to its roots in historical accuracy. For denial is not the exclusive preserve of the victim.

By exploding the myth that nobody ever complained, it is possible to start understanding the damage that is caused by adults' disbelief.

A child who has been plucked from a cocoon of innocence to be violated for the sexual gratification of an adult who, society ordains, is somebody entitled to respect, needs great courage to depend on another adult to make it stop. Trust in authority is low, with justification, and there is embarrassment to be overcome for a child broaching a conversation strewn with the language of genitalia and sexual contact. When that second investment of trust is betrayed, the hurt and the fear must be all-consuming. International research has found that children who received supportive responses after disclosure showed fewer symptoms of trauma and were abused for a shorter period. Conversely, negative reactions have been found to have caused further harm to the child.

'The term "complaint" can, of course, be taken in a narrow sense to mean what the IASA constitution says it to mean,' the Murphy Report elaborates, 'that is, a formal expression in writing of dissatisfaction with an action of any person in connection with the sport within fourteen days after the incident which gave rise to it, subject to the Branch Executive extending the time where good cause is shown for the delay. Witnesses have testified to the Inquiry that they told a teacher, officers of clubs, executive members of the Leinster Branch and of the IASA and, indeed, one named coach in respect of the alleged abuse by the other named coach. In a broad sense, this telling equates to notice of improper behaviour. It is clearly a complaint, an expression of dissatisfaction. There is a position of trust implicit in the relationship between young swimmers and their club and the swimming organisation generally. From a consideration of the pattern of transfers and defections of young swimmers in the context of rumours in 1991-92 [from Trojans] there were indications that there was something wrong which needed investigation. There is an obligation on every authority, voluntary or professional, who direct young people towards exceptional performance to secure their health, safety and welfare.'

The pools fished by Gibney, O'Rourke, Bennett and McCann were populated with children who had the word 'vulnerable' writ large on their foreheads. They were in the care of these men at that fragile stage of their development between childhood and adulthood. They were scantily dressed. They were competitive, ambitious and idealistic and they believed that their attackers could help them make their dreams of triumph come true. These were children who got out of bed at four and five o'clock on the most wretched winter mornings and watched each other with the hawk eye of rivals. They were growing up in a culture that rewarded sacrifice; the greater the sacrifice, the more glittering the reward. A study by Professor Celia Brackenridge and Dr Rod Jaques published in the British Journal of Sporting Science in October 2004, which found that one in five athletes had been abused by their coach, noted that the stage just before peak performance, known as the 'stage of imminent achievement', is a critical period. At that juncture, coach-athlete relationships are at their most intense with the athlete's desire to succeed making them more likely to disregard any abuse suffered. The report maintained that sports in which this stage coincides with puberty, such as 'the touchy-feely sports' of swimming and gymnastics, pose the greatest risk of exploitation. The gymnast Olga Korbut claimed she was raped by her coach the night before she competed in the 1972 Munich Olympics, but her coach, who maintained she concocted the story, was never prosecuted. The former Scotland and Manchester United footballer Alan Brazil has spoken about the sexual abuse he suffered from his coach when he was a teenager, a victim of institutionalised maltreatment at the Celtic boys' club in the 1960s.

Time and again, swimmers who were abused by Gibney and

O'Rourke reiterate how acutely conscious they were as children that their families were depriving themselves to nourish their dreams and how they could not contemplate shattering their illusions. The 2002 SAVI (Sexual Abuse and Violence in Ireland) Report recorded that the vast majority of abused children who were surveyed were targeted in pre-pubescence: 67 per cent of abused girls and 62 per cent of abused boys. Of those who took part in the study, 47 per cent had never reported their abuse to anyone. Young swimmers were forced into a reversal of roles by their abusers. They were children protecting their parents from the big, bad world. Many of them did not even know they were being abused. It was unnecessary for the abusers to threaten them into silence. Nearly all of them, at first, thought they were being groomed for greatness. Some thought this was love. In the transition from child to adult, sexual sensations can be mistaken for affection. 'I thought he loved me,' says a swimmer who was persistently abused by Gibney. Many thought too that they were the only one. Their abusers were masters of subterfuge. Not only were they adroit at concealing their activities from adults, but from other children as well. As Michelle Smith de Bruin said: 'I really did think he thought the other girls were better than me. That drove a wedge between us.' By such divide-and-conquer stratagems does a child abuser hunt, undetected. Isolating a victim from family and friends is a weapon for increasing the child's emotional dependence on the abuser. 'Swimmers who alleged that they had been abused stated in their evidence to the Inquiry that they believed themselves to have been the only victims,' wrote Roderick Murphy in his report. 'This was another inhibiting factor in reporting or complaining.'

The British Journal of Sporting Medicine report warned that one of the reasons why sport remains a bespoke refuge for the child abuser is the opportunity it provides to exploit a uniquely intimate adult-child relationship. They spend hours together, training and travelling, sharing meals and accommodation, their innermost fears and dreams. There is ample physical contact, with the added lure of the coach's shoulder to cry on when things go wrong. 'The abusing coach uses this dependence, creating a climate of favouritism, secrecy and closeness with malice afore thought,' according to the report. 'Abusers in sport evade detection by operating behind a wall of silence and approval, partly because they are deemed good coaches and "nice men". Brackenridge and Jaques interviewed more than five hundred sportsmen and women. One in five said they had been abused either by a coach or another authority figure. Most of them never reported their abusers. 'In a solo sport, you crave attention and the only one who can give you attention is your coach because he's the only one watching you perform,' Gary O'Toole explains. 'Swimmers ... never really evolve from a nine-year-old doing exactly what they're told to do in the water. At nineteen, they still do not question. When I was swimming, it was unthinkable that you would sit there and suggest to the coach "Why don't we do it this way?"' Brackenridge and Jaques reached the verdict: 'It is our belief that the cases that do come to light are the tip of the iceberg.' Reacting to the disclosure that police investigated a hundred cases of abuse and bullying in football and sixty cases in swimming in Britain in the 2000 to 2001 period, Celia Brackenridge, who has spent more than fifteen years researching sex abuse in sport, said: 'It's probably the biggest problem confronting sport today. Everyone talks about the perils of doping, but if there were a hundred drugs cases under investigation in football, or sixty in swimming, or forty in tennis, there would be uproar. Yet that's the scale of the problem with sex abuse today.'

In its chapter 'Why did victims not complain?' the Murphy Report deals with the varying degrees of abuse endured by different children who were targetted. 'If one compares the first complaint [Chalkie White's] against the first named coach [George Gibney], which was made many years after the abuse took place, with the third complaint [the girl who informed King's Hospital club in November 1992] against the second named coach [Derry O'Rourke], which was promptly reported to the club within days, one can understand the difficulty that there exists, in general, for an abused child to complain, even where he or she has grown into adulthood. The less serious the complaint the easier it is for the victim to react and to complain. The more serious and persistent the abuse, the more it compromises the victim and effectively blocks any complaint being made or delays its articulation.' In other words, the worse the abuse, the safer the abuser.

This finding is borne out by the SAVI Report. When participants in the survey were asked to rate the effect of the abuse on their lives, their responses were 'largely dependant on the type of abuse reported, with those experiencing more serious abuse rating their experiences as having a greater effect'. But it would be wildly simplistic to translate this finding as a rigid paradigm of cause and effect. The extent of a victim's suffering is not only dictated by the frequency, duration or invasiveness of the attacks, but also by the child's own state of mind and other factors at the time he or she is swooped upon. An especially vulnerable child – one, perhaps, with low self-esteem or poor communication at home – will be badly scarred by even a fleeting, superficial sexual contact because it will unleash a hailstorm of corrosive emotions: fear, guilt, shame, the hurt of betrayal and confusion. One study (Prescott and Kendler, 2001) found that the risk of psychological injury increased if the perpetrator was a relative, if the abuse involved intercourse or attempted intercourse, or if threats or force were used. Other studies have found that the risk of adverse outcomes was reduced for abused children who had supportive family environments.

When a person eventually plucks up the courage to make a formal complaint against an abuser only to find that the criminal justice system will not follow through with a prosecution, the effect is akin to being abused all over again. Ireland is one of 149 jurisdiction-signatories to the United Nations Convention on the Rights of the Child which requires each country, under articles 34 and 35, to protect its children from all forms of sexual exploitation and sexual abuse. The low rate of prosecutions and convictions in cases of alleged child sexual abuse in this country constitutes a perturbing verdict on Ireland's performance in upholding the tenets of the UN Convention. Professional child protection advocates have warned repeatedly that inertia in the criminal justice process can transmit a subliminal message to abusers that a country offers safe harbour for their crimes. The swimmer who was raped by George Gibney in Florida in 1991, having been routinely abused by her neighbour's grandfather as a child, is as much a victim of the Irish State's reluctance to administer justice as she is of her attackers. (SAVI found that a quarter of women and one-fifth of men had been abused by different perpetrators as both children and adults).

Even those who are convicted and imprisoned are released back into society potentially more dangerous than they were when they went in. In 1998, the year Derry O'Rourke was jailed, there were 247 sex offenders in Irish jails, but there were only ten places available on treatment programmes in prison, all optional. The Department of Justice provides the State's only sex offenders' treatment programme in Arbour Hill Prison in Dublin through a psychologist and officers of the probation and welfare service. It began in 1994. By 2002, the prison population of sex offenders had risen to 319, but by 2007, the number of treatment places on penal treatment programmes had fallen back to eight a year, following the closure of the Curragh Prison. When O'Rourke rejoined society on 1 March 2007 he had received no treatment whatsoever for his history of abuse, despite paedophilia being, according to the consensus of expert opinion, a highly recidivist offence. Instead, he had been corralled for nine years with fellow child sex offenders. This policy of segregation has been condemned by many childcare professionals as a hot-house for re-offending. 'They are all together in prison and they use that to exchange information on the children they have abused so that when they come out of prison they will be able to identify those children,' argues Ian Elliott, the inaugural chief executive of the Catholic Church's child protection office in Maynooth. The dearth of therapy provided by the Irish penal system is testament to the State's denial of the prevalence of child sexual abuse.

The international Catholic Church has been forced to confront some of the most discomfitting aspects of the phenomenon – including aspects from which even hard-bitten, pulpit-thumping journalism recoils – the post-mortem of numerous scandals involving priests. In some quarters of the Church, the views and prescriptions are far more radical and bold than the instant-fix, crowd-pleasing recommendations trotted out on the airwaves and in the press. The 2007 report of the Dublin archdiocese's prison chaplains, for instance, had this to say:

'Daily we accompany people convicted of sexual offences and those who have been abused. We are aware of the trail of pain and disaster that such actions and crimes cause to victims. It seems, however, that the only way the state will help is after someone has actually offended. He/she is then eligible for treatment – but this is not guaranteed and in many instances will not be available. Should they succeed in availing of the one programme currently available in Arbour Hill Prison they will receive help. There are eight available places each year! Services for those who realise they are at risk of offending need to be set up and made available. At present, no such services exist. Some look for help privately only to find that the prohibitive cost is beyond their means ... Again, without in any way diminishing the gravity of sexual offending or the pain caused to victims, we need to ask the question as to whether prison is the best way to deal with it. This complex issue will not be resolved by a single one-track response. Families of victims and of perpetrators alike have been destroyed and will continue to be destroyed unless and until some positive interventions are made. ... Child protection issues are best served by prevention. As a society issue, education as opposed to media hype is what is needed to come to some understanding of this malaise of our nation. This complex issue calls for a human response and not a response of labelling, marginalisation or isolation.'

In May 2008, a senior law lecturer at NUI Galway, Tom O'Malley, proposed that the State prioritise the treatment of offenders over custodial sentences on an experimental basis. He told a conference of the National Organisation for the Treatment of Abusers in Galway that there was a lack of resources for offender treatment, even though such treatment had proven to be more effective than prison. When courts handed down lenient sentences there was 'the usual hullabaloo' and the standard calls for the 'removal of the judge', he said, but society had to be prepared 'collectively' to take responsibility and allow for greater latitude in applying remedies. His speech provoked no shrieks of outrage. It was met by a silence of unease. So too was a report in 2005 by the visitors' committee for Arbour Hill Prison, the chief sex-offenders' place of detention in Ireland. The committee recommended 'active sentence management for sex offenders combined with a structured release system for prisoners who successfully completed relevant courses of therapy. It urged that prisoners participating in such courses have it acknowledged in any review of their sentences and in the consideration of temporary or early release. 'At present, participation in these programmes does not give a prisoner any reduction in time to be served,' the report stated. 'Consequently, the uptake of places is disappointing.' Experience elsewhere has shown that the inducement of a sentence-reduction attracts offenders onto these courses for reasons of pure expediency but that, once they have been recruited, they can be susceptible to rehabilitative treatment.

In determining the plethora of alternative ways of addressing child sexual abuse, it is imperative to keep the feelings and sensitivities of victims at the forefront. That means walking a tightrope between the balance of victims' rights and the essential needs of society. While it may sound more sympathetic to demonise all perpetrators as evil perverts, it does not assist either those who have already been injured or those who are targetted in the future. That is the soft option. Child sexual abuse is a riveting journalistic story in itself, hitting all the human buttons of horror, wonder and introspective examination. It asks for no embellishment. Editors are often loath to colour in the shade when something is this black-and-white. It's the classic good-versus-bad morality tale and trespassing beyond that central theme means stepping into a zone where paedophiles must be regarded as human beings in order to understand why they do what they do and to attempt to find solutions that work. Avoiding serious public analysis might save people who have been abused from further hurt, but it compounds the problem in the long term. It creates stigma, secrecy, taboo and a climate where the victim's rights get stuffed into the to-do ledger and left on a shelf to gather dust. In reality, it is more detrimental to survivors. A serious deficiency in the State's response to child sexual abuse, for example, is that Ireland's national child protection service does not provide a tailor-made treatment programme for victims of child sexual abuse.

'One of the failures is the non-availability of therapeutic recovery programmes for victims,' says Ian Elliott, the former director of the National Society for the Prevention of Cruelty to Children in Belfast. 'This is absolutely critical, particularly in Ireland. It is true to say that individuals who have been abused may go on to abuse others, although it is not true to say that it will inevitably follow, but you are much less likely to move along the continuum and harm others if you have had access to therapeutic programmes. We are woefully bad. The Department of Health sponsored research in 2005 that looked at sexual abuse and the availability of treatment programmes. Chapter seven of that report records that there are no dedicated treatment programmes for abused people in Ireland. There are five *ad hoc* programmes that have been developed in some individual hospitals. We're not doing enough in a number of areas. I am constantly amazed at the lack of understanding, despite there being loads of information available. For instance, people in pivotal positions talk about 'historical abuse', as if it will not happen again. These individuals who offend have high libidos. They will be sexually active for very much longer so that in their eighties and nineties they can still be a risk to children. It is absolutely wrong to say they are not a risk to children anymore.'

The word 'victim' is not only a reductive term, but a narrow one too. Child sexual abuse affects more people than the targetted child alone. Parents, siblings, spouses, partners, future children all suffer to some extent. K, whose mother drowned herself after Derry O'Rourke was convicted of sexually abusing her only daughter, is adamant that her old coach brought death and despair to her entire family. 'What he did to me has affected everyone,' she says. 'My brothers have lost their mam. My dad has lost his wife and partner. My brothers found me on the floor and had to watch me being brought into John of God's. My mam only got to see one of her six grandchildren. He's spent nine years in prison. I'd have swapped with him. I'd have done his nine years and I would have been an awful lot happier than in the prison I've been in.'

Esther and Jessica McCann were victims. They got in the way of Frank McCann's secret sex life and he made them pay for it with their lives. Esther's sister, Marian Leonard, and her extended family are all victims. Asked if McCann's colleagues in swimming – some of whom have continued to visit him in Arbour Hill – ever contacted the family after his conviction, Marian replied: 'Heels for dust. The swimming association never came near us. I contacted House of Sport at one stage, but I got no response. It would have meant a lot to Mum. The only reason he killed them was to protect his own image in the swimming association. There was no monetary gain. He wasn't with anybody he wanted to spend the rest of his life with. None of the normal motives were there. His was the most unthinkable motive – his image and the swimming association.'

The sport of swimming was a victim. Sponsors fled from it. Acrimony flared. Writs flew. Competitions were called off. Elite swimmers were curtailed. Worst of all, it threw up an iron curtain between adults and children. 'Gibney and his ilk destroyed any potential for trust between adults and children,' says Derek West, the former principal at Newpark Comprehensive School. Roderick Murphy decried the IASA's requirement under its Rule 33 that all complaints had to be formally made to both a swimmer's club and branch. 'Indeed it is difficult to interpret the evidence given by victims and by parents other than by finding that Rule 33 discouraged complaints,' he wrote. 'There appears to have been an attitude of disbelief and a desire that the problem would go away, which was justified by reliance upon the view that a person accused of serious abuse is entitled to his good name until convicted in criminal proceedings. This was compounded by a reliance upon the use of such phrases as "the matter is *sub judice*" to remove the need for action by the Branch and the IASA on receipt of such complaints of abuse after the matter was being investigated by the Gardaí.'

The inaugural chief executive of Swim Ireland, Sarah Keane, says: 'I think it's a very good thing all this has come out. How are we supposed to change society unless people come out and talk about these things? What we are trying to do in Swim Ireland is create a positive atmosphere for the people who are there now and to recognise what happened to people before now. We're trying to deal with it as best we can. People aren't trying to make excuses. If the sport helps bring this issue out in the public, that's a good thing. We're trying to allow the sport to put its head above the parapet, to let people recognise the good parts of it and be proud of it. We have to get the balance right between recognising what's wrong and doing our best to ensure it never happens again, but also to put some sort of closure to it. The people who were abused could have got so much good out of the sport if that hadn't been done to them. When you're involved in swimming, it almost becomes who you are. You make friendships that last forever. Because it happened in that environment makes it so much worse. The problem is that abusers don't walk around the place with Xs on their foreheads.'

As for Chalkie White, the swimmer and coach whose courage exposed the sport's sordid secrets, it has been like a bomb exploding in his family. He and his wife have separated after nearly thirty years of marriage and he has gone to live abroad. 'I had to get up and get out of swimming. I had to leave the country to stop seeing people who constantly reminded me of him. People who worked with him. People who looked like him. Everything was a constant reminder,' Chalkie says, on the phone from his new home. 'The effect of what he did to me as a child is still going on in my head. You see, I thought I loved him when I was a child. I didn't hate the sight of him. I didn't hate the sound of the door opening, like other people did. I had to deal with all that. I got out of swimming. I went to work abroad. I stopped seeing cars I thought were his and people who looked like him, but there are times I regret doing what I did because it's had such a big impact on everyone around me. In my head there's a big part of me that says I wish I'd never done it.'

He continues to swim in a pool every day for two hours. For those 120 minutes, he forgets. The rhythm of the strokes soothes him. It is his only escape. He may have left his wife and children in Ireland, but his memories have followed him across the world.

'People think "God love that child being abused", but it's not just him. It's the whole family. It caused an awful lot of problems,' says Chalkie's wife, Val. 'I found out in 1991. It's had a devastating effect on our family. I can't deal with it anymore. It's not just the victim who suffers. It's your wife, your children, your parents, your brothers and sisters, your friends. Everyone suffers. When Chalkie told his mother she said "You certainly were not abused by George Gibney. Your father was always with you". It's hard when your mother denies it. He went in the car with him. He stayed nights alone in the house with him. I remember when Chalkie had his accident in Switzerland, George coming to the house in Killiney to tell me the morning after it. George got an emergency passport for me and I flew to Switzerland. When I got there, I was using George's official pass. He had got money for me and made sure the IASA insurance would cover the costs. Chalkie'd had an eight-hour operation by the time I heard. Nobody else had bothered to tell me. I thought George was so charming and nice, but when I told Chalkie in the hospital how good he'd been to me he looked like he was going to cry. When he told me, I decided we had to tell the kids and he had to tell his mother. Our eldest son was ten, going on eleven – the same age Chalkie was when George started abusing him.

'Chalkie was sacked from Glenalbyn soon after that.

'I remember when he came home from Villanova in 1976; he was swimming in King's Hospital, training for the Moscow Olympics. Derry O'Rourke was your typical father figure, but there was always something … There was always talk going around about Derry and little girls. There used to be a mattress on the floor in the boiler room. I remember going to Paris on a swimming trip and walking into a room in the hotel. There was a physio's table in the room and a girl swimmer lying on it being massaged. Frank McCann was at the top end of the table. Derry, Chalkie and I were at the other end. I said to Chalkie I thought it was a disgrace that that girl is in there having a rub down and all these fellows in there. Everything was brushed under the carpet. They had these men up on pedestals.

'Chalkie was always fairly quiet, but very honest. If he said he'd do something for you, it would be done. He was always true to his word. He went to school with my brother at the Marists. We were teenage sweethearts. I still love him. You don't live with somebody for twenty-eight years and stop loving them. George Gibney has an awful lot to answer for. I remember going to the theatre – the Project – him and Brona and Chalkie and me. He was a charmer. He definitely was. Jesus, when I found out afterwards. An awful lot of people didn't believe Chalkie. They said "No way would George do something like that" when he told them. I think the individuals in the association who refused to believe it should be called to account for what they did. Everybody wanted to be on George's good side. It's a disgrace the way Chalkie was dealt with by the swimming association. He gave so much to swimming and to swimmers over the years. Nobody has even privately approached him to say sorry. Why else is he suicidal? Nobody believed him. Oh, they do now, but what did it take? He's such a good person.

'When it all came out, I went to a victims' meeting in a hotel and I couldn't believe how ruined so many lives were. All these girls I'd known from way back. One girl, her marriage had just broken down and I thought, "Oh Jesus, is this the road I'm going down?" I supported him through everything. There were so many times he tried to end it. One day – he'd moved out of home and into an apartment – he was taken by ambulance from Grafton Street. When he was released from the hospital, I sat outside his apartment to make sure he didn't try to come out. The next day, he rang me and said "sorry". I said, "Chalkie, you're in the gutter. I sat in that hospital with drug addicts and alcoholics and you're in the gutter. You need to get yourself help." Later, an opportunity came up at work for him to go to Japan. I drove him to the airport and that was it. It ends up with all of us being upset. At first, he'd ring me from Tokyo and say "I've taken thirty tablets. I'm ready to go to sleep now". He'd say it's a compliment to me that I'm the one he rings. And I'd be out of my mind with worry. He had a habit of writing things down during the years. After he left, I found a notebook in which he had written all about how he'd told Gary the whole thing on the plane to Perth. I lived with him for twenty-eight years. I loved him and I still love him. Nothing changed for me, but it all changed for him. He's a very good father. He supports us totally. That's the way he is. I think it would help him and the other survivors if George was brought back to face the charges. I don't know if Chalkie could take the pain of what he'd have to go through to bring him to justice, but he deserves to be shown that at long last, after all he's been through, he's believed.'

Child sexual abuse is outlawed in every developed country. In some jurisdictions, life imprisonment and even capital punishment are the mandatory sentences. In Ireland, the crime is commonly prosecuted at the level of the Circuit Criminal Court (though statutory rape and aggravated sexual assault are allowed to be tried in the Central Criminal Court, as well as adult rape and murder). Judges determine the sentence on a case-by-case basis. It is notoriously hard to convict abusers for all sorts of reasons: the antiquity of complaints, the absence of witnesses, the familiarity of a child with an abuser (in four-fifths of cases, the perpetrator is known to the victim), continuing menace and threats, and the abuser's skill at covering his tracks. The failure to prosecute can have devastating consequences for the victim because knowing you are believed can be crucial to the recovery of a survivor. International studies show that the tactics employed by George Gibney to elude prosecution are standard behaviour for abusers facing court charges. 'They never admit to anything until there is categorical proof against them,' Celia Brackenridge states. 'They know how difficult it is to get evidence against them to convict.' When Ireland's Director of Public Prosecutions is considering bringing charges in a case, he is primarily concerned with the provability of the case and the attendant obligations to be prudent with taxpayers' money and the courts' time. Over the border in Northern Ireland, his counterpart is beholden to give greater weight to consideration of the public interest, which means that a decision is taken when there is a case to be answered for the good of the wider community.

The SAVI Report revealed a disturbingly low success rate in

pursuing allegations of abuse. Of those surveyed, only ten of the 178 men and twenty-eight of the 290 women had reported their cases to Gardaí (8 per cent in all). Just six of the thirty-eight reported cases (just over 15 per cent) resulted in prosecutions, with only four of those culminating in a guilty verdict. Such dismal results can act as a deterrent to others who are contemplating disclosure of abuse they suffered, adding to the difficulty in measuring the extent of child sexual abuse in society. SAVI found that 60 per cent of its male respondents had told nobody prior to participating in the study. That statistic lends credence to Gary O'Toole's belief that other male swimmers, apart from Chalkie White, were abused by George Gibney, but that they have never felt able to disclose it. Society's reluctance to fully discuss the gamut of complexities relating to the crime – our selective blind eye – means that, in general, it remains harder for males to report child sexual abuse in any context and for child victims of either gender to report abuse by a female perpetrator.

'I always thought Chalkie blamed himself because no other males came forward, but there were a few men I thought it could have happened to,' O'Toole confirms. 'I went to them and asked them straight out. I said: "He abused males as well". They all shook their heads and said "no". Do I believe them? Not all of them.'

Carole Walsh agrees: 'There were other boys, no doubt about it, but Chalkie was the only man who ever came out. There was a huge stigma attached to a man saying he had been abused.'

One way of creating a climate conducive to the reporting of child abuse crimes is to make it a crime for adults who suspect it not to voluntarily report it. There is no statutory obligation on Irish citizens to report suspicions or allegations of child sexual abuse though a 1997 act does provide legal immunity for anyone who does so. Other jurisdictions, however, have specific laws obliging citizens to do whatever they can to stop abuse, unlike the black hole that exists in the Irish statute books. Recommendation number fourteen by Judge Frank Murphy in his acclaimed Ferns Report published in October 2005 was that this flaw be rectified. 'The Inquiry believes that consideration should be given by the Legislature to the introduction of a new criminal offence which would apply to situations where any person "wantonly or recklessly engages in conduct that creates a substantial risk of bodily injury or sexual abuse to a child or wantonly or recklessly fails to take reasonable steps to alleviate such risk where there is a duty to act." (General Laws of Massachusetts Part IV Title I Chapter 265). The Inquiry believes that the implications of such a law on teachers, childcare workers and professionals whose work brings them into contact with children would have to be fully explored and the parameters of any such legislation would have to be clearly outlined.'

Ireland has an abysmal track record in tackling the crime of sheltering criminals. Only two cases involving the charge of accessory-after-the-fact appear in the Law Reports. A new criminal offence of reckless endangerment of children was created by the Criminal Justice Act 2006 as a result of the Ferns Inquiry, but nobody has yet been charged with the crime. It came into effect on 1 August 2006. Under the law, a person with authority or control over a child, or an abuser, can be found guilty if it's proven that they intentionally or recklessly endangered a child by putting him or her in a situation where there was a risk or by failing to take reasonable steps to prevent that risk.

The State's standard for reporting suspected child sexual abusers, 'Children First', remains no more than a guideline. An official review of procedures followed by Gardaí, childcare workers and other professionals under the Children First guidelines reported in 2008 that they were being implemented haphazardly, even within the same HSE areas. Just 9 per cent of respondents working in positions governed by the guidelines felt there were adequate structures and agencies in place to successfully implement the guidelines. Fine Gael's spokesman on children, Alan Shatter, said the report had 'confirmed that our child protection services are chaotic, uncoordinated and grossly inadequate.'

In urging that 'every effort should be made by legislation and publicity to preserve and strengthen the more open environment of reporting', Judge Frank Murphy wrote in the Ferns Report: 'Criminal wrong-doing will not cease, but the extent of the misery created by unchecked child abuse by adults in a position of power or privilege will be greatly reduced by the creation of an open and informed environment that will encourage a willingness to report promptly inappropriate sexual behaviour towards children.'

Had his proposed law been in place in the 1970s, there is a strong chance that George Gibney, Derry O'Rourke and Fr Ronald Bennett would have been exposed and children whom they went on to abuse could have been saved. 'OK, Derry O'Rourke went to prison but was he the only one at fault?' asks K. 'The sport didn't make the paedophiles. They were in the sport because it gave them access to vulnerable kids. We all paid our capitation fees and our insurance to the IASA. They were supposed to mind us.'

Carole Walsh, who worked alongside George Gibney as a coach in Trojans, believes: 'There are people who were associated with swimming and who were aware of what was happening and who have not put their hands up. You know what they say about hindsight, but they saw kids changing, they saw their personalities changing and they should have gone to somebody about it. There is too much of this, "Oh, we could be sued".'

Swim Ireland's chief executive, though, is keen to emphasise the changes the sport has adopted in the aftermath of its serial scandals. 'Our rules have changed radically,' Sarah Keane asserts. 'We don't allow over-18s to share rooms with under-18s, for instance, even if they are best friends. Coaches and managers are not allowed on their own in dressing rooms with swimmers, only in certain circumstances and they they must be accompanied by another official. You're not allowed do a swimming teacher's course until you've done the Irish Sports Council/Sports NI child protection course, which is based upon the HSE Children First guidelines. There were a hundred recommendations in the Murphy Report, but even those have been overtaken by time and we now must operate to current best practice. If you teach or coach for more than two or three hours a week you can't be on a committee because of the concern around the possible dominant effect of a coach. They can be very passionate, very committed, and they have a very high level of expertise, which means some parents will listen to them about everything. You cannot stay on the board of Swim Ireland now for more than four years in a row. There are specific children's officers nationally, regionally and in the clubs. One of the problems we have is that the [swimming pool] facilities are not owned by us. Do the facilties have training for child protection? That's something that needs to be looked at. Any criminal abuse allegations we get are dealt with through the recommended HSE reporting procedures. This means we automatically inform the HSE and the Gardaí. If there is an allegation of abuse, the accused person is automatically stepped down. The people in swimming now are prepared to stand up and do something about this. We almost doubled our members' fees to put money towards the compensation of swimmers. The members voted that in.'

Gary O'Toole suggests that the swim authorities in Ireland should take their lead from the example set by Chalkie White for blowing the whistle on what was going on. 'I think they owe an awful lot to Chalkie and to the man [the husband of the swimmer] who came to the meeting with us in the Ashling Hotel. They refused our specific request that night to stop George Gibney coaching at a scheduled event. You know, it is true that power corrupts. I was very lucky that I had very protective parents who didn't say to me: "How can you say these things?" After all, George has never been convicted of anything but, if he was sitting there beside you, I would say the same thing. George Gibney sexually abused children. You can take me into any court in the land and I'll say it. I'm very glad I did what I did. I think the Association did their best to talk down what I was saying; that it wasn't as serious as I was making it out to be. If the *Sunday Tribune* hadn't published the story based on the affidavits, the IASA would never ever have believed that any abuse had taken place at the hands of George Gibney. Because of that, as a society, as a sport and maybe personally, we are truly indebted to the newspaper.'

14. Was There A Paedophile Ring?

On the eve of Derry O'Rourke's release from the Midlands Prison in the spring of 2007, while Swim Ireland was still contesting his victims' High Court actions for compensation, the divisions and high emotions in Irish swimming caused by successive scandals burst onto the national air waves.

RTÉ Radio One's audience-participation programme, *Liveline*, was debating the death penalty in certain US states when it took a call from a woman who introduced herself as Hilary Hughes. She talked about a twenty-year pen-friendship she had maintained with a condemned man on death row whose execution by lethal injection in the Southern Ohio Correctional Facility she had attended a year earlier as his nominated witness. Glenn Benner II had protested his innocence for twenty years after twenty-six-year-old Cynthia Sedgwick was found murdered in woodlands in 1985. Six months later, the body of his second victim, twenty-one-year-old Trina Bowser, was found by her family in the boot of a burning car abandoned on the side of a highway. Both women had been raped and strangled with their underwear. Bowser pleaded guilty to the rape of a third woman after breaking into her home. Shortly after ten o'clock on the morning of 7 February 2006, while strapped to the execution chair, Benner, then aged forty-three, finally confessed his guilt and apologised to the families of his victims. As he died, Hilary Hughes prayed and kept vigil with him in the execution chamber. When it was over, she read a statement to journalists congregated outside the prison, describing Benner as 'a beloved friend' and railing against the death penalty. 'I'm sorry, but I cannot get my head around the logic,' she said. 'To show it is wrong to kill someone, it is acceptable to kill someone else?' She said Benner had 'turned to God for help and forgiveness' and that he had 'made many friends, touched many hearts and become the kind, gentle and loving man God intended him to be'. On returning to her home in south Dublin, she continued to correspond with death-row inmates in the US, she told the *Liveline* audience. She spoke compassionately, eliciting calls from listeners who praised her for her concern and humanity.

But when she mentioned that she had also visited a double-murderer called Frank McCann in Dublin's Arbour Hill Prison, one man who had been listening to the radio with angry disbelief picked up his phone and called *Liveline*. Aidan O'Toole told the programme team member who answered that the Hilary Hughes who was advocating mercy for convicted killers was the same Hilary Hughes who had served as secretary to the Leinster Branch of the Irish Amateur Swimming Association for ten years, while the sport was in paroxysms over George Gibney, Derry O'Rourke and Frank McCann. Hughes had also spent seven years as secretary to Glenalbyn Swimming Club, which sacked Chalkie White as its coach. She was also the person who informed Gary O'Toole that officers of the Leinster branch would not meet him when he wished to address them with his concerns about George Gibney in the early 1990s. Aidan offered to go head-to-head with Hughes live on air the following day to debate the response of the swimming authorities to the discovery that its two most senior coaches were child sex abusers while, at the same time, the most senior official in Leinster murdered his wife and his sister's child. He said he wanted to talk about the repercussions of rape and child sexual abuse for the victims, not the perpetrators.

Hilary Hughes did not make a return visit to the programme the next day, but Aidan O'Toole spoke at length, followed by his son, Gary. They talked about Gibney and O'Rourke and how the two sexual predators had continued to enjoy access to young swimmers even after swim officials were aware that they were being investigated by Gardaí. They talked about McCann, who had murdered Esther and Jessica to cover the tracks of his sexual liaison with a young swimmer whom he made pregnant. They did not mention Ronald Bennett whose suspended jail sentence was about to be successfully appealed by the DPP. The conversation soon arrived at the question that is omnipresent for survivors of abuse in swimming, but which hardly dares articulate itself in public. Was it possible that a ring of child sexual abusers had been operating in Irish swimming for half a century or more? 'I don't think O'Rourke and Gibney were in cahoots or that there was a ring,' Gary O'Toole replied, true to the belief he has consistently expressed in private. 'The two of them hated each other, probably because they were of similar character. The environment around swimming at that time was extremely competitive, to such a degree that the club Gibney coached and the club O'Rourke coached rarely mixed.'

In an interview for this book, Gary expounded on his theory, 'I think they're all individuals, all rotten individuals, who just happened upon a situation where they could thrive. There was very little monitoring, very little supervision, and these guys could get away with anything. Derry and George hated each other and were very competitive.'

When it comes to the question of whether there was organised child sexual abuse in swimming, there are nearly as many opinions as there are ripples in a pool.

'The three of them [Gibney, O'Rourke and McCann] were very pally. They were very macho,' remembers a woman whose children were swimmers during the trio's reign. 'There were always lots of suggestive remarks being made about girls in their swimsuits.'

An abuse survivor acknowledges that it would have been easy for the coaches to swap victims, but does not believe they did.

'I wouldn't be at all surprised if they knew about each other, that they recognised it in each other,' she says, 'but I don't think they were passing children around among themselves, no.'

There is significant overlap in the careers of Gibney, O'Rourke, McCann, and Bennett. Gibney served as coach to the Irish Schools Swimming Association, founded by Bennett. O'Rourke regularly held overnight training camps at Bennett's workplace, Gormanston College. According to some former swimmers, Gibney, O'Rourke and McCann were frequently on the pool bank simultaneously during galas and one swimmer says she felt 'it was like running the gauntlet having to pass them, one after the other, going to and from the [swimming] lanes'. There were incidents too when, in retrospect, the abusers appeared to cover up for one another. When Chalkie White told Frank McCann in February 1991 that Gibney had abused him, the then president of the Leinster branch did nothing about it. Later, when a written complaint against Derry O'Rourke was posted to the IASA's head office, McCann took it upon himself to visit O'Rourke informally at King's Hospital pool. The complainant received no response to her letter.

The Murphy Report recorded two instances of victims being shared. Witness number four to the inquiry alleged that, in 1977 when she was aged twelve, someone who had previously abused her suggested she accept a lift home from 'the first named coach' [Gibney]. She said Gibney abused her in the car taking her home. 'The evidence of one of the witnesses that a previous abuser suggested she take a lift from the first named coach was most disturbing,' Roderick Murphy concluded. In Chapter 3.6 of the Report, Murphy records that witness number six alleged she had been frequently abused at the [Trojans] pool when she was aged from eleven to thirteen. She too was advised to take a lift home from Gibney after training and he 'touched her inappropriately' during the journey.

Evidence has also come to light that in one family, several siblings were abused over a period of years by two swimming coaches. The coaches acted separately and targeted different children within the family.

Swimming is awash with opportunities for child molesters, providing an unending supply of victims and lending an aura of institutional authority to predators. When Kings Hospital club president, Michael McCann wrote to the Garda Commissioner, Patrick Culligan, on 17 September 1993, questioning the nature of the investigation into Derry O'Rourke, and alluding to the cases then before the courts involving George Gibney and Frank McCann, he said,

'While I can accept the sheer coincidence of two sets of unrelated criminal proceedings referring to high ranking officials in the Irish Amateur Swimming Association in the space of one year, it would stretch my credulity, and that of the public at large, were a third incident to arise in this our Centenary Year.' This illustrates how hard it is for people to believe that several abusers could be on the prowl at once in the same milieu, and demonstrates the inherent danger of this disbelief.

It is now known, in fact, that there were four men molesting young swimmers while enjoying exalted positions in the sport's hierarchy –

George Gibney, Derry O'Rourke, Frank McCann and Ronald Bennett. Other coaches from outside Ireland also had occasional access, such as the physical education teacher and former British national swim coach, Paul Hickson, who was jailed on fifteen charges of child sexual abuse in Wales in September 1995. He was one of three of Britain's top swimming pool coaches convicted on child sex abuse charges, bringing to seven the number of abusers operating at the highest echelon of the sport in Ireland and Britain. The two countries have traditionally enjoyed a neighbourly relationship in the sport, with young Irish swimmers often travelling across the Irish Sea for training and competition and British coaches working on contract in Ireland.

'It's hard to believe they wouldn't have known about each other,' says journalist Johnny Watterson. 'Hickson and Gibney knew each other well. They were both national coaches. They would have had a lot of contact and, because of the geographical proximity, there was even more than usual.'

In a paper entitled 'Government-Sponsored Professional Sports Coaches and the Need for Better Child Protection' written by welfare-in-sport researcher Yvonne Williams in the law department of the University of Wales, Aberystwyth and published in 2003, the similarities between the handling of abuse cases in Ireland and England are explored. Under the heading 'Closing Ranks', Williams writes:

> No evidence was given at the trial to suggest that Hickson came into sport in order to gain access to children, rather he was in the sport from a young age, had graduated into coaching and chose to abuse children he coached. Hickson was not one of the 'dirty old men brigade … in raincoats and mucky

hats' ... that is often believed to be typical of child abusers; instead, he was a well-educated, well-qualified professional person who, although not necessarily liked by some other adult swimmers, was nevertheless held in some considerable esteem by officials in his governing body. At the time of his arrest he was also married with an eight-year-old child. A particularly disturbing feature of the case, however, is the lack of attention paid by Hickson's governing body officials to his activities, as it was made clear at his trial and in later newspaper reports that, although complaints had been made about him to officials of the Amateur Swimming Association, they had been reluctant to intervene. ... A similar reluctance is illustrated in a case identical to Hickson's in the Republic of Ireland in 1990, where again allegations of sexual abuse had been made about an Olympic swimming coach and the sport's governing body had ignored them. The coach, George Gibney, was charged with serious sexual complaints in April 1993, but was not prosecuted. Hickson's trial followed in 1995; and at the same time a second Irish Olympic swimming coach (Derry O'Rourke, the successor to Gibney) was sexually abusing children and young people he was coaching. Complaints against O'Rourke had been investigated by the governing body in 1992 and the finding had been that the incident complained of had 'resulted from a misunderstanding'. [The complaint Williams is referring to is one which was actually made to the Committee of King's Hospital Swimming Club, and not to the IASA, as she implies.] He was allowed to continue coaching and abusing. The result of the two Irish cases was a government inquiry in 1998 into child protection in sport, in which the Joint Committee on

Tourism, Sport and Recreation [sic] could find no links between Hickson and the first Irish Olympic coach apart from the fact that they had both been at the Seoul Olympics at the same time. However, it is particularly disturbing that at least three Olympic swimming coaches were sexually abusing young people in their care during a given period of time, especially as a fourth coach, Mike Drew, and Mike Edge, a British Olympic diving coach, had both been recently convicted for the sexual abuse of children they coached.

Williams makes the point that these Olympic coaches would very possibly have crossed paths, despite the fact that the official Irish inquiry did not prove there were links between them. Many swimmers remember them being together at competitions, both in Ireland and abroad.

Despite Gary O'Toole's argument that Gibney and O'Rourke 'hated each other', there is evidence that they also facilitated each other. Carole Walsh remembers walking into Gibney's office in Trojans and hearing him on the phone, arranging to have O'Rourke replace him as national coach when he stepped aside at the commencement of the Garda investigation. In normal circumstances, it would have been an uncharacteristically magnanimous gesture by a notoriously arrogant coach to a colleague whom he appeared to despise. Similarly, several sources remember occasions when Frank McCann filled in for Derry O'Rourke on away trips if O'Rourke was otherwise engaged, and at his express request. 'I don't think Derry ever actually told George he was abusing girls,' says Carole Walsh. 'I couldn't see them ever having a conversation about it, but there probably was a silent acknowledgement that it was happening. Those coaches saw as much of the swimmers as they saw of their own kids;

morning, noon and night and on away trips for up to three weeks at a time.'

Fr Ronald Bennett was sports master and bursar at Gormanston College, the fee-paying County Meath boarding school. Gormanston boasted a twenty-five-yard, four-lane pool and during the Easter and summer holidays, its dormitories were occupied by highly-focused young people attending the residential training camps frequently run by Gibney and O'Rourke.

Chalkie White says he was aware at training camps in Gormanston of rumours about Bennett molesting boys. 'Because all three of them were doing the same, none of them was going to jump up and say 'Hey, do you know what he's doing?' because they were doing it themselves. So, within the climate, it was very easy for it to go on. I think the word 'ring' might be too strict. I think they were able to keep within the same circles without necessarily having much contact with each other, but, maybe, because they were all operating they understood which swimmers they could pick on. As far as I know, there wouldn't have been any victims abused by all of them, but what they would have been constantly doing was picking up on the technique, because there is a technique to it.'

Chalkie's analysis mirrors academic research on paedophile and child sexual abuse rings. The often nebulous nature of a 'ring' makes it harder to prove its existence. A ring can run the gamut from a highly-organised, internet-based collaboration of offenders engaged in abuse, to an informal structure of abusers operating singly and with nod-and-wink approval from other abusers that would be imperceptible to anyone else; abusers may never meet or share details, but may use the internet to 'normalise' their behaviour through discussions with others.

Linda Jones of Howard House, a child abuse therapy centre in north London, has described organised networks as working 'in cells, like terrorist cells. No paedophile who is linked knows of more than one other, so they'll use a child, then tell him to go to someone else – there are huge rings, with children passed from one to another to another.'

Ray Wyre, one of the most respected child sexual abuse experts in the world until his death in June 2008, wrote in *Prison Reform Trust* (1990) about how offenders seek each other out to share memories and contacts while in jail. 'Paedophiles [attracted to pre-pubescent children] in particular tend to congregate in groups. They often swap addresses and [prison] units can be the breeding-ground for sex rings.'

Chalkie White's description of the casual and almost invisible understanding that existed between Gibney, O'Rourke and Bennett is a pattern of abuser behaviour recognised by the eminent child care advocate, Norah Gibbons. 'Just as pornography offenders talk to each other, O'Rourke and Gibney could have talked to each other about what they were doing and got a vicarious thrill from talking about it,' she says. 'Or, it could have been a subtle communication: that one picked up on what the other was doing, indicated they knew and they approved, and the other felt the need to share the spoils. Paedophile rings are uncommon. You come across them where there are people who are in the position to pass children one to the other. These people are normally in their positions in a particular organisation at the same time as each other, rather than in a time line,' explains Gibbons, Barnardos' director of advocacy, a member of the Child Abuse Commission and chairwoman of the Roscommon child neglect and incest inquiry. 'There are three main types of abuser. There's the type who abuses within the family only. There's the type that abuses only boys or only girls and only outside the family. And the third type who abuses boys and/or girls inside the family and outside and wherever they find children. You do wonder why some people get away with abusing children for a very long time in a particular organisation and you have to wonder if there was somebody in the organisation protecting them or somebody who had something else going on in their lives. Not that they were abusing too, but maybe they were compromised by a drink problem or money problems or an affair with a parent. Something that made them vulnerable and there was then mutual protection; not explicit. Of course, naturally, we don't like to think that people we know are capable of that sort of behaviour and, if you're vulnerable yourself, your mind might be more closed. What does that circle do? They deny, because there is nothing else.'

Gibbons' analysis evokes memories of the most notorious child sexual abuse ring uncovered in Ireland when three staff members at Kincora Boys Home in East Belfast were convicted in the 1980s of the sexual abuse of boys in their care. One of the offenders, William McGrath, a prominent Orangeman and Born Again Christian led a double life as an MI5 agent. Speculation persists that he was allowed to continue his abuse spree in Kincora and other institutions in Northern Ireland as long as the information he was passing onto his spy handlers proved useful. It was a clear-cut case of the sort of mutual protection Gibbons outlines.

'It is difficult for people to take on board that people like Derry O'Rourke will target positions where they know they have access to children,' she continues. 'They can be the most helpful people. They'll work late hours and come in extra early and are prepared to do anything for anyone. The other element that lets them get away with it is when a parent is pushy – as opposed to encouraging their child, which is perfectly right. Such parents tend not to have their eyes as open as they should be. That's not to criticise parents. You have a coach saying "your child is doing really well and I'll take him or her for extra classes". People who sexually abuse children are charming. They inveigle their way into families' lives. They go out of their way to help families. It is the most appalling betrayal of trust. It leaves parents feeling so guilty and older siblings often feel guilty too. You feel conned.'

Ian Elliott, a fellow leading child protection professional agrees with Gibbons that the swimming environment may have allowed the abuse to flourish. 'Abusers are driven by the obsession to observe and access children in order to gratify themselves. That leads on to an ability to detect and make contact with other individuals who have similar tendencies,' says the chief executive of the National Board for Safeguarding Children and former head of the Society for the Protection of Children in Northern Ireland. 'A ring occurs where you have a group of these individuals who have similar interests and who realise that by working together they can have greater access and they start to organise together. They may never meet. What they would do is have communication with each other, either face to face or on the internet. They have an ability to recognise each other in a crowd of people. They also have an ability to detect children who have already been abused. I'm not surprised to find a group of individuals who have a sexual interest in children and young people in an activity like swimming. Any activity that provides access will be of interest to these individuals. Usually they are not unintelligent people. They are proficient. . . The details of what happened in Irish swimming, as you have presented them, would be a typical situation of a group of people with a shared interest in children and who are supporting each other in terms of exchange of information. I would say it is certainly a situation of organised abuse. How many other victims are around, you have to ask, in an activity that offers so much access to children?'

It is debatable whether the people who ran swimming during the unmasking of Gibney and O'Rourke can justify their inaction because of the weak guidelines that prevailed, but their obdurate failure to reach out to victims in the aftermath is less easy to explain away. Swim Ireland pursued a legalistic attitude to survivors and their advocates, defying O'Rourke's victims to see them in the High Court for a full decade after his conviction. There was intensive political lobbying behind the scenes to extract a commitment from the government that the State would pay the victims' compensation but, after a number of cabinet meetings on the matter, the advice from the Attorney General was that such a move would set a financially unsustainable precedent for other abuse cases. Only in the spring of 2008, after negotiations spanning nine days, was a settlement of 2.5million (excluding legal costs) in total finally agreed with fourteen plaintiffs, and then only after the plaintiffs faced a further wait of three more years pending a potential Supreme Court appeal. Another two plaintiffs, including the US-based woman who had been frequently raped by O'Rourke from the age of twelve and who made the first complaint to Gardaí – waited a further six months before their settlements were reached. An attempt by King's Hospital to stitch a confidentiality clause into the first agreement, prohibiting the victims from publicly recounting their stories, was rejected by the plaintiffs. Instead, they insisted that, as part of the settlement, Swim Ireland and the King's Hospital School issue a written acknowledgement to them of the suffering they had endured since they were children. Fourteen months after the compensation cheques came through their letterboxes, that written acknowledgement, in the name of Swim Ireland alone, finally materialised. The letter, received by the survivors on 30 April 2009, read:

Dear ——,

The Irish Amateur Swimming Association trading as Swim Ireland wholeheartedly and unreservedly apologises for the unspeakable wrong done to you by Derry O'Rourke. We are very aware that you have suffered significant trauma and personal injury as a result of the abuse you suffered at the hands of Derry O'Rourke while participating in swimming, the sport which this association represents. It is deeply regretted within Swim Ireland that these events took place and it is our hope that now the litigation has been settled you can move forward with your life.

Over the past decade Swim Ireland has developed significant new structures, procedures and safeguards to ensure that all aquatic activities with its remit can continue to operate and develop in a safe and healthy environment. We hope that this acknowledgment will help you to close the chapter in the painful experiences which you have suffered.

The letter was signed by Pat Donovan, Swim Ireland's secretary, and Sarah Keane, chief executive.

The attitude of the authorities since the scandals has potentially acted as a deterrent to other victims who might have considered coming forward to report their abuse, as often happens when cases of child sexual abuse are reported in the media.

Undoubtedly, stricter rules have been adopted in the running of the sport for its 12,000-plus members nationwide. Such requirements as the presence of two parents at the poolside during training are welcome, but the institutional mindset has been slow to change. Swim Ireland continues to charge a fee to receive complaints of abuse, something Norah Gibbons says is 'absolutely wrong because it militates against people making complaints'. Most remarkably, the organisation did not appoint a full time national children's officer until January 2007; exactly nine years after O'Rourke was jailed. According to Swim Ireland's annual accounts for 2006, it spent almost twice as much on public relations (34,178)as it spent on child welfare (18,178)for that year. The PR bill had trebled from 12,401the previous year.

'A lot of work done on child welfare is not paid-for work,' argued Padraig McKeown, managing director of Drury Communications, the firm contracted to represent Swim Ireland. 'People on the ground have been trained and are responsible individuals working on a voluntary basis. If you want to put a value on that, it would be very substantial.' But Gibbons warns that child protection 'cannot be voluntary'.

Whether or not there was a child sexual abuse ring operating in Irish swimming, what happened before can happen again. It only takes one abuser.

'Vigilance will prevent it, but it won't prevent it completely,' Norah Gibbons warns, 'We must have systems to knock back people who are determined to abuse children. No institution will get destroyed if it errs on the side of the child. You can't risk it because the costs for the child are too heavy.'

15. Where Are They Now?

For every child abused, there are many victims. Families and whole communities suffer. It is impossible to say how many people have suffered the consequences of sexual abuse crimes committed against children in Irish swimming. In the minds of those survivors who have told their stories there is no doubt that many others were abused who have never spoken out. From those stories that have been told, we know there has been appalling suffering. Marriages have disintegrated, there have been suicides and attempted suicides, severe mental illnesses, lost friendships, ruptured families, financial hardship and unemployment. The perpetrators' loved ones are among the victims. So too are many others peripherally involved, either in the sport of swimming or in the wider community. The children who were sexually abused by their coaches have come through a protracted darkness that they will never fully escape but, in most cases, sheer resilience has helped them to survive and to become extraordinary adults.

GEORGE GIBNEY: His last reported fixed abode was a condominium in Orange City, Florida. In January 2008, a former elite swimmer, while on a New Year holiday in New York with his wife, stepped outside the door of his Manhattan hotel and feels sure he saw Gibney walking by, accompanied by a young male. The swimmer attempted to follow them, but Gibney melted into the crowd.

DERRY O'ROURKE: After serving nine years of the total 125 years imposed by the courts, he was released from the Midlands Prison on 1 March 2007. While in prison, he received no treatment for sexual deviancy. In the week following his release amid intense speculation in the media as to his whereabouts, a male caller left a voice message on this author's phone, wanting to reassure those abused by O'Rourke that he would not be returning to live with his family, in the neighbourhood where some of his victims still lived. When the *Sunday World* revealed that O'Rourke was living near Baltinglass, Co. Wicklow and producing religious oil paintings, local people mounted a public protest against his presence among them. It was later reported that he had moved to Co. Cavan.

FRANK MCCANN: Since unsuccessfully challenging his murder conviction in the Court of Criminal Appeal, Frank McCann has spent much of his incarceration working in Arbour Hill Prison library and producing Braille text. He has also acquired a PhD in computer science while in jail. He was turned down for release at his first parole hearing in August 2006.

RONALD BENNETT: After serving ten months of a two and half year jail sentence, he was released at the age of seventy-four in January 2009. Dismissed from the priesthood on the order of the Congregation for the Doctrine of the Faith in Rome, he remains a member of the Franciscan order, residing under restrictions at their Killiney, Co. Dublin house. He received no treatment for sexual deviancy while in prison.

CHALKIE WHITE: He moved to the Far East on a long-term work contract and occasionally comes home to visit his wife and children.

VAL WHITE: She continues to live in the marital home and says, 'Chalkie and I have a strong relationship.'

GARY O'TOOLE: Now an orthopaedic consultant at St Vincent's and Cappagh hospitals, with private rooms at the Beacon in Dublin, he is married with twin daughters. Having once admitted that, were he ever to have children, he would find it hard to get them involved in swimming, he was moved to receive matching pairs of Speedo swimsuits from a well-wisher when his daughters were born. He occasionally takes them swimming at weekends at his local pool.

KAYE & AIDAN O'TOOLE: Aidan resigned from the Leinster Branch of the swimming association in protest against its inaction over George Gibney. He has never been invited to a gala since and his club, Triton, has been disbanded. He works as the facilities manager of Ireland's largest schoolboys' football club, St Joseph's in Sallynoggin. He and Kaye have eight grandchildren.

BART NOLAN SENIOR: A grandfather of three, he still goes to Swim Ireland's annual general meetings, voicing objections and generally being a thorn in the side of the organisation. His reputation as an advocate on behalf of child abuse victims has spread and he is often to be seen in courtrooms lending support to people who were abused beyond the sphere of swimming.

BART NOLAN JUNIOR: Married with two children, he manages two swimming pools in Dublin.

SWIMMER A: She moved to a rural part of Ireland where she lives with her husband and children.

K: Since her mother's suicide she has lived at home with her father. She has a young son and says that, while every day is a struggle, her son gives her reason to live. She continues to attend St John of God's Hospital and is on prescribed medication.

SWIMMER B: After her evidence helped jail O'Rourke in 1998, she was sacked from her job as a coach with a Dublin swimming club. The day she heard he was being released nine years later, she was in a shop trying on her wedding dress.

SWIMMER D: She has resumed an involvement in swimming as a parent. When she contacted officials to tell them that a coach had shouted abusively at one of her children during a Gala, she was required to pay 50euro to lodge a formal complaint. She made the complaint while her own High Court case against Swim Ireland and King's Hospital was being contested by the defendants. The child was not interviewed as part of an inquiry. The complaint was adjudged to be without foundation.

THE WOMAN WHO MADE THE FIRST COMPLAINT TO GARDAI ABOUT DERRY O'ROURKE: She lives in the rural US with her husband and children and seldom comes back to Ireland.

THE GIRL RAPED BY GEORGE GIBNEY IN FLORIDA IN 1991: She lives at home with her parents, is unable to take up a full-time job, is addicted to cough medicine and has made numerous attempts to take her life since the DPP decided not to seek Gibney's extradition. She is still pursuing a legal action for damages.

PROFESSOR MOIRA O'BRIEN: She retired from Trinity College and took up a position as an orthopaedic consultant with a private clinic in Smithfield, Dublin.

MARIAN LEONARD: She has returned to work at a full-time job she enjoys and continues to assist journalists whenever the murders of Esther and Jessica surface in the news.

RODERICK MURPHY: He was appointed to the bench of the High Court in 2000. He was the judge in the celebrated 'Lying Eyes' conspiracy to murder trial of Sharon Collins and Essam Eid and was one of the three appeal judges who refused Joe O'Reilly's appeal against his conviction for the murder of his wife, Rachel.

MICHELLE SMITH DE BRUIN: After officially retiring from swimming in 1999, she qualified as a barrister in 2005 and had her first law book, *Transnational Litigation: Jurisdiction and Procedures*, published in 2008. The previous year, she came second in an RTÉ reality TV show, *Celebrities Go Wild*.

MICHAEL MCCANN: Since the demise of King's Hospital Swimming Club, he has no longer played a high-profile role in the sport but remains an active committee man in other walks of life. He was elected chairman of the Kildare branch of Trinity College's alumni organisation and served as chairman of the Irish Translators' & Interpreters' Association in 2004.